Dear Dr. Menninger

Dear Dr. Menninger

Women's Voices from the Thirties

EDITED WITH AN INTRODUCTION BY

HOWARD J. FAULKNER AND VIRGINIA D. PRUITT

University of Missouri Press
Columbia and London

Copyright © 1997 by

The Curators of the University of Missouri

University of Missouri Press, Columbia, Missouri 65201

Printed and bound in the United States of America

All rights reserved

5 4 3 2 1   01 00 99 98 97

Library of Congress Cataloging-in-Publication Data

Dear Dr. Menninger : women's voices from the thirties / edited with an
   introduction by Howard J. Faulkner and Virginia D. Pruitt.

      p.   cm.

   ISBN 0-8262-1111-9 (pbk. : alk. paper)

   1. Women—United States—Social conditions.   2. Women—Health and
hygiene—United States.   3. Psychiatrists—United States—
Correspondence.   4. Sex role—United States.   5. Women—United
States—Psychology.   I. Faulkner, Howard J., 1945–   .   II. Pruitt,
Virginia D., 1943–   .

   HQ1420.D42   1997

   305.4'0973—dc21   96-40209
                                                                 CIP

∞™ This paper meets the requirements of the
American National Standard for Permanence of Paper
for Printed Library Materials, Z39.48, 1984.

Designer: Stephanie Foley
Typesetter: BOOKCOMP
Printer and binder: Thomson-Shore, Inc.
Typeface: Palatino

Material published in *Ladies' Home Journal,* © 1932
Meredith Corporation. Used with the permission of
Ladies' Home Journal and the estate of Dr. Karl Menninger.

In affectionate remembrance of
Dr. Karl and Jeanetta Lyle Menninger

Contents

Acknowledgments

*W*e owe appreciation to numerous people for supporting our research and editing efforts. Special thanks go to Robert D. Stein, Chair of the Department of English and Dean of Honors; Paul Sanford Salter, Dean Emeritus of the College of Arts and Sciences; and Wayne Sheley, Vice-President of Academic Affairs, Washburn University, for granting us released time to complete this project and for their warm support. We also wish to thank the research committees at Washburn, which provided financial assistance.

Much gratitude is also due to Mrs. Walter (Connie) Menninger, archivist of the Karl Menninger Archives, and to the superb editorial staff at the University of Missouri Press: Beverly Jarrett, editor-in-chief and director; Jane Lago, managing editor; and Clair Willcox, acquisitions editor.

Editorial Practices

*I*n almost every case, we have printed the letters, from both inquirers and Dr. Menninger, in their entirety. We have, however, sometimes deleted Menninger's recommendations for further reading when such advice was repetitious of previous suggestions. Such deletions are indicated by spaced ellipses; unspaced dots indicate the use of a series of periods by one of the letter writers. We have also deleted the names of correspondents, and any family members mentioned in the letters are designated only by initials. In most cases, we have provided the city and state in which each letter writer lived, but if the location was a small town, thus making identification of the writer possible, if unlikely after all these years, we have simply noted the state.

Most of the letters were remarkably free from spelling and punctuation errors. We have silently regularized such minor punctuation conventions as placing commas and periods inside quotation marks but have generally left punctuation and spelling as written; thus, for example, the frequent spellings "thru," "tho," and "enuf" suggest a short-lived but rather consistent tendency in the early thirties. We have used *sic* sparingly, though when a correspondent writes "I'll have to omit" for "I'll have to admit," or "precautious" for "precocious," it seems worth indicating that the slip was the writer's.

Editing, annotating, and writing were all truly mutual efforts; we shared equally in the pains and pleasures of preparing this volume, and the ordering of our names on the title page reflects nothing more than the exigencies of printing.

Dear Dr. Menninger

Introduction

In 1929, Topeka psychiatrist Karl Menninger, then thirty-six years old and the father of three children, began a column of advice directed at parents troubled by their children's behavior. That column, in *Household*, a locally published but nationally prominent magazine, became such a popular feature that it continued for more than a decade, ending finally in 1942. A year after the *Household* columns first appeared, Loring A. Schuler, editor of the *Ladies' Home Journal*, approached Menninger about becoming mental hygiene[1] adviser to the *Journal*, suggesting that he write a monthly column that would address specific problems related to mental health and perhaps answer letters that readers would be invited to contribute.

Sixty years after that interview with Schuler in the Philadelphia headquarters of the *Journal*, Menninger reminisced about his impressions: "I just remember his office seeming bigger and bigger, while I was feeling smaller and smaller." Schuler offered Menninger a dollar a word, and he accepted the proposition; the first of his columns on "Mental Hygiene in the Home" was printed in the October 1930 issue of the magazine. Menninger, always a proselytizer for mental health causes and an advocate of improving psychological understanding among the lay public, discussed his motives in writing the column: "Fifty years ago, we were trying to popularize the idea that a person's mind could be healthy—coordinate with the specialized idea that it could be unhealthy and need psychiatric services. To that end, the *Journal* offered to publish some articles on what was healthy and what was unhealthy. I wrote those articles, published month by month, and in

---

1. The term *mental hygiene* was coined during the first decades of the twentieth century to describe the theory and practice behind the maintenance of mental health. According to the *Psychiatric Dictionary*, the dual purpose of mental hygiene is "to develop optimal modes of personal and social conduct in order to produce the happiest utilization of inborn endowments and capacities, and . . . to prevent mental disorders" (*Psychiatric Dictionary*, ed. Robert Jean Campbell, 7th ed. [New York: Oxford University Press, 1996], 332).

connection with them an invitation went out to readers that if they wanted to write me, they shouldn't hesitate to do so."[2]

Schuler and Menninger were unprepared for the response that the invitation elicited. Nearly two thousand letters from readers have been preserved in the Menninger archives, but originally many more existed, until one afternoon Mildred Law, a longtime Menninger employee, decided to clean a storage room and discarded the *Journal* letters she found there.[3] To cope with the onslaught of appeals for help, Menninger advertised for an assistant. One of the applicants, Jean (Jeanetta) Lyle, had been working as a textbook writer and journalist in Kansas City. She talked first to Menninger himself, then was interviewed by John Stone, the Menninger business manager. During her conversation with him, Stone asked her whether she thought she could handle the job. Jean Lyle, who eleven years later was to become the second Mrs. Menninger, remembered answering rather blithely, "Yes. Dr. Karl showed me how, so I think that I can do it."[4] Although Stone suggested that she not tell Menninger she considered the task as perfunctory as her reply indicated, she recalled thinking that Menninger's ego was not of a sort to be so easily wounded. She was quickly hired.

The collaborative effort initiated with the mental hygiene column was to last through almost fifty years of marriage and more than thirty years of Jean's work as an editor of the *Menninger Bulletin* and author of professional publications with her husband. The *Journal* column, however, survived only eighteen months, as Menninger had just entered into psychoanalysis in Chicago and found that in addition to his other professional obligations, he did not have time for both of these new undertakings. Moreover, only a few of the thousands of letters he received were used in the column; rather, he preferred to spend his monthly allowance of words in writing an essay of a page or more on a single theme, illustrated more frequently, if less convincingly, by hypothetical cases than by letters from his readers.

From our point of view sixty-five years later, however, no hypothetical case could provide the exactness of detail found in the actual letters women sent to Menninger between October 1930 and May 1932, when he stopped writing the column. Menninger often began his responses with the line, "Yours is one of the most remarkable letters I have received," and indeed these letters, almost none of which was even excerpted in the columns,

2. Interviews with Karl and Jeanetta Lyle Menninger, fall 1989.

3. Ibid.

4. Because there were three Dr. Menningers in Topeka, the father was usually referred to as Dr. C. F., and his sons as Dr. Karl and Dr. Will.

are remarkable documents, providing intimate glimpses into the most personal recesses of women's experiences. Delineating problems of love and sex, of finance and career, of the struggle to achieve a balance among the often competing demands of society, family, and self, the letter writers reveal the central concerns of their existence. Some of these concerns are different from those one finds now in the appeals to contemporary advice columnists. The tough Depression years and the more confining mores of the early 1930s demanded different choices and exacted different penalties from those of the 1990s. Many of the depictions of lives during these lean times belie a romanticized view of extended families living in domestic tranquillity. However, family strife, as well as a plethora of other problems aired in the letters, is a timeless issue, though the perspective articulated in these letters and the language in which it is voiced are often significantly different from current-day expectations. No one frets, for example, about "low self-esteem," "codependency," or "recovered memories."

The appeal of advice columns had first been apparent nearly 250 years earlier, shortly after newspapers as we know them originated. In 1691, John Dunton, a London bookseller, came up with the notion of a journal concerned exclusively with readers' questions. These queries, along with the responses to them, were printed in his paper, *The Athenian Mercury.* Unlike contemporary readers who write to Ann Landers or Abigail Van Buren chiefly on such topics as love affairs and personal relations, inquirers to Dunton's journal, as well as those to similar journals in the eighteenth century, solicited both advice and information: whether rooks fed on carrion, whether fleas possessed stingers, whether anyone could identify Cain's wife—these were among the early questions.[5] Indeed, matters of natural science comprised 20 percent of the queries, whereas marital inquiries accounted for only 4 percent of them.

Perhaps the most famous of these early advice columnists was Daniel Defoe, who in 1704 began a journal of public affairs, *A Review of the Affairs of France,* a title soon abbreviated to simply the *Review.* Defoe incorporated an advice column in his paper, but like Menninger he was quickly overwhelmed by the cataract of requests, receiving up to fifty letters a month (at the time evidently a startling number) and soon accumulating a backlog of nearly three hundred letters. The *Review* lasted nine years, but Defoe had long before severely reduced the space devoted to advice.

By 1930, Americans had developed their own more personal style of advice column. There were several immediate models for Menninger's

5. W. Clark Hendley, "Dear Abby, Miss Lonelyhearts, and the Eighteenth Century: The Origins of the Newspaper Advice Column," *Journal of Popular Culture* 11 (1977): 345–52.

new column, including of course his own *Household* column. Another, "Diet and Health," was written by a friend and colleague of Menninger's, Kansas City physician Logan Clendening, for the *Kansas City Star*. The most important nonmedical model to come to Menninger's attention was probably "The Chaperon," a column of information and advice that also ran in the *Star* during those years, informing its readers that "Questions on social customs, beauty aids, and affairs that come up daily in the experience of busy people will receive prompt answers Mondays from THE CHAPERON."[6] Signed with such epithets as Troubled Twenty-Four, Wanting to Know, Broken-Hearted, Disgusted, Inexperienced Mother, Perplexed Suitor, and Lonely and Blue, the letters solicited assistance on questions of etiquette, grammar, diet, and housekeeping, as well as the expected romantic quandaries. An amalgam of Heloise, Dr. Ruth, Ann Landers, and Miss Manners, "The Chaperon" typically printed one long letter a week with a response and then devoted the rest of the space, perhaps half a page or so, to a series of brief questions, comments, and quotes. The writer struck a commonsensical tone, often chastising the reader for her, or more rarely his, own failures. The answers to questions that weren't strictly practical tended to reflect a rather conventional morality. To the woman who wrote in August 1929 describing life with a man she didn't love and asking if she should remain in the marriage for the sake of the three children, "The Chaperon" replied without equivocation that she should cheer up, be thankful for the kids, and stop pining for perfect happiness. To another woman who wondered about the etiquette for going single to a public dance, "The Chaperon" replied that a girl should not "go stag" to such an event under any circumstance. And when a wife complained that her husband seemed to be taking excessive notice of one young woman who visited their farm, "The Chaperon" chided the wife for being deficient, arguing that the husband must be seeking in the young girl qualities that the letter writer herself might have lost.[7]

Advice columns, then, were attaining a widespread following in 1930, perhaps because they provided a unique forum in which the risks were minimized and the confrontation with the adviser distanced by the preservation of anonymity, while the writer could still expect a personal and expert response. "Mental Hygiene in the Home" also originated at a moment when Menninger was experiencing, as was the mental hygiene movement itself, immense popularity and prestige. After receiving his M.D. from Harvard University in 1916, Menninger had interned at Kansas City

6. This invitation was printed each Monday with "The Chaperon" in the *Kansas City Star*.
7. The last two examples were from the columns of February 4, 1929, and February 11, 1929.

General Hospital, but in 1918 he returned to Massachusetts to continue his work with Elmer Ernest Southard, his professor of neuropsychiatry at Harvard and the superintendent of Boston Psychopathic Hospital, where Menninger had done postgraduate study. It was Southard who had turned Menninger's medical interest to psychological disturbances, so that in 1919, when Menninger came back to Topeka to enter medical practice with his father, it was the ills and hygiene of the mind that increasingly occupied his attention.

Although Topeka was far from centers where American neuropsychiatry was burgeoning, during the decade that preceded Menninger's *Ladies' Home Journal* column he was staking out a prominent place in American psychiatry. In 1920, Menninger and his father founded the Menninger Clinic, the forerunner of today's institution called simply Menninger, internationally acknowledged as a preeminent psychiatric institution. In 1926, father and son opened a children's division of the hospital. Meanwhile, during the 1920s Menninger helped found two important psychiatric organizations: the Central [States] Neuro-Psychiatric Association in 1922 and the American Orthopsychiatric Association in 1924. Between 1926 and 1928, he chaired the American Psychiatric Association's Committee on Legal Aspects of Psychiatry, the first attempt to define the important relationship between law and psychiatry and to establish guidelines for psychiatrists' testimony in legal proceedings.

In addition to the demands of the clinic and of family life (it was during the 1920s that Menninger and his wife, Grace, became parents of three children), Menninger assumed another responsibility, launching his lifelong project of educating the lay public about mental health by teaching courses at the local Washburn College, which he had attended his freshman year before transferring to the University of Wisconsin. He taught his first classes in the fall of 1920; they were listed in the catalog as Mental Hygiene, Abnormal Psychology, Psychopathology of Social and Industrial Relations, and Psychopathology of Delinquents and Criminals. That same semester his father taught a course required of all entering students, Freshman Hygiene. By 1921–1922, Psychopathology of Social and Industrial Relations had been absorbed into Abnormal Psychology, and the course on Delinquents and Criminals was renamed simply Criminology. Mental Hygiene was described as "an introductory lecture course designed to acquaint the student with the fundamental facts of mind in relation to its proper use and normal development." Abnormal Psychology involved "a description and analytical study of the phenomena accompanying abnormal mental states."[8]

8. Information gathered from Washburn College bulletins of the period.

This was clearly an elaborate and ambitious venture, especially at a college as small as Washburn. But just as obviously, this undertaking, like Menninger's advice column in the *Journal*, represented his belief that psychiatry ought to address itself not merely to the maladjusted or to other professionals, but to a lay audience that would benefit from acquiring the psychiatric tools of self-understanding. One important result of his teaching was the writing of a book, developed out of class outlines and lecture notes, that was to propel him into nationwide fame. His chief handicap as a teacher at Washburn, he felt, was the lack of appropriate texts for his courses. Medical texts were too specialized and too sophisticated for introductory courses, yet they were the only texts available. It was to fill this gap that Menninger wrote his first book, *The Human Mind*, designed not only for his students but also as a companion volume to Clendening's book *The Human Body* and as a general introduction for lay readers to "the views of the younger group in American psychiatry."[9] In today's world of best-selling pop psychology books, it is perhaps difficult to imagine what an unlikely prospect for widespread readership this work would have been, yet it achieved amazing success, becoming a best-seller. In addition to regular sales through its publisher, *The Human Mind* was selected as the February 1930 book choice by the Literary Guild of America, and thereafter seventy thousand subscribers received it. Carl Van Doren of the guild stated, "At last . . . the editors have been able to select a scientific work of which they feel that the appeal is almost universal."[10]

Part of the credit for the book's reception was due to Menninger's vivid style. His writing, as it does in these letters, clarified and hence made accessible complicated human and psychological concepts. He delighted in the use of imaginative and metaphorical language to dramatize his points. Indeed, the book opens with an analogy to explain the working of the human mind:

> When a trout rising to a fly gets hooked on a line and finds itself unable to swim about freely, it begins a fight which results in struggles and splashes and sometimes an escape. Often, of course, the situation is too tough for him.
>
> In the same way the human being struggles with his environment and with the hooks that catch him. Sometimes he masters his difficulties; sometimes they are too much for him. His struggles are all that the world sees

9. *The Human Mind* (New York: Knopf, 1930), ix.
10. Quoted in *Washburn College Bulletin, Alumni Edition* 15:3 (March 1930): 6.

and it usually misunderstands them. It is hard for a free fish to understand what is happening to a hooked one.[11]

More striking even than his employment of metaphor was the insistent use of illustrative case histories. Virtually no complex idea was simply defined or explained: it was concretized through examples drawn from Menninger's more than decade-long experience with the "hooked fish," the mentally ill. There was also something at once confident and reassuring about Menninger's tone that must have appealed to readers. He comforted them with the thought that "it is ignorance which makes people think of abnormality only with horror. . . . For surely anyone who achieves anything is, *a priori*, abnormal. . . . I presume that most of the people in *Who's Who in America* would resent being called normal."[12] As in all of his writing, he advocated greater understanding of mental illness and the mentally ill—and of mental hygiene and the principles that might prevent mental illness or at least modify its effects. All of these characteristics of tone and style enabled Menninger to achieve a popular notice quite different from that garnered by any other of his American colleagues.

Thus, when in 1930 Menninger began his column for the *Ladies' Home Journal*, it was as a published author widely known for the quality of his ideas on mental hygiene and for his ability to give them lucid and colorful embodiment. But Menninger's success in reaching the American public also reflected the temper of the times, since by 1930 what was then known as the mental health (or mental hygiene) movement had captured the interest of a broad segment of Americans. Indeed, though *The Human Mind* was the first such book to become a best-seller, a number of self-help psychology books had previously appeared on the American scene. Menninger was aware of them, and in his columns and letters of advice he frequently recommended not only works of fiction and philosophy but also such psychology books as a means for readers to better understand their problems. Menninger's obvious favorite among these works was Josephine Jackson's relentlessly uplifting *Outwitting Our Nerves: A Primer of Psychotherapy*, which had been published by Century in 1921. With Menninger, Jackson shared a positivistic faith in the power of psychotherapy to heal mental illness. She compared its therapeutic powers to those of surgery, a metaphor Menninger himself utilized in these letters. Although her central image for the workings of the human mind—that of a mental

11. *The Human Mind*, 3.
12. Ibid.

machine that sometimes slips a cog—was more mechanistic and implied less adaptability than Menninger's own model, she shared his notion that most difficulties originate in childhood experiences, that their causes are often obscure to the sufferer, and most important that understanding these hidden causes is the primary and biggest step toward attaining mental health. Like Menninger, she was an optimist and an educator. With the proper knowledge we can choose our emotions, she argued; thus, we can choose to be healthy.

Jackson's work was one popular expression of the developing interest in mental hygiene as a public concern. It had been Clifford Beers who first attracted the public's attention with the publication in 1908 of a compelling autobiographical description of his own recovery of mental health, *A Mind That Found Itself*. A graduate of Yale who had suffered a nervous breakdown, Beers described the draconian treatment he witnessed during his three-year incarceration in private and state mental hospitals. He pledged the remainder of his life to ameliorating abuses in these institutions and to supporting measures to prevent mental disorders. He quickly acted to establish in Connecticut the first mental hygiene society for the purpose of improving the quality of care for the mentally ill, for the prevention of mental diseases, for the conserving of mental health, and for the distribution of accurate information about the subject. A year later, in 1909, Beers established the National Committee for Mental Hygiene, which dedicated itself during its initial three years to fund-raising and attempted to enlist the support of educators, physicians, and other pertinent professionals. Adolf Meyer, a Baltimore psychiatrist, had suggested to Beers that the term *mental hygiene* conveyed both the major theme and essential purpose of his book. Meyer's own pioneering work, a dynamic life history chart for diagnosing mental problems and monitoring their course, significantly influenced Menninger's early view of mental illness and his conviction, evident throughout these letters, that mental diseases are not fixed or static conditions that can be isolated from environmental factors but rather can be understood only in the total context of an individual's history, relationships, and continuous attempts at adjustment.

The post–World War I period also saw the birth of the Child Guidance clinics—offspring of the mental hygiene crusade. If education, or guidance, was the key to mental health, then the proper education of the child was a necessary preliminary to securing it. Indeed, Menninger's original and longest-running column of advice published in *Household* was intended for parents concerned about the appropriate upbringing of their children. And the emphasis on child guidance evolved not only out of the mental health movement but also out of Americans' increasing fascination with the ideas of Sigmund Freud, whose psychoanalytic theories also stressed the importance of childhood experiences in the etiology of psychic distress. In September 1909, the same year that Beers founded the National Committee for Mental Hygiene, Freud made his famous first visit to the United States, giving a series of lectures at Clark University. In the two decades that followed, his influence was evident in heightened sensitivity to the contributing roles of the environment and society in the genesis of mental illness, an awareness that nicely complemented the efforts of the indigenous mental hygiene movement.

Thus, by the time Menninger began his *Ladies' Home Journal* column, the general public had had two decades to familiarize itself with ideas regarding mental illness and to replace the view that the mentally ill were marked by a permanent difference that could best be dealt with by their separation from the mainstream of society in custodial institutions with the view that we all share vulnerability to mental sickness, just as to physical maladies, but that knowledge and acceptance of the principles of mental hygiene could minimize the suffering that such illness entailed. Menninger's column offered this public a further chance at self-education, both those readers who solicited his personal advice and those who benefited more indirectly.

When we discovered the approximately two thousand letters addressed to "Dear Dr. Menninger," we were quickly engaged not only by the drama of the letter writers' lives but also by the clear and affecting presentations we found in letter after letter, correspondence from a generation of American women giving voice to their dilemmas. From such an embarrassment of riches, we have chosen more than eighty letters on the basis of only two criteria: that the letters be interesting and that they be representative of the spectrum of problems confronted by the women who wrote.

All regions of the country are represented, as are all types of communities: farms, small and medium-size towns, suburbs, and large cities. The vast majority of the women who wrote were housewives. Single women, when they worked, were typically secretaries or teachers. Although many of the latter were forbidden by state laws to be married, there was an occasional married teacher or secretary, and one woman was a married journalist, but we found virtually no questions about careers, an area that is largely ignored, even though for many of the inquirers money was short during these hard times.

The family members described in the letters resolve themselves into a typical cast of characters. Usually the letter writer proclaimed herself defenseless, or weak, or suffering from a bad case of "nerves," though to a modern reader these "neurasthenic" women seem often to be quite stoically bearing a great deal of suffering. Frequently in-laws were the source of complaint, since this correspondence was generated during the Depression, and in-laws were often living under the same roof with the letter writer. Commonly it was the mother-in-law with whom the correspondent had difficulty, often finding her interfering and domineering. Both the husbands and fathers of the letter writers are typically portrayed either as exceptional in character yet failures, disappointments to their wives, their lack of success possibly due to their very fineness, or as philandering or abusive, inflicting disappointments of a more serious nature. Descriptions abound of husbands who deserve to succeed, because they work hard and have decent values, but who are not getting ahead, much to the dismay and sometimes resentment of their wives. Children, too, tend to be either lavishly praised or seriously despaired of.

Probably the most common tactic employed by Menninger in his responses was to analyze what the correspondent had written to bring to the surface what the questioner knew intuitively but not consciously; in doing so, Menninger pointed out underlying motives and unwitting contradictions. As he wrote in a letter of November 19, 1931, "I do not like to give advice beyond indicating some of the factors not always seen by my correspondents." That becoming aware of subconscious motives constitutes the important first step toward mental health was a conviction consistent with Menninger's growing acceptance of Freudian theory and therapy.

Throughout the 1920s, Menninger's philosophy and practice had increasingly reflected Freud's influence, and he came to see himself more and more as one of Freud's champions in America. Tellingly, he rewrote later editions of *The Human Mind* from a largely Freudian perspective. Yet he kept references to Freudian concepts and hypotheses to a minimum in his column, preferring to use the more widely accepted terms of mental hygiene. He led off his first column by quoting his own definition of mental health from the recently published first edition of *The Human Mind:*

> Mental health is the adjustment of human beings to the world and to one another with a maximum of effectiveness and happiness. Not just efficiency, or the grace of obeying the rules of the game cheerfully; it is all these together. It is the ability to maintain an even temper, an alert intelligence, socially considerate behavior, and a happy disposition.
>
> Great numbers of people are interested now in mental hygiene—more everyday. It appears reasonable that mental health is something which can be largely controlled—like physical health—by a proper distribution of the available scientific knowledge which pertains to it.
>
> We all know enough, now, to avoid public drinking cups and to be vaccinated against smallpox and to drink lots of water when we have a cold. Why

shouldn't we be equally fortified against temper tantrums, depressions, and such things as "nervous indigestion" and "nervous headaches"?

But Menninger's Freudian outlook is nonetheless visible in his responses to many of the letters: he equated miserliness with impotence and linked many somatic difficulties, acne for one, to psychic causes. Stuttering and alcoholism alike were best cured, he argued, by psychotherapy. Homosexuality ought usually to be left alone, since few homosexuals wanted to be cured, but Menninger viewed homosexuality as an illness, or as an arrested stage of psychic development, a phase that everyone experienced, but that healthy people passed through. Numerous of his letters end with the counsel that the correspondent should search out the nearest psychotherapist, though in the early 1930s analysts were often geographically remote from the troubled letter writer. It is worth noting, for example, that until the forties, all the psychoanalysts west of the Mississippi River worked under the Menninger aegis. The San Francisco Psychoanalytic Society was not founded until 1941; the Los Angeles Society not until 1946.

Despite his avowed predilection for merely pointing out underlying motives, Menninger could be prescriptive and judgmental, even harshly so. He was particularly outspoken on the subject of in-laws who lived with their children, always deploring the arrangement and urging the writer and her family to move out—or move the in-laws out. His reaction to letters from women whose husbands were having affairs (and there were many such letters) might seem even more surprising: time after time he admonished the wife about her shortcomings, implying that she had driven her husband into another woman's arms; he often suggested that the husband be forgiven without further ado. The tangles of Menninger's own life at this time, however, go far to explain his advice. Unhappily married to his first wife, Grace, Menninger was having an affair with Lillian Johnson, the wife of a Topeka judge. Grace had discovered the affair, and she was sometimes finding consolation, and doing so at Menninger's urging, with Lillian's husband, Beryl.[13] When Menninger's affair with Lillian ended, he and Jean Lyle became lovers, a relationship that extended through much of the 1930s until Menninger finally divorced Grace in 1941 to marry Jean. A further complexity in the situation was posed by Jean's role as an adviser on the responses to the *Ladies' Home Journal* letters. As the letters continued

13. For a discussion of Dr. Karl's marital difficulties and extramarital relationships during this period, see Lawrence J. Friedman, *Menninger: The Family and the Clinic* (New York: Knopf, 1990).

to pour in and as Jean proved her competence and writing skill, she quickly shifted from assistant to coauthor. Although it is now difficult to determine who was actually responsible for which responses, it is clear that often Menninger simply read the letter seeking advice, scrawled a few diagnostic notations, perhaps underlined some indicative phrases, and then turned the letter over to Jean. While they were alive, Menninger was more willing than Jean to insist on her critical role in answering the correspondence. What is certain is that they thought alike and worked as a team, creating the seamless body of responses.

Menninger's own view of what made a woman attractive—an undemanding cheerfulness seems to have headed the list of attributes—is by contemporary standards off-putting. In fact, in his column of April 1932, he regretted the gains in power by women as "an inversion of the biological relationship." Thus, it seems at first ironic that he should have divorced Grace, who was a good cook, mother, housekeeper, and host, for Jean, a career woman. Yet despite her domestic virtues, Grace was highly strung, and it was with the competent and professionally assured Jean that Menninger found a more congenial partner for the second half of his life.

In some cases, the advice that Menninger and Jean gave sixty-five years ago seems enlightened and modern. In response to a woman whose father enjoyed dressing in women's clothes, Menninger dismissed the cross-dressing as of no serious consequence and emphasized instead the writer's own unarticulated problems. Unlike "The Chaperon," the Kansas City advice column that always encouraged women to stay with husbands for the sake of children, Menninger often tacitly, and occasionally explicitly, suggested that a divorce was the better solution for a woman and her children. Again, his personal situation at this time may have shaped this then unconventional viewpoint.

What seems most notable about these letters that six and a half decades ago provoked Menninger's responses is the precision and clarity of the women's voices. The letters convey a variety of tones—from recriminatory to defensive to apologetic; the inquirers adopt varying strategies for presenting the issues: many letters first praise the writer's husband before advancing the complaint, as if it were necessary to give a balanced view; others are laments. Against the backdrop of the Great Depression, the stories related are sometimes tragic, often desperate, and occasionally comic. The problems range from the trivial to the catastrophic, and the appeals from the pathetic to the profoundly dignified. Unlike the letters one reads in newspaper advice columns today, these are often long and absorbing, the details selected with the instinct of an artist. Most striking is the insight they give into the way the women saw themselves, formulated their problems, conceived the world. It is for this reason that we have left the letters uncut, for in addition to assuring the coherence of the dramatic stories they tell, the letters in their entirety present cohesive voices with wonderfully revealing asides of seemingly extraneous information: one woman worried that her husband's "flat back head" might be the cause of their difficulties; another agonized over her ugly face, but consoled herself with her "small hands and feet."

We have arranged the letters chronologically within thematic groups. Of course, many letters deal with more than one issue, and the nature of the problem as perceived by the letter writer may be different from the perception of Menninger or of a modern reader. Clearly, all the letters in the section on unconscious hostility suggest a problem somewhat different from that which the writers saw and consciously delineated. We tried, in each case, to choose what seemed the crucial issue of the letter as a reader would see it. The first sections deal with problems primarily of individuals and are followed by sections dealing with marriage and the family.

When we first came across these letters during our research into Menninger's professional correspondence, we stopped the work we were doing. Captivated by the candid and uncensored glimpses of American women in the early 1930s, we marveled at our luck in gaining such a privileged look at a world now distanced from ours by momentous decades of changes in cultural and individual consciousness.

Even Menninger, ninety-six years old when he reread these letters, was enthralled by the unfolding stories. He wanted to identify those who were still alive and write to them. "Did I do them any good?" he asked several times. Of course, the idea of tracing the women was impractical: even if there were survivors, we had only an address from nearly sixty years before, and few Americans remain in one spot so long. Yet the favorite letter of one of the editors (dated June 18, 1931, and included in the section "Interfering In-Laws") was written by a woman in a small town in central Iowa near where he had grown up. She describes with gallows humor her dreadful life as the second wife of a weak husband, who dotes on his equally doting (and domineering) mother. She wrote to Menninger to ask whether she should divorce her husband, but he refused to tell her what to do, though he said that the answer was implicit in what she had written. In 1989, back in Iowa for a visit, the editor asked the widow of a rural letter carrier if she knew anyone in the community where the letter writer had lived. Astonishingly, she knew the man who had been postmaster there since the end of World War II, and though that was still fourteen years after the writing of the letter, her lead seemed a good place to start. We found the postmaster, who began to call longtime residents of the small town, asking if they remembered the family, the woman, the outcome of the story. The woman was evidently as memorable as her letter would suggest, for several people recalled her, remembered that soon after the letter would have been written she had indeed left her husband—though he quickly found a third wife to shoulder the drudgery.

We hope that you find the letters as engaging and revealing, as touching and inspiring, as we did, and we invite you to step back with us into this fast-receding era.

1.

Sexual Conflicts

Milford, Conn.
Nov. 1930

Doctor Menninger:

It does not seem possible for one to give another a really clear picture of one's problems—but fools enter where angels fear to tread—so . . .

The "special" problem is excessive masturbation. It warrants lengthy discussion, I suppose.

I am eighteen years of age—a grammar school teacher; and for the past three years have been indulging in this habit, until I am really frightened. I have consulted numerous doctors—including one nerve-specialist three times as old as I, who decided that the only cure was "more than fatherly embraces" etc. Now I apply to you.

But I can analyze the problem to a certain limited extent: You see, I had absolutely no sex information except for that which I pried out for myself. And at home it has always been taken for granted that desire for the other sex, desire for the companionship of both sexes, has never been present. Sex is never discussed.

Religious education has been—shall I say intensive as well as extensive? Consequently, at the present moment I have no faith in people, in a God, in prayer—just a hatred for living. This lack is discouraging when one attempts to "grow up" sexually and emotionally.

And I just happened on this habit myself. I know no girl who does it or ever did do it, altho I did know two fellows who became insane because of it. (I knew them only by sight—nothing more.) In fact, I abused myself for a month or so—as I remember it vaguely, before I knew what I was about. Then—it had grown to such proportions.

As to the habit itself. There is always the orgasm, with accompanying fantasies as a rule.

An apology: there is an absolute lack of logical sequence in this letter, I am writing as I think. Sorry.

At times I am able to control myself for weeks at a stretch, but I always— invariably return to it.

Physically, I am all right, except for the nervous tension, lack of sleep. But mentally I am a mess. I believe that I always did desire to be different—and bored individuals held the most charm for me. At last I, too, have thought myself into a morbid outlook, a confusion of right and wrong, an entire lack of self-respect, the recurring ideas of suicide. All the things that are making for extreme discontentment, unhappiness, mental unrest.

But I am pretty much in a fog. You are really a sort of last resort. So far, doctors have done nothing but disillusion me—and now, if you are able, will you help me?

Nov. 29, 1930

My dear Miss:

Your letter of recent date addressed to me in care of the *Ladies' Home Journal* interests me very much.

The first thing that impresses me about your letter is your abundance of false and incorrect information. Strange as this may sound to you, I think you are giving yourself airs, I think you are greatly exaggerating the importance of *your* masturbation. You go so far as to say that you know of no girl who does it or ever did do it. Let me assure you that nine-tenths of the girls that you know have done it and many of them are doing it right now. I say this because repeated investigations have shown that the vast majority of women as well as men go thru a period when they get their sexual satisfaction out of masturbation. So don't think you are having experiences which no one else ever had or that you are the victim of a temptation which no one else ever had. You are not.

To be sure most people do grow up and get over it because it is an infantile kind of satisfaction which ought to be replaced with something better. Either it ought to be replaced with the right sexual sort of satisfaction in the form of sexual relations with a man, or else it ought to be sublimated into work and play and hobbies and sports and other things which take you outside of yourself. Most people are able to accomplish this with varying degrees of success. So far you have not accomplished this but it does not mean that you are not going to.

The next thing which I feel that I must correct you about is the statement that you know two fellows who became insane because of it. I am quite certain that you are wrong about this. I have studied insanity for fifteen years or more and I have never known a case of the many thousands which I have seen whose condition was caused by masturbation. Masturbation never causes insanity. It is perfectly true that some people who masturbate become insane for the very reason that I have already told you, namely that practically everyone masturbates, or at least the large majority of people, and since a good many of us go insane, some of those who go insane will be found to have masturbated. But it is just as absurd to say that their masturbation was the cause of it as to say that their red hair was the cause of insanity or the fact that they were fond of gooseberry pie. And so get over that delusion too.

You say in the last paragraph of your letter that doctors have done nothing but disillusion you. I don't know just what you mean by this. If they really did disillusion you, I should think you would be grateful. I think the trouble is that they did not disillusion you. You have the illusion of the dreadfulness of your great sin. It is neither dreadful nor unique nor is it a sin. It is a kind of childish performance which indicates that you don't have enough external outlet for your libido but it is nothing serious, nothing terrible and nothing in fact to occasion you anything like the anxiety and grief which it seems to be doing.

Look at it from this standpoint and I think it will lose some of its intense attraction for you. To the extent that it gives you satisfaction, why forbid yourself? The thing you should regret is the fact that other things do not interest you more. I think they would if you would give them a chance, give it a try.

Sincerely yours,

New Orleans, La.
Nov. 18, 1930

Dear Dr. Menninger:

Have just read your page in December *Ladies' Home Journal* and feel that I'd like to unburden my mind to you.

I shall go back to the very beginning of my life—from a tiny child, I have always been super sensitive and very morbid and melancholy. When quite little I'd worry about the world ending and various other things when I should have been out playing.

As I grew older I got out of this somewhat, but not altogether.

From childhood days I have always had girlfriends usually one very close friend whom I liked very much and of whom I was intensely jealous (only in regards to girls), we went out together with worlds of young men. In the work I do, I have traveled quite a bit—so when it would become necessary to go to another city—I'd leave—and soon I'd have another girl I liked and palled around with. I have always liked men tho—and before my marriage usually had quite a flock around me. I'm very feminine and quite attractive in a soft way. (This just for your information.) Am now 24 and have been married 6 weeks to a man I love very much.

Now here is the point in my life that has worried me incessantly and which I want to lay open, in the true light to you for your advice.

About two years ago I met, in an apartment house where I lived, a young woman about five years my senior—very fascinating in a mysterious way and extremely interesting—we were attracted to each other immediately or at least I to her—and became quite good friends. It wasn't for some time that I found out that she drank liquors in a wild, continuous way, staying drunk in a stupor for days sometimes. For neither of us had people here, and as I was new in the city and lonesome we were together regularly. The love I had for her was a kind of sympathetic love and lonesomeness and nothing of a sensuous nature at all, although we each went out with young men. All the time I was intensely jealous of her other girl friends and could almost go out of my mind when she would disappear on one of her drinking orgies. Up to this time I had never had any familiarities with any girls at all. Had never found there were such people as homosexualists. But one night we were sleeping together she said she would like to kiss my breast. Because I loved her, I allowed her to do this and other things—but that was about all. Even tho I still liked her I soon put a stop to this with just a mutual understanding. Let me say here that I believe she is perfectly normal and just lonesome and for myself that I didn't feel her attentions at all sensuously. Just because I loved her I reciprocated. Because of her drinking we broke up—but a year before we broke up we had ceased any relations of this kind altogether.

Now I'm married and crazy about my husband and the thought that perhaps because of this regrettable experience I am one of those terribly unfortunates designated as being "queer" preys on my mind; my relations with my husband seem perfectly normal. I'd like for you to please tell me something in a personal letter to me. Several times lately I've been at the point of telling my husband and more times than one of self-destruction. Dr. it has me crazed. I can't free my mind from this obsession. Please don't print letter in magazine under any circumstances but write me personally at your earliest possible convenience and I shall gladly pay any remuneration you deem just.

Sincerely yours,

Dec. 19, 1930

My dear Mrs.:

I am very glad indeed you wrote me on November 18 in care of the *Ladies' Home Journal.*

In the first place let me assure you that we will not print your letter in the *Journal* and also that there is no charge for my answering your letter as that is what I have agreed to do for the readers of the *Ladies' Home Journal*, and it is made possible by the *Journal*.

I think I can give you a great deal of mental relief. The experience that you have been thru is a perfectly normal and very common experience. It does not mean that you are homosexual. It does not mean that you will ever become homosexual. It does not even mean that your friend was a homosexual.

To understand exactly what happened to you I must tell you a little about the theory of sexuality. Most people assume that the quality of being male is one thing and the quality of being female is another and that men are all male and that women are all female. Now that is not correct at all. It is more nearly correct to say that men are mostly male but have some female element and women are mostly female but have some male element in their makeup. If it were not so, there would be no such things as fraternities and men's clubs and women's clubs and so forth. There would not be much friendship among men for other men and among women for other women. On the other hand, the mixture of male and female traits is not exactly the same in all individuals. Some women are more mannish than others, as you know, and some men are more feminine than others. The woman you describe was evidently more mannish than you and you are evidently a very feminine type of woman, with very little mannish element. Therefore, it is apparent that she was attracted by you and you were attracted by her to some extent.

But this is nothing serious at all. It is a very common experience and whenever people of the same sex are thrown together a good deal and denied the company of the opposite sex this experience is exceedingly common. It is very common, for example, for girls who are thrown together in dormitories and schools, and so forth. It is sometimes carried quite far and violent love affairs come from it which are unhealthy as you know. You may have heard about the play *The Captive* in New York a year or two ago. In this play the attachment between two girls had gone to such an extent that they could not break it and it meant more to them than anything else in the world. This, of course, is abnormal. This is what we call frank, outspoken homosexuality.[1]

---

1. *La Prisonnière* by Edouard Bourdet had opened in Paris on March 6, 1926. An American version, *The Captive*, translated and adapted by Arthur Hornblow Jr., opened at the Empire Theater in New York on September 26, 1926. Among the original cast were Basil Rathbone and Helen Menken, who was then married to Humphrey Bogart.

The affair you had with this woman was not a full-fledged case of sexuality. It was indeed a kind of homosexual attraction but homosexual attraction is not a serious thing and usually means only that the individual is denied normal sexual outlet and is given a peculiar and particular opportunity.

I would certainly not discuss it with my husband if there was any possibility of his misunderstanding as I think there is. I do not see that there is anything that you need to tell him because I don't think it is abnormal, I don't think it is wrong, I think it has done you no harm, and I think the best thing in the world to do is to regard it as a natural experience and forget about it. The fact that you have normal and enjoyable sexual relations with your husband is proof that you are not sexually abnormal at the present time and I don't believe you ever will be. It is nothing to be ashamed of but it might be misunderstood by your husband. On the other hand, if he is a very intelligent sort he would probably laugh it off and wonder why it worried you so much. Don't be worried any more.

Sincerely yours,

Florida
Mar. 22, 1931

Dear Doctor Menninger-

Your help is very much needed in our family, tho it will be for you to decide whether my husband or myself is the most needy.

It is necessary that I give you an outline of our lives so you can judge our reactions. My husband is a man of sterling worth—almost too honest for his own good. Very clever in his lines of business. He has always made a success of his business. His word is his bond. All the men admire his ability and reliability—but he has no men friends. He belongs to clubs and entertains many men but the fact remains that he does not like them for friends, tho they would be willing to be closer friends if he allowed it. When I met him his home life seemed singularly cheerless because the men were extremely quiet and taciturn and the mother was so clannish that they rarely entertained any except relatives. I realized from the start that W. was starved for ordinary friendliness and companionship and that he liked girls better than men. He isn't sissy and his friendship is of such a shy quality, tentative, as tho expecting a rebuff, that everyone exerts themselves to show they like him. I have met only one woman who didn't like him. The older women mother him and the others treat him as a brother. He likes to come home in time for tea or even take a rubber or two of bridge and it is characteristic of his friends that the women make a fuss over him and go on talking as they would not talk before other men. They tell him things for they know he will take no wrong meaning out of their confidences. Do you see him now? Just a wholesome man of thirty-eight who frankly enjoys women more than he does the company of men. He doesn't hunt or fish or play poker but he likes bridge, swimming, hiking, tennis and all the sports our women friends like.

My mother died when I was very small and my father and two brothers brought me up with the aid of a nurse. Our home was the center of all the social doings of the younger set. My father was a genial, humorous host— one of the most popular men in our city. I was sent off to school at the age of six and grew so lonely that after a few years my father married an estimable woman of good family, solely, I believe, on my account—in order to make a home for me. He idolized my mother and would have put no one in her place if I hadn't complicated things. I loved my father intensely and my brothers too—we had so many men about all the time. When my step-mother arrived things took a sudden change. Instead of keeping open house we had stated evenings when we were allowed to invite our friends. My father had to entertain at his clubs; my brothers couldn't stand the strain and eventually left home. She was a very good woman—so very good that we hated the word. I immersed myself in music in order to try to forget her. I wrote a little and had a number of articles accepted and she ridiculed my efforts so I've never attempted any writing since. In short she gave me an inferiority complex not only about my person but about everything I did. As you may guess most of my friends were boys for my brothers brought home their college chums and now she made herself such a pest that the boys rebelled. She wouldn't let me snowshoe or skate unless I dragged an older person with me. Thus grew my antipathy for women and it strengthened my love for men. As was to be expected I married soon after my father died. Married a man who was so jealous of me life was unbearable. So unbearable that I left him before our honeymoon was really over. Thinking my new estate would at least make her let me manage my own affairs, I found on my return from abroad that I was still a child in her estimation. I had stayed long enough to take another musical degree and so had told her my intention was to leave my home and be absolutely independent of her. She was aghast at this—what would people say? She had never given me a single caress in her life.

Then I met my present husband. He was as hungry for friendship and love as I was afraid of jealousy. I had watched many married couples and seen them let their love degenerate into bickering. It seemed to me that the women demanded too much. Of course they expected attentions from their husband but so many demanded all his time and attentions—were truly selfish for they didn't let the poor men have any interests outside of them. I believed in fifty-fifty. I saw when a man got tied down too tight, begin to wriggle loose. The bit doesn't hurt until it is cutting, then when there's a ditch to jump—then comes a cropper. I was absolutely convinced that to hold a man and make him want to be held—one must give him his head— let him have friends of his own choosing, and make all his own decisions.

That is what I've done with my husband. Many have told me I was wrong, but I like men better than women so why shouldn't he like women best? I entertain women solely on his account and he has been just as cordial to the men as I have been to the women. We have been married fifteen years—are the same age, have an attractive hospitable home. We love each other more now than we did then for we've been thru so much together. Our friends say we laugh and joke and are REAL friends—they envy us our confidence in each other. We tell each other all we can tell— for our friends seem to load their troubles on both of us and we do not violate confidences. My husband asked me once what I'd do if he fell in love with another woman. He knows if he TRULY loved her—I'd give him his freedom at once. He also knows that I realize that men are men and that if he did anything which he afterward regretted, that I would not judge him spiritually disloyal because of a physical lapse. He knows with my nature that I would be as open to temptation as he would be. I absolutely trust him and despite the freedom he has been accorded I feel he has been loyal to me in every way, for tho he likes women he is no flirt.

I forgot to say that I am far from beautiful—in fact even my best friends agree that the Lord must have been visiting the day I was born. My face is ugly, tho I have small hands and feet and a really good figure. Just last evening a man asked my husband who the woman was with the stunning figure. In short my only proper claim to notice is my son and daughter.

Now after all these years the serpent has entered our Eden. My only disappointments in my husband until now have been his refusal to own a home of our own or to study in order to advance himself. He is advancing in experience but is neglecting certain educational benefits which I feel he should not overlook, but these things did not spoil my happiness. Since the boom broke here our Real Estate investments disappeared and taxes ate up the others—due to three bank failures we are poorer than we were fifteen years ago—but I feel it isn't the experience, but how you receive it that counts. We have even missed our vacation for two years and had a lot of illness. I know these money worries are apt to make any man queer. All these years I have had a few men friends, mostly from other parts of the state or from abroad. I've had but one close friend right here—the only man my husband really likes really well. It is a small place and gossip thrives. When I heard this one friend mentioned I decided to tell him not to come without his wife but my husband laughed at me for his wife lives in another city—he said it was nobody's business but ours and that he approved of this friend and added that he knew I didn't like women because so many of them are selfish and trivial. So that was that, until recently. I am afraid history is repeating itself. W. SEEMS to be getting jealous. NOT of my one or two close friends—but of the queerest sort. We live in the country and I market in town once a week and W. thinks I talk too much to the GROCER. A piano-tuner raised his ire. He thinks I shouldn't play or sing when asked because the men hang around the piano. He objects to my dancing with certain men. He said when I was buying furniture that it hardly seemed necessary to go look at the same suite three times. I have a friend abroad who helps me keep up my French by writing me in that language—he is a happily married man. W. objects after all these years. This same friend returned north three different years—about five years apart—just when we did—and because he was a very old friend my crowd teased W. about it and it has evidently rankled. He has even objected to my wearing certain dresses because they fitted too well. What shall I do? Humor him? It has lasted eight months now and is getting worse. I go out rarely without him as he objects if I do. I have refrained from seeing many friends I like because of this. I know he has a load of money worries but I'm doing all my own work and being so economical he praises me for it. I believe in fifty-fifty but it would be silly for me to ask him to give up all his friends just in order to retaliate. The children miss people dropping in and it embarrasses me considerably when my friends act mystified by my actions. I am not religious—Pantheism suits my mind best, I guess, but my real belief is that the best thing in this life is the friends you have. I hate to lose friends but if this goes on W. will lose friends too. Are we incompatible because he likes women and I like men? If we give love to others—it is like the widow's oil, the more we give the more we have. If our lives have been happy for all these years, what is wrong now? I have asked if I've done anything to hurt him—have offered him his freedom, thinking there was someone else, but he doesn't want it and avers he loves me more than he ever did. It seems all trivial to me—tho lately he seems to want me to be more possessive. Is it possible that he wishes me to demand that he give up his friends—to be with me ALL the time? It doesn't seem possible but when I asked if he wished his freedom he was horrified and said in a hurt tone "I believe you'd give me to the very first woman who asked for me." Is my theory of a loose rein wrong? Then why did it work so well for fifteen years? I am so confused that I do not know whether the trouble is my fault or his. If I were beautiful I could understand it. If it is best for him I'll gladly give up all the men in the world.

I am signing my own name, naturally, but if you MUST print my letter, please sign not only another name, but also another state for my husband reads your articles too.

Very sincerely,

May 9, 1931

My dear Mrs.:

Your letter of March 22 addressed to me in care of the *Ladies' Home Journal* is a very remarkable one for several reasons. In the first place it is written in a flowing, readable, vivid style which is a great relief after some of the drab documents I have to pore thru. In the second place, the case as you describe it is an exceedingly interesting one. I shall do my best to make some suggestions that will prove helpful to you but I want to warn you in advance that anything as complicated as your situation is not likely to prove easy to correct.

I must tell you at the very start of your letter I am very suspicious as to the significance of your husband's peculiar preference for women. I really do not think that he seeks women as much as you think. I wonder if you realize how definitely you give the impression in the first paragraph of your letter that your husband is somewhat like a woman himself? You say "he isn't sissy" but he associates with women at tea parties and bridge parties and they go on talking with him just as they would talk before themselves and not before other men.

Now I think what has happened is something like this. Your husband is, as you say, jealous because you have taken an interest in the man whom he regarded as his best friend. I think his jealousy is really toward this man altho he appears to project it upon other people. Furthermore, I think the thing that he is jealous about is not the fact that you like the man but the fact that the man likes you.

This may seem unreasonable to you but I think for the sake of the best outcome of the case you had better take my word for it on the basis of a great deal of experience. Let me warn you first of all, however, that it would be very unwise for you to attempt to discuss with your husband the psychological motive. You are not a doctor and it will be quite impossible for you to help him in this way by any appeal to his intelligence. What you can do, however, is to drop the friendship of this man immediately and see to it that your husband and this man are together more and you and the man less. It might even be a good idea for you to take a little vacation from one another for a while. Above all, I think it wise for you to make every effort to keep your temper and tolerance and poise in spite of his absurd notions and behavior.

I am frank to tell you that I have some serious misgivings about the subsequent developments of his mental state. It may become steadily worse to a very serious degree. Yet if he were aware of the psychopathological nature of his symptoms, I think something might be done. In that case I would strongly advise that he go immediately to a psychiatrist somewhere in the North or West where he could be treated. Under the circumstances, however, since he does not recognize it, I doubt if it is wise for you to push the matter. If he makes any opening at all for it, I think I would recommend it.

Once again let me urge you not to attempt to do any amateur psychoanalyzing on him yourself. Tell him, if you like, that you think his notions are quite absurd but do it in a kindly or humorous way: give him as little provocation as possible; cut out your contacts with the man of whom I suspect him to be jealous and curb your disapproval of his business dealings and so forth down to a minimum. By sitting very still you may keep the boat from rocking and conditions may subside. If they get steadily worse, there will be nothing for you to do but to take him to a psychiatrist. I am telling you the worst because this is my one and only contact with you and I think it is only fair that you be warned of the possibilities.

Sincerely yours,

Ft. Worth, Tex.
Apr. 6, 1931

My dear Sir:

Your articles in the *Ladies' Home Journal* have interested me intensely, particularly the one on "Self-Adoration." I believe you can give me valuable information and advice—hence my appeal.

Perhaps there is no better way than coming directly to the point, though the unvarnished truth in this case is not beautiful. Is there hope of becoming normal, through psychiatric or any other kind of treatment, for a man, thirty-five years of age, who has never known sexual satisfaction except through contact with men? He can feel passionate affection for a woman, but much more for one of his own sex. He is very high-strung, has an abnormal appetite, suffers from indigestion, is subject to violent fits of temper, at which times he says things he does not mean and often does not even remember. He is very critical of people, even his best friends. He becomes angry or disgusted over the most trivial occurrences or remarks and then says the most unkind things to or about the friend or relative involved.

He seems to realize his condition but fears it is impossible to change it. If you can give us any hope and direct him to the best place for consultation he will go. He prefers not to consult anyone here. Is there someone competent along this line in Dallas? This man is planning a trip west in June. Can he find someone in that part of the country? Or should he go somewhere else? Will his case require the constant personal supervision of the doctor handling it?

May I beg of you to give my letter most thorough consideration and send me the help you can. It is indeed a matter of vital importance to him and to me.

Thanking you, I am
Very truly,

May. 2, 1931

My dear Mrs.:

I have read with a great deal of care your letter of April 6 in regard to the man who has so much difficulty in his sexual life.

Everything you describe about this man indicates that his homosexual tendency is of neurotic origin. I must explain to you what I mean. There are in general two kinds of homosexual men. In one case the preference for a person of the same sex arises on the basis of constitutional or physical factors which cannot be changed by psychological treatment. In the other type the preference for persons of the same sex is a kind of perverted or distorted psychological development which can be successfully treated.

The nervous symptoms which accompany this man's condition and the other symptoms which you describe all indicate, as I have said, that he is under an enormous psychological stress which indicates that his homosexual satisfactions are not giving him real happiness and could, therefore, be relieved by the right kind of psychological surgery. In my opinion the best possible treatment for this condition is psychoanalysis. Unfortunately, I do not believe there are any psychoanalysts in your near vicinity. The man will have to make up his mind that he really wants to be treated, that it is the most important thing in his life for him for a while. It may take him a year and it may even take him longer. It will necessitate his going wherever the psychoanalyst is and staying there. It will require daily personal contact with the doctor until he sees the thing thru. It will cost him a great deal of time and some money but a successful outcome in a case like this is immensely gratifying and is worth many, many times what it costs to everyone concerned. I very much hope that you will be able to guide him to treatment of this sort. May I give you a final word of warning in regard to the particular psychiatrist you pick out. There are many claiming to be psychoanalysts who are quacks. This has brought psychoanalysis into rather bad repute in certain quarters. Unfortunately, however, it has not eliminated the quacks. Therefore, be sure that the man you wish to go to is a member of the American Psychoanalytic Association.

Upon re-reading your letter I notice you ask if there is anyone doing psychoanalysis so far West. Unfortunately I think not. I do not think it would be possible for this man to combine business and treatment. He will have to give up everything for a time and do nothing but follow out the treatment. If it is not worth that sacrifice, it isn't worth doing at all.

Sincerely yours,

Pennsylvania
Apr. 23, 1931

Dear Dr. Menninger:

After reading your article in the May issue of the *Ladies' Home Journal* I decided to write and ask you to enlighten me, if you will, on the motives which impelled me to wreck my whole future six months ago. I have always been mystified as to the reason for my sudden change of mind; it does not seem possible that any woman in her right mind would burn her bridges behind her and deliberately refuse happiness for a mere whim. Two days before the wedding was to have taken place I was truly in love with the man (and am yet, for that matter); the night before, cold panic seized me and I felt compelled by a force I do not yet understand to call it off.

Needless to say, the man is thoroughly angry with me; I feel sure he hates me; we both exchanged angry words and harsher letters, for in the perverse mood which held me, I tried to blame him! Not until I acknowledged to myself some few weeks ago that I still loved him did I have any peace of mind. And so far as this peace of mind is concerned, what does it mean without completion? I am frustrated, balked; yet it is all my own doing.

To attempt to make him believe I still love him is, I fear, impossible. He judges me by my actions; he is a business man, not a psychiatrist. How can I expect him to understand? While he is generous, kind, and honest, yet he is sensitive and is one who finds it hard to forgive or to forget. I have hurt his pride by refusing to marry him.

We met a number of years ago and for several years past carried on a correspondence which culminated in plans for marriage six months ago. The meeting involved a long journey for both of us and great expense for him. I left my job, my family and friends, perfectly content to make my home with him many miles away. There were certain religious difficulties which I knew about and which I agreed not to let stand in our way. And the night when I called off the marriage, I seized on these religious matters as a desperate excuse for the postponement—and this after telling him previously they should never stand in the way. The best way I can describe my state of mind at that time is to say that I suddenly developed a notion that he did not look like the man I ought to marry; he seemed like an utter stranger, and the thought of intimacy with him frightened me. I could not explain my feelings to him, for he was in no mood to listen. He tried to tell me there was another man, back home perhaps. He could not understand it. He finally reached the conclusion that I wanted a sight seeing trip at his expense, and has written me since to this effect. He knows in his heart that this charge is unfair, but one can hardly blame a man for reaching such a conclusion by pure logic.

Doctor Menninger, what is wrong with me? I want everything that a real woman wants, yet there is always some barrier, in this case of my own making. Is it because I had the wrong concept of marriage in my girlhood?

My father died when I was 11 years of age; I was the oldest of 6 children, and the chief breadwinner for many years. Until I was 26 (I am now 38) I had never had a real love affair. And as for marriage my mother always discouraged such talk. The model sons and daughters of her acquaintances were those who stayed with their parents, especially if the parent was a widow; those who married in their youth (if they had a widowed mother) were labeled "ungrateful," or the criticism took the form of condolences and laments as to their foolhardiness in courting misfortune, for they "didn't know what they were getting in to," or "they'd be sorry they didn't stay single," and so on ad nauseam. And this in spite of the fact that she was happily married during the 12 years of her own married life. I hate to criticize my own mother unnecessarily, but it is a fact that she did not realize the social responsibility which was hers with a family which included 4 daughters. Only 1 of us is married and not too happily at that. While we were poor, the lack of means should not have kept cheerfulness and neatness from the home; I have yet to find both present in our home, altho' financial conditions have greatly changed. Her indifferent and sometimes hostile attitude towards the young men who did call is, I believe, the real reason for her indifference to the condition of the home.

I idolized my father; I was the only one of the family who could recall him. I can remember shutting myself up in my room and weeping bitterly for him on the occasion of a clash with my mother, and such occasions were frequent when I was a young girl. He was a very kind man, and loved his children intensely.

The man to whom I was engaged recently is the exact physical opposite of my father. In character he is very much like my parent; he is kind, honest, gentle, and reliable. But he is dark and of Latin blood, whereas my father was fair and a Celt.

To go back to the subject which impelled me to write you, do you think I can expect this man to forgive me? Shall I take him into my confidence, tell him of my unhappy, thwarted girlhood, and ask him to give me another chance? Or shall I make up my mind to forget him?

If you can help me I shall indeed be grateful, for I am in need of sound advice. My whole future depends on it.

Respectfully yours,

May 11, 1931

My dear Miss:

I have read with a great deal of interest your letter of April 23rd addressed to me in care of the *Ladies' Home Journal.*

I think your case illustrates very well the way in which inhibiting factors may arise out of our unconscious and prevent our doing something which we consciously believe, and have reason for believing, that we want to do. It is not always so clearly accomplished as in your case. What I mean to say is that many people are inhibited from doing something they should or are compelled to do something that they should not without understanding how reactional it is and how it represents an unconscious rather than a conscious wish. They attempt to explain it on the basis of circumstances and they distort the fact and strain their intelligence and logic to prove it.

In your case you understand the origin of it geographically but you do not understand it psychologically so to speak. Just why you declined to go thru with it at the last minute we can only guess at. Your letter makes it so clear that your attachment to your father was unusually great and persistent that I should think that you were prevented from a happy fulfillment of your marital plans by an unconscious feeling that it was disloyal to your father. I think you more or less recognize that yourself but you do not recognize how strong such a motive could be.

As to the final questions as to whether or not to return to the man, I should certainly do so if I still could. I think I would tell him all about it and try to get reinstated if I could but I am afraid that you will again defeat yourself in spite of your good intentions. It occurs to me that it will be quite necessary for you sooner or later to get a little better understanding of yourself or you will be continually wrecking your plans inadvertently and in one sense unintentionally just like this. I don't know just where your city is in Pennsylvania but I would strongly suggest that you go to Philadelphia and have a talk with a psychiatrist who can make these things very much clearer in conversation and consultation than I possibly can in a letter. He can inquire in more detail as to certain features which you do not mention.

I suggest that you go to see Dr. Earl Bond, Philadelphia, whom I regard as one of the best men in our profession and whom you will find to be a gentleman as well as a scientist.

Sincerely yours,

Portland, Ore.
May 8, 1931

Dear Sir:

Please advise me. I am so disgusted with myself and so miserable. Until recently I didn't know there was such a thing as homosexualism and now that seems to explain my past and present unhappiness. It is too hideous.

My mother died when I was three. During childhood my craving for motherlove found an outlet in worshipping different women. I would "play" I was the loved child of whichever charming woman held my fancy at the time.

This unnatural make-believe continued through high school, where I had "crushes" on my teachers. I no longer pretended to be their child, of course, but wanted their friendship, their attention, even their love, more than anything in the world and was naturally very unhappy over real and imagined slights.

In college my infatuation turned to upper classmen, and I knew periods of exaltation and despondency over these "cases." It was late in my college life before I began to feel the normal interest in men.

After graduation from college there was a blessed period of five years— blessed because it was free from what now seems so perverted an emotional life. I had the usual friendships with men, and married.

Now, after two years of comparatively happy married life the old curse is back. I have fought against it this time in view of my later knowledge of psychology. Yet, even while I tell myself how revolting it all is, my interest in this older, charming woman supplies me with a satisfaction I cannot explain. It seems the one absorbing thing in life. Infantile as it is, I carry on imaginary conversations with her, and she is constantly on my mind.

I feel my love for my husband disappearing. I am critical of him. Perhaps I should say that he is not passionate and we have had sexual intercourse only at rare intervals. I have told him this is not normal.

This is all revolting to me and I hate myself more every day. Is there something I can do to rid myself of this complex, or whatever it is? Am I going crazy? Sometimes I think so. Am I really that awful thing, a homosexualist? Be frank with me. I need it.

Sincerely yours,

Jun. 30, 1931

My dear Mrs.:

I have read with much interest your letter addressed to me in care of the *Ladies' Home Journal.*

I think you have probably made a correct diagnosis of yourself but I do not believe that you understand the diagnosis. Homosexuality is a phase of psychological development thru which all people go. In the normal person it is relinquished or at least submerged in favor of a preponderant degree of heterosexuality. Why this has not occurred in your case or why it has not occurred to a more satisfying degree, I cannot say. I am sure, however, that it is not something for you to reproach yourself about but rather something for you to attempt to get rid of in the interest of a happier union with your husband and a better motherhood.

I think the best way to get rid of it is by submitting oneself to psycho-analysis and I would recommend that you go to any length necessary to have a consultation with a psychoanalyst. . . . Take his advice and work out the reasons for your clinging to this infantile emotional attitude.

Sincerely yours,

Georgia
Sep. 28, 1931

Dear Dr. Menninger:

Perhaps this does not come under the head of *Mental Hygiene*. I hardly know where to turn since, under the conditions, a psychiatrist is out of the question. Properly speaking the problem is not mine, and yet it touches me nearly, so that I am giving you the part of the story with which I am familiar.

I met the girl I shall call W. two years ago. She was one of the younger children in a family where, figuratively speaking, "dementia scholastica" was apparently inherent. The parents were unusually strict: reading comic strips was forbidden on the grounds of vulgarity. Discipline was enforced by a leather belt. The child admired her big, handsome brothers above all others, and she competed with them for the parents' attention in vain. The father, who was a teacher, died just before W. entered college, leaving the family finances in a precarious condition. She secured a scholarship to a small, Southern teachers' college, took a degree in Manual Arts, and has the best job of any one of her class. As a high school girl she was in no sense a social success. As nearly as I can gather, her curiosity concerning the other sex earned her a punishment at the age of five that she never forgot; she was never curious again. As a freshman and sophomore she took quite an active part in campus life; president of her class, officer in her sorority and the glee club, and Art Editor of the annual. The next two years the glow wore off of being collegiate, she dropped out of everything pretty well and earned the name of being a little "queer." When she was a senior and I was a junior I knew her only by sight as a heavily-built, attractive looking girl, whom the voice instructor had discouraged because there are no songs written for women written low enough for W.'s voice. She was easily the brainiest girl in her class.

We were thrown together often and soon became very good friends. After a while I began to be aware that an unpleasant situation was shaping itself. We had a very definite physical attraction for each other. Neither of us is a simpleton; one doesn't live three years in a girls' school without a working knowledge of "crushes," besides a thorough grounding in psychology had showed us the reasons for such. I was quite confident of my own control and sense of humor, and counted on our approaching separation to clear the air. In January of the following year (we had not seen each other since May) she became ill and one of her friends wrote, asking me to come to see her in an effort to lift her depression. The intimacy of that three-weeks' visit proved too great a strain for our resistance; I am afraid things went much further than is generally the case. She was so upset when I left that I knew there must never, under any circumstances, be a repetition of that particular brand of idiocy. When W. came to see me in June I assumed the responsibility for our good behavior— and averaged one hour's sleep out of the twenty-four during those two weeks. The fact that I was not financially able kept me from a nervous breakdown.

Ours was only one of a series of similar affairs for her, beginning when she was thirteen. A year is about the average duration, and there is one every year. Before I left college, I went to one of the instructors in whose common sense I had much confidence and indirectly asked for her opinion of W. She said: "W. is one of our problems on the campus, a case of delayed adolescence." I happen to know that W. had asked for, but received no intelligent direction. This summer she took a course in psychoanalysis at the University of Illinois, and in desperation at the beginning of another affair with a woman, conducted an experiment with a man who had "biological doubts" concerning himself to see whether she had any attraction for the other sex. Though it was not consummated, she got the response. Consulting her family physician, W. was told that she had done a wise thing but the experience should have been completed and suggested that she do the completing. The man is kindly, reputable, middle-aged and married, but W. can not make up her mind even in the face of obvious attraction for him. Back in the small, university town, teaching school, she is tormented by a sort of super-susceptibility to obvious masculinity regardless of size, shape or previous condition. There is danger of her marrying the first man who inspires her with confidence.

Dr. Menninger, as nearly as I am able to judge, W. could no more make a go of a marriage than she could fly to Jericho. She is absolutely self-centered, though as unconsciously as a child. She has no conception of the give and take that makes for successful marriage, and [is] incapable of sustained interest in one person. Though she does not realize it [her] attitude of living is masculine rather than feminine, if such delineation is possible. Because of an unsympathetic mother and an uninterested older sister, she turns to me for advice, and I am getting distinctly out of my depth. Where does she go from here? Is she to waste so much of her time and brain fighting a recurrent homosexuality all her life? What do you think of marriage as a remedy? Any direction that you can give us as to where to find help and any suggestion you would be kind enough to give would be deeply appreciated.

Sincerely yours,

Jan. 3, 1932

My dear Miss:

I am very sorry to have been delayed in answering your letter of September 28.

I think you have analyzed the factors entering into your friend's case quite well.

My comments on your final paragraph would be these: I have the impression that you are still too anxious to control your friend. You seem to think it is up to you to decide what she should do and I get the impression that you are rather too much concerned as to whether or not she marries. Your logic may be correct but I do not see how one can make logic take any effect on a person who is so obviously driven by her emotions and her unconscious impulses.

Of course the girl needs help. Anyone who is struggling with homosexual tendencies needs help because society is constituted to favor only heterosexual investments. I do not think you are in a position to give her very much help because aside from your own personal difficulties which you frankly confess you cannot see the case clearly and dispassionately. Moreover, it is a technical job for which I presume you have had no training, and I can assure you it is very wise to turn such problems over to people who have had training.

Naturally one cannot withdraw interest from one's friends but I think you could do her the greatest favor if you would help her to see that she needs help from someone other than you, especially a psychiatrist and preferably a psychiatrist who is recognized as a competent psychoanalyst. Whatever it costs her in time, comfort, money, etc., must be measured against the happiness of her entire future.

Sincerely yours,

New York, N.Y.
Oct. 13, 1931

My dear Doctor Menninger:

I am anxious to have your opinion as a doctor and psychologist on a problem of mine on which I have never before asked advice. You will doubtless understand what has caused it, and you may be able to tell me how to cure myself of my "habit of mind."

I am 24, graduated from Smith College in 1928, and have been doing secretarial work in New York since graduation. My mother teaches piano and my father, voice. They taught in Smith College from 1907–25 and then left because of college politics. I lived in Northampton all my life until I graduated from college and came here.

I had an uneventful childhood. I am an only child and was ill most of the time until I was twelve. I played some with other children but most often by myself.

In High School I was carefully kept from the society of boys. (I had gone to a girls' private day school until then.) I was not allowed to go to the local dancing school because my parents did not like the crowd that went there. Consequently I have never yet been at ease at a dance. I never had a date with a boy until my freshman year at college. There I developed two or three crushes on boys—crushes entirely on my side.

In my sophomore year at college I became very friendly with a classmate my own age. (Also an only child.) She was the first real friend I had ever had. We used to lie in bed, talking late into the night and soon discovered that we were physically attractive to each other. Neither of us knew the implications of this. We were entirely uninstructed, and believed that we were unique and sinning horribly when we put our arms around each other. We went no further and we had no idea how to do so. We fought against our inclinations and they increased.

During my junior year we quarreled because of jealousy and did not speak to each other for the whole year. For nine or ten months I suffered terribly and continuously. Even now, looking back, I would rather die than go through it again. Of course I know that the same circumstances would not hurt me as much another time.

At the beginning of my senior year I set about getting back on speaking terms with my friend, whom I may as well call X, and by the end of the year we were back on a casually friendly basis.

During the first year after graduation we discovered that our physical attraction for each other was still very much present. By now we knew in a general way what was wrong with us. I had learned by reading *The Well of Loneliness*.[1] X had learned through personal experiment.

Two years ago, in another fit of jealousy, I tried desperately to break myself of what seemed more than a schoolgirl infatuation. I decided that I needed the society of men so I "gave myself" perfectly deliberately to a man several years older, thinking that by that one act my whole outlook would change. Of course it didn't. I never gave my theory a fair chance to work, because I never repeated this experiment. On the other hand, X herself "came around" exactly as might have been expected. In the years I have known her I have learned that she always behaves along the most elementary emotional lines, but I rarely have the will power or the heart to turn this to my own advantage.

In the three years since college I have met several men who have seemed to be attracted by me, but none of the type that could really help me. They were usually ten to fifteen years older, brilliant, artistic, heavy drinkers, and promiscuous with women. There has not been for one minute a man whose company I have preferred to that of X.

We are congenial in every sense: the same tastes—athletics, books, music. By now we have almost a code of language—bywords and phrases that have come to mean one thing or another to us and are perfectly unintelligible to anyone else.

I am really looking forward to marriage—with my mind. But I can't forget X long enough to react normally to such men's society as I do have. And I don't really want to except that I don't feel that this can continue forever.

I've tried to write this dispassionately. But it is a fact that my feeling for this girl is no crush. This is the seventh year I've known her and I love her more each year. There hasn't been one day in the seven years when I haven't thought of her.

Can you suggest a cure? Or will you tell me that this must come from "within myself"? There is nothing within myself that can tear me away from her except a very small voice that tells me that I want a home and husband and children. But the prospect of a home without her is heartwrenching. And I would like my children to be very much like her. Is this outrageous? What *can* be done if a person happens to fall in love for once in her life, and with a person of the same sex? Or do you think that seven years is only a little time?

1. Radclyffe Hall's famous book had been published in London by Jonathan Cape in 1928.

I'm afraid this is a very difficult and unpleasant letter to read. I wish I could have typed it so it would at least be legible.

I enclose a stamped addressed envelope, and trust you will reply at your convenience.

Very truly yours,

Dec. 9, 1931

My dear Miss:

I am very sorry that I have been so tardy in replying to your letter, because I think your problem is a very important one, but my correspondence has been a little bit beyond me.

Since you are familiar, as you say, with the general nature of homosexual attachment between girls and have read such books as *The Well of Loneliness*, I do [not] need to explain to you that your problem is a well-known one, a very common one, and a very perplexing one. Society, of course, regards it with extreme moral disapproval but with this point of view science has little sympathy. The serious drawback from the scientific point of view is that it thwarts the possibility of much greater happiness which is only possible through the fulfillment of the biologically and psychologically normal functions.

That you have strong yearnings to lead a more normal and therefore happier life is quite apparent from the various efforts you have made and the psychological struggle which you say you are now experiencing. I must warn you however that the attractiveness of your present situation is probably more powerful than you recognize. I should think the greatest obstacle in helping you to be happier is that you think you are happy enough already and that anything else would be misery. In other words, although you know intellectually that sooner or later you are bound to suffer exquisitely, in fact more terribly than you suffered while in college which you say you wouldn't live through again for the world, unfortunately in spite of this I think the greatest obstacle in helping you is the fact that you don't altogether want to be helped.

Of course I hope I am wrong about this and I hope you will find it easy to carry out the purposes of your intelligence and your better judgment but I think it is only fair to warn you of my fear that you will put stumbling blocks in your own way. I am quite certain that you cannot do it alone. You will have to have professional help. Now if you are in a position to take advantage of psychiatric or psychoanalytic help, which fortunately is easily available to you in New York City, I shall be glad to make some suggestions as to whom you might see if you do not already know of one. But that you should see a psychiatrist and put the whole problem before him or her, I think there can be no two opinions. Personally, I strongly favor psychoanalysis as a method of therapy but some psychiatrists prefer to use other methods and do so successfully. That, too, I shall leave to your preference.

Sincerely yours,

2.

Depression and Anxiety

New Orleans, La.
Oct. 23, 1930

Dear Sir:

I have just finished reading your article on "Mental Hygiene" in the *Ladies' Home Journal.* My case may not come within your jurisdiction yet l am hoping you can help me some way.

I am a young woman of 23 years. I married one year ago. On the 20th of August 1930 my husband disappeared. The night before he left he told me that I was not like he thought I would be—that I was pessimistic. That may or may not be what he meant to say. Anyway it has left me in a terrible state of mind. I can't seem to get a new lease on life. It is all I can do to keep from ending it all. Beyond leaving one with a terrible sense of loss—I have a terrible inferiority complex, combined with inertia and indifference to everything. I have tried coming to a new place to live—I have tried everything, but nothing helps. I am on night duty here at the Y.W.C.A. and of course it is confining. I try to get out for an hour or two each day in order to get some fresh air.

I just can't seem to get myself out of this terrible state I am in. Would going back to the place we lived help? What must I do? I feel so sordid. I feel soiled—another ex-wife—among the many—broken dreams—cut off from friends—because in my sensitiveness I hate to be pitied so I came away. Please try to help me if you think you can because unless help comes from some source, I feel like I shant be able to keep on living. Can you suggest anything? I have lost my ambition. Everything seems useless. I will appreciate anything you can do for me.

Sincerely,

Nov. 5, 1930

My dear Miss:

I have just received your letter of October 23 addressed to me in care of the *Ladies' Home Journal* and am very glad indeed that you wrote me.

I can fully understand the state of depression and despair in which you find yourself. It is, as you say, a mixture of emotions. Some of these emotions, however, I think could easily be eliminated. Let us look carefully into the problem.

In the first place I am impressed by the fact that in your entire letter you do not once say that you love your husband or that you ever did. If he left you so suddenly, I am quite sure that there was some unhappiness before he left. You say nothing about this. While it seems to me to be a cruel way to do it, perhaps your husband thought that he was leaving you in the kindest way possible. What I mean is, he may have thought that by breaking off suddenly without any anguish of gradual separation he would be doing both you and himself a kindness. He may have been right. It may be much better for both of you to be separated, particularly if you don't really love each other, as some things in your letter lead me to believe.

Even if I am wrong about that, however, let me point out some other things to you. You say frankly that you are suffering mostly from a sense of loss and a feeling of inferiority that something must be wrong about you. Both of these are very selfish things, aren't they? What I mean is that you indicate that you are thinking how you have been injured because it is your self-love that is hurt, not your love for someone else. This is further borne out by your great sensitiveness about having been deserted. It is not a matter for sensitiveness; it is a matter to look at very frankly. If you were partly responsible, I would try to change myself in those respects so that I would be a better wife next time for there is certain to be a next time in your life. If it was entirely his fault I think I should take the position that it was good riddance and that I was glad to be freed if I was tied up to that sort of man.

I can't understand the reason you should feel sordid and soiled as you call it. Perhaps that comes from the wrong attitude toward sex on your part. I don't know just what your attitude is and if you were here I should talk that over with you in considerable detail. It may have had a great deal to do with your marital unhappiness. But it is certainly wrong of you to consider yourself soiled. It is quite natural for you to be depressed and upset by this thing but I feel sure you can get on your feet if you will examine yourself a little bit and think about your problem with your intellect instead of feeling about it with your emotions so keenly. Then I should certainly take a little diversion. If it is books you like best, read as much as you can. If you like movies, or even if you don't like them very much, go to all the good ones.

And now that you are in New Orleans, you are in the most wonderful place in the world for good food and even if you do not have much appetite for it, we all have to eat and you might as well amuse yourself by interest in eating.

I wish you would write me again and tell me how you react to these suggestions. I am sure you will find changes taking place in yourself and I think we can help you over this hard time and it ought to make a better woman of you than ever before.

Sincerely yours,

Mantanzas, Cuba
Oct. 23, 1930

Dear Sir:

I am a reader of the *Ladies' Home Journal* in Cuba. I know a little English and I'm always interested in the beautiful readings of the charming review of the journal. On page 101, the issue of November, is your very interesting article, "Mental Hygiene in the Home." How good that is! How needful are we, the Cuban girls, of that kind of hygiene. How needful I am, Dr. Menninger! That's my problem. I must be happy, for I'm rather young, only 24 years old, I'm pretty and sweet and tender, have my parents alive, six brothers, I've a very nice sweetheart, I'm a teacher and that lets me earn my living. However I'm not as happy as people expect I am.

What's the reason of my unhappiness? I think it is I have a machine instead of a brain. I'm always thinking and thinking of all things: house, school, marriage. I can not amuse myself, for these three things occupy all my thoughts and my whole life.

How can I get rid of these things at least for five minutes? Can you give me some advices? Can you tell me how can I be happy and laugh at the life as other girls do?

Pardon me, for I've been too extensive, and excuse me all the mistakes I've writing in the beautiful language of Shakespeare. Can you understand my English? Oh! that English that have cost my parents so many sacrifices. Eight years at an American school.

Good bye, Dr. Menninger. Please answer me as soon as you can. Tell me all you think I must do in order to be happy, to be gay as I wish.

Thanks you very much.
Sincerely yours,

Dec. 9, 1930

My dear Miss:

I think your letter is a very beautiful one, and so I have printed it all, as you see. You need not worry about the little mistakes in English; there are not many, and our readers will love your clear, simple, honest way of writing, so different from our conventionally evasive speech. And they will, at least thoughtful ones, sympathize with you in your very familiar kind of unhappiness.

Your letter sounds to me as if it were written by a very healthy-minded girl, one who has looked kindly and gratefully at life, one who appreciated things and was glad for her opportunities, one not burdened by false modesty or enviousness or malice. Perhaps a bit too serious, too hard-pressed by the hard realities of life, somewhat torn by the conflicts of many criss-crossing necessities. But these, Maria, are the burdens of a civilization that forces us all along faster than we can travel.

The things which fill your mind so incessantly . . . "home, school, marriage" . . . home, work, love . . . these are what life is made of. No wonder you think of them constantly; so does anyone else who thinks about what he is doing (as many do not). But I know what you mean. You mean you want to be able to play, sometimes, to quit living for a spell and just "laugh at the life." So do we all, Maria. And it's fine thing to do; after we have looked at it and laughed at it we can go back and live it better. I had a teacher once who called it "washing the mind." He played chess to wash his mind, he said.[1]

It's a thing one learns, partly . . . and perhaps some of it is temperamental, whatever that means. Anyway some learn to do it ever so much better than others. Life has been hard for you . . . strenuous . . . serious. I can read that between the lines. It will take you a little while to realize that you have reached a point now where you need not press on quite so fervidly, quite so anxiously. You have, as you say, happy prospects, soon to be more completely realized. Perhaps when your "very nice sweetheart" has made you his wife you will feel a little less tense, a little more contented, and even "for only five minutes" gay. I think so.

Do you know that your problem is the problem of most Americans, Maria? Most of us haven't learned to play, at least not with any grace. When you were here in school you saw the immense palaces erected to the pursuit of joy. You saw hundreds of millions of dollars invested in places in which to dance and in places in which to see moving pictures, and in places in which to play. All this for people who want to be gay, who want to stop thinking about home, work, and love, and just play. Some can find it in books, and some in golf and some in chatting with friends and some in movie palaces; some find it only in alcohol and some never find it at all.

I think you can learn to play, to be gay and laugh at life, but with your earnest, serious, honest heart you may always find it a bit hard to forget the

---

1. Elmer Ernest Southard, Menninger's mentor at Harvard.

world or stand very long outside of it. You know too well its bitternesses, its tragedies, its disappointments, its rigorous demands upon us. That seems to be part of the heritage of civilization which came to us along with "the beautiful language of Shakespeare," and may I add, the beautiful language of Cervantes, El Greco.

Perhaps, in your American school, you discovered a poet (Wordsworth) who wrote about your problem this way:

> The world is too much with us; late and soon,
> Getting and spending, we lay waste our powers:
> Little we see in Nature that is ours;
> We have given our hearts away, a sordid boon!
> This Sea that bares her bosom to the moon;
> The winds that will be howling at all hours,
> And are up-gathered now like sleeping flowers;
> For this, for everything, we are out of tune;
> It moves us not.—Great God! I'd rather be
> A Pagan suckled in a creed outworn;
> So might I, standing on this pleasant lea,
> Have glimpses that would make me less forlorn;
> Have sight of Proteus rising from the sea;
> Or hear old Triton blow his wreathèd horn.

Sincerely yours,

Florida
Oct. 24, 1930

Dear Karl Menninger:

Have read your articles in *Ladies' Home Journal* and was specially interested in the last one. I wonder if you can help me. I've been unhappy so much and I seem to be a misfit in life somehow.

I was born of middle-aged parents 38 years ago. I was a timid, shrinking child. My father was a retired minister—an old-fashioned kind—intolerant and very unreasonable. My mother feared him, as I did. As a child I was happy enough. I had a few girl playmates—never boys. I have never understood the relations of men and women and was always taught to keep away from boys. When I entered the teens I began to want some social life as other girls had, to go out occasionally at night. It was not allowed because I might meet boys. My father taunted me, sarcastically, with being crazy to go with the boys, etc. All innocent pleasures appeared to him to be invested with some "ulterior motive." I was allowed not quite two years of high school. We lived in the country and mother was sick so I must quit and do all the work. This nearly broke my heart. For many years I was secretly rebellious because of this. It was my only contact with the world. Then mother died—I was 16 at the time—and for four lonely years I kept house for father. In my dreams yet the loneliness comes back to me. Bitter and rebellious, yet never daring to show it, I hoped on and on that somewhere, sometime I would have the good times that other girls had—have beaus and go places, laugh and be carefree. I had 2 or 3 girl friends who came to see me now and then when there was nothing better to do. I often cried at night but I took refuge in a dream world and hoped that some day my dreams might come true. Then I met and married an older man just to get away from it all. I never cared for him. He was *good* enough but commonplace and not ambitious. In a year the boy was born. Twelve years I lived with him before getting up nerve enough to leave. I had taken up a trade and worked for several years. I have a lot of pride and I hated the debts and penny-pinching and I hoped to get some new clothes. And still I had my dreams. But not happiness. I thought if I were free I could still have my chance at a few wholesome good times. Four years, and more, I have been alone, with the boy of course, and the good times are farther away than ever. I work hard to support us, for the father works only a small part of the time and does not help us. I have not seen him for four years and I never want to see him. I have my divorce but I am not happy. I am old and tired. When I leave my shop I come home to our small apartment, and cook and wash and iron and sweep etc. that my boy may go with the crowd. He is my one compensation and yet we are not close together and I don't know why. He is very popular and has many friends, both young and old. He is kind and agreeable. I suppose I should ask nothing else of life. I try not to but I work so hard and have no play. All my life long I have longed and yearned to wear an evening dress and go to a dance with a man who would know how to act at a dance (my husband never would and I was always more or less ashamed of him). There are dances around here, small affairs at the Yacht Club etc. but there are no men here (single) and there are many single women. Anyway, I couldn't afford an evening dress. My son must have clothes and he goes to all the young folks' dances. Even if there were men here I have never appealed to men. I don't seem to know how to act with them, I have been so shielded from them. I think I must be emotionally unbalanced. It isn't that I want to get married. I want to play around a bit, as I said before, and have a good time. Why can't I give up this foolish notion and just grow old gracefully and find pleasure in my son's pleasures! I often hear my acquaintances talk of their girlhood and their good times and their beaus, etc. It makes me so bitter because I cannot say one word. I have nothing to tell. I am a woman's woman. They seem to like me tho' I don't make friends quickly. But I don't understand men or they me. I am not strong and I so often work beyond my strength. And all days are alike, all years alike. I am beginning to realize now that my dreams will never come true—and I don't dream much anymore. But I am still bitter and I often cry into the night. I could go out occasionally with a few gabbling gossipy old maids whom I know but somehow they bore me. I know people think I am "queer." My mother always reminded me that I was "queer." I have no pleasant memory of my youth or of my parents. My father died shortly after I married. I've brought my boy up differently and, I'm sure, more successfully. He is not afraid of me even tho' he doesn't quite understand me.

I get quite morbid sometimes and I believe if it wasn't for him I would find a way out of life. I am *very* emotional. I never can speak of anything that seems pathetic to me because I cannot control my voice. I cry very easily. I weigh less than I ever have since I am grown—116. And I am 5 ft. 7½ inches in height and large-boned and awkward. This has always been a source of humiliation to me for even if I had nice clothes they wouldn't look well on me.

I have written to so-called psychologists a time or two and they say don't do this or that and think thus and so. That is easy to say. I have been as I am for nearly 25 years. I cannot say "I will change myself" and so change. I am not a good business woman because of my early life and impressions. I was never allowed any contact with the world and I am still timid, still afraid I am not doing the right thing, etc. Not so much so as I used to be but still fearful. Everything is so hard for me. Nothing comes easy. Even when I pray it is always in agony. Why can't I "let loose" and just live! So many people bore me so. I am always waiting and watching for something to happen to me—something worthwhile. Twenty-five years I have waited and in vain. I don't believe now that I will ever be happy. I am always uncertain. I never know what is best to do. I guess I just didn't get started out right and now it's too late. My life seems so empty. I cannot speak about my past to anyone. It is not pleasant and I do not care to recall it. Somehow it has made me abnormal. I've never been very close to anyone and the older I get the more I withdraw into myself. I don't want anyone to see the queer creature that I really am. I have moods of course. Occasionally I am hilarious for a brief time, then I go to the depths again, then I go along awhile dull and listless.

Pardon my lengthy letter. You may laugh at it and I will not know but it helps sometimes just to be able to tell things. I think it is too late to really help. I thank you.

Sincerely,

Nov. 6, 1930

My dear Mrs.:

I have read very carefully your long letter of October 24 addressed to me in care of the *Ladies' Home Journal*. I want to reassure you that I certainly did not laugh at it as you suggested I might. I think anyone with any heart at all could not help but be very sympathetic with the pathos of it. Because obviously, as you may know, you have had a very tragic life. Life at best is hard; no one is justified in being as happy as they are probably, but you have even fewer illusions and fewer justifications for happy moments than the average.

I think it must have been some help to you to put it down in this fashion and talk it out to me. It gave you an opportunity of looking at yourself somewhat more objectively. That is usually a help. You don't like to talk about it, you say, you don't care to recall it and yet it is sometimes a good thing to do so in just such a way as you have done in this letter.

Considering the way in which you were treated by your father and by your mother's illness, we cannot really be very much surprised at your life, can we? Because it is surely very natural and logical that you should have become embittered at them, your father because of his attitude toward you, your mother because she interrupted the one opportunity that you had had thus far in life to transfer your interests from yourself and your home into representatives of the outside world. This bitterness has never had an opportunity to leave your heart. The proper kind of a love affair might have done it for you; a psychoanalytic washing of your mind might have done it for you. But you didn't get the right kind of a love affair, partly because of the pressure under which you made your selection, I think, and you probably cannot afford either the time or the money for psychoanalysis.

But let us look at some of the hopeful aspects of the matter. In the first place, you have backbone. If you didn't have, you would not have left your husband when you finally made up your mind that he was not the satisfaction to you that you had hoped for. It takes guts to do that and you evidently have them. It takes guts, if you will pardon my using the familiar American word, to run your own shop as well as your own home, raise a son and do the work for him as well as yourself and create for him an opportunity better than your own. It is not quite clear to me why you are not quite satisfied with your relations with your son. You say you are not close together. I imagine you are close enough. Remember that it was because your father held you so close to him that your own life was ruined. You will have to be very philosophical and comfort yourself with the idea that while he may not be as dependent upon you as you might like, it is probably much better for his future. I think this thought will make you a little happier.

As for your wanting to go to dances, etc., most of that is just fantasy. Dances are just as boresome as most of the rest of things in life if one feels a bit worn down at the bone as you have been. It would be difficult. I can suggest a very much better emotional outlet for you than this particular fantasy. Instead of imagining yourself going to a dance and having a good time with the other girls, why not substitute an illusion which you can more easily acquire? I mean you can surely afford the indulgence of an occasional moving picture show, and there is a vast world of books in which many people lose themselves with a greater happiness than any of the real things of life would ever have given them. You didn't mention anything about books in your letter and I am quite certain from your literary style that you would be capable of enjoying them greatly. Are you familiar, for example, with Goethe's *Faust*? If not get it and read it. Read *Of Human Bondage* by Somerset Maugham, and *The Brothers Karamazov* by Dostoievski. Read Dickens' books. I think you could have a great deal of vicarious pleasure in this way that you are denying yourself at present, because you are wasting your energy in imagining pleasure in a thing in which you would find nothing but boredom and emptiness once you had the opportunity. It is like someone sitting by a brook at the foot of a mountain and fancying that it would be lovely if one could be on the other side of the mountain or on top of the mountain. When you got there you would find that it was only rocks, and scenery very much like that which now surrounds you, seen from another angle. All the time there is a brook right by your side. I feel that way about books and movies. I think books and movies are a necessity and not a luxury. I think you ought to try to lose yourself in them. They are one of the ways in which life is made tolerable for us.

Finally, let me refer to the matter that your mother and others think you are queer. You must remember that they think most everyone is queer. If you have happened to see my book *The Human Mind* you will remember that I pointed out in there that there is really no such thing as a normal person but it is always the other fellow who appears queer. The reason you know yourself to be queer is that you are somewhat more intelligent than the average and more introspective.

Won't you please write and tell me how you feel about things after you have read this letter and thought about it a while and put into operation some of the suggestions?

Sincerely yours,

Missouri
Nov. 15, 1930

Dear Sir,

I am coming to you with my own mental problem, whether it is based on a bodily ailment I do not know, anyway I think my problem is one commonly known as "nerves."

I am twenty eight years old, the wife of a farmer in very moderate circumstances and the mother of four children.

My first mental trouble came upon me when I was sixteen years old. After a busy day I went to bed, only to experience a feeling that I had never had before, that of a great oppression coming over me; I could not get my breath and I thought I was dying. I rushed to my parents' bedroom in great fear and tried to explain to them what I was going through. Then I was afraid to go to sleep for fear I would die. The next morning I had a headache and temperature and suffered an attack of the "flu." That was the year during the war when influenza was so prevalent.

After I was well again I resumed my high school work, but that awful fear came over me when I went to bed at night. Some of the same sensations came over me. No one whom I told seemed to understand me. So my nights were horrors and my days came to be days of brooding. I dreaded to be by myself for my thoughts seemed to always turn toward that "something the matter with me." I constantly sought something to take my mind off of my troubles, somewhere to go or something to do. I was a rather high-strung child, my parents always said, my father was on that order, too. I had diseased tonsils which were removed just a few months before the occurrence which I have already mentioned.

I gradually overcame my trouble within the next few years. At the age of twenty I married. When I was twenty-one my first child was born. Then by the time three years and eight months had elapsed I had had my fourth child.

When my second baby was four months old I again had a similar experience to that of my girlhood. Lying in bed one night I thought I was dying. Then after that sensation was over, everything seemed blurred to me, that is, my senses were dulled, my head having great pressure in it, a horrible depression came over me, and I decided then that I must be losing my mind or having something happening to it. I went into hysterics one day and the doctor was called. He told me it was just my "nerves" and not to worry. He told me also that I had a simple goiter.

It took me a year to gain much strength and I had that feeling that there was something the matter with me and I was different from others. I was so afraid I would not be right.

My husband was not very sympathetic with me. I realize he did not understand my trouble. Every winter since I have had more or less trouble in the same manner. Every once in a while I have one of those sinking, swimming, "falling away" sensations but I try not to let them frighten me.

Last winter I became so depressed one night that I went into hysterics. Then for a couple of months I was dull and depressed. Horrible thoughts entered my mind. I was afraid I might lose control of myself and harm someone. At times my spirits would rise and I would be happy.

Now this winter I am threatened again with thoughts which come without my bidding and almost paralyze me. I have a sharp pain in the region of my goiter at times, and often a feeling as if I had something tied around my neck. I am also constipated most of the time.

It is my desire to make a happy home and rear good Christian children. But I do not seem to be able to handle children right, and they quarrel so, which only upsets me and makes me nervous and weak. I suffer far more in a way than I did a few years ago. I like beauty, neatness and order in my home and it is not possible. That frets me. I work hard, do every bit of the housework and laundering and help my husband when he needs me, out-of-doors.

I teach a Sunday school class and am the president of the Neighborhood Club. I like to do these things, but so often I find myself dull and weary, irritable and cross. I feel that my life needs adjustment. I want to learn to know the true values of life.

For years I felt that my marriage was unsatisfactory for all my friends were starting professional work, while I was drudging away bearing children too fast and working too hard, worrying and fretting, with it. My disposition changed from one which was seldom ruffled outwardly to a "crosspatch."

I am getting away from some of those old ideas and now I want a set of mental hygiene rules which will help me to be happy. I know happiness is in the reach of all, but I do not seem to know how to find it.

May the Lord greatly enrich you if you can help me.

Yours truly,

Dec. 12, 1930

My dear Mrs.:

Your letter of November 15 addressed to me in care of the *Ladies' Home Journal* has been carefully read.

From your description I should say that there is not very much doubt about the type of trouble from which you suffer. Your description is almost classically that of the nervous disease which we know as anxiety neurosis.

Now that I have told you the name of it I don't know that I have helped you very much. You may want to read about it; I have written about it myself in my book called *The Human Mind* which is about the mind and its afflictions and which I think you might enjoy reading.

The particular things that you ought to know about your trouble are these. In the first place, you will never die in one of these attacks, terrible as they seem at times. You will be amused at the story about the policeman in my book on page 251, who was not afraid of anything in the world and yet used to get so frightened at nothing at all. You will not die, you will probably not do anything horrible either to yourself or to anyone else, you will not lose your mind. But you will suffer the tortures of the damned. Nothing is more distressing than this sense of anxiety and fear which is so typical of these attacks or panics.

They are caused by disturbances in the depths of the mind, the part which is known as the subconscious or unconscious part of the mind. A good deal can be done by a skilled specialist in the way of eradicating the cause of them. But you do not live anywhere near a good psychoanalyst and if you can possibly get along without taking treatments I know you want to do so. I think perhaps my reassurance that nothing terrible will come of them, in spite of the way you feel, will help you some and then I also want to make another suggestion which is rather difficult to make clear in a letter but which I shall attempt. In some instances these attacks come because of the lack of satisfaction in the sexual life. You did not mention anything about this in your letter and of course I know nothing about it in your particular instance. Sometimes, however, it is very helpful for the husband to talk this over very frankly with a doctor and get him to help you both to arrange your sexual life in such a way that it gives you complete satisfaction if possible. Some husbands do not realize how important it is for their wife's health. They are apt to be so engrossed in their own satisfaction that they forget their wives. This is not due to unkindness or meanness on their part but usually due to a lack of understanding. I think, perhaps, if your husband had his attention called to it and perhaps had a little help in the matter, it would do you both a great deal of good. There are a number of books discussing such things; I often refer people to some books by Dr. Robie; next time you are in Kansas City stop in to a second hand bookstore and any book by Dr. Robie is a good one. I believe one of them is called *Rational Sex Ethics* and another one is called *Love and Life*[1] or

---

1. Menninger has conflated the titles of two of Walter Franklin Robie's books, *Sex and Life: What the Experienced Should Teach and What the Inexperienced Should Learn* (Boston: Richard G. Badger, 1924) and *The Art of Love* (Boston: Richard G. Badger, 1921).

something of the sort. I don't remember just the titles but the books all deal in general with the same thing. Most sex books are not very satisfactory in their discussion of it. Of course, I have taken a long shot in the dark because I don't know whether this applies in your case but it does in some.

May I add a final word about your children. All children quarrel; it is a part of the battle of life on a small scale. They have to learn the technique of fighting as well as other forms of life. Don't be too disturbed about it. I think it might reassure you and help you a little to read some of the books on child culture which are now so numerous. Particularly one by Garry Myers called *The Modern Parent* and one which Mr. Crawford and I have edited called *The Healthy-Minded Child*.[2] If I can find one I will enclose a circular describing it.

Sincerely yours,

Syracuse, N.Y.
Nov. 21, 1930

Dear Doctor Menninger,

I read your articles in the *Home Journal* and enjoy them, and as goodness knows I am a mental misfit or something thought I would write you. Hardly know how to tell you my feelings now that I have started to write however.

To begin with, I think I must have a terrible inferiority complex as I can't see a thing in the world about myself that is right, and I am about to worry myself crazy over getting old. I am thirty-three years old and people say I am nice looking, but all I can see every time I look in the mirror is a face that is getting older and tired looking. Oh yes, Doctor, I will tell you why perhaps getting old is so dreadful to me. I am married to a young man seven years younger than myself, have been married three years and very happily, but I worry constantly about the difference in our ages, and for fear he will fall in love with some young girl. When I am out in public all I do is look at the young faces all around and think to myself that there is the one my husband should have married. He is grand to me, but it seems that when we are in company of younger women he is not so tender to me, like perhaps he is sorry he is married to me or a little ashamed of me. Doctor, you have no idea how I feel, really sometimes I think of suicide, yet I know hundreds of people that would be glad to exchange places with me. My husband is so considerate of me and all, especially so when we are alone

---

2. Gary C. Myers, *The Modern Parent: A Practical Guide to Everyday Problems* (New York: Greenberg, 1930); Nelson Antrim Crawford and Karl A. Menninger, eds., *The Healthy-Minded Child* (New York: Coward-McCann, 1930). Menninger in these letters consistently misspelled Myers's first name.

or with older people. I expect you will consider this the silliest letter you have ever gotten but I cannot help it. I do so want to talk to someone and have no one to talk to. I would not dare breathe these things to any of my friends. And, Doctor, I want to ask your advice on the subject of face lifting. Do you think it is practical and does it really make one look younger, or do you consider it dangerous? My husband would be quite willing I had it done provided I could find someone reputable, but we are strangers in this part of the country and how would I go about finding a good plastic surgeon say in New York City? I know one in Chicago that I would trust; however he is so far away. I do not suppose you would recommend one, but if you could please tell me to whom I could write for this information I would be very grateful. Doctor, I will be very glad if you will write me and perhaps help me to adjust myself. I am blue and depressed nearly all the time. Thanking you in advance, I beg to remain,

Your truly,

Dec. 19, 1930

My dear Mrs.:

I have read with a great deal of interest your letter of November 21 which you thought was so silly. I don't think it is silly at all. I think it indicates some wrong thinking on your part in places, but I think it was very sensible of you to write to me as frankly about it as you did.

In the first place let me express my feeling that you are doing everything you can to bring about the thing you fear. You say you are afraid you will become unattractive and that your husband will like someone younger and so you are worrying yourself into a very fine state of unattractiveness. It is a curious thing how people do that but they do it. They do the very thing and bring on the very thing they say they are afraid will happen.

I think you ought to remember that the chief thing a man wants in a woman is not beauty and youth but the things that beauty and youth represent, namely, cheerfulness and happiness. If you could be cheerful and happy and gay and encouraging and reassuring and peaceful with your husband, you are going to have him until Judgment Day. But if you are gloomy and anxious and weary and anxious about your looks and talking about having your face lifted and all that sort of trash, you are going to lose him. He will put up with it for a while, and love you in spite of it, but ultimately it is going to bore him to death and he is going to hunt for someone else. Now you had better make up your mind right now to cut it out.

That is precisely what I would say if I were talking to you and so I shall say it in writing and hope it will not sound too severe. Get over your enviousness of younger people. You were young once and had your chance. You are still young for that matter. You feel a little guilty about the fact that your husband is younger than you. You shouldn't feel guilty about it. It was his choice as much as yours. For some psychological reason or other he preferred someone a little older than himself. Well, that's your good luck and his too. So call it quits. If I were you, I would forget about this face lifting business. It may be all right, I don't know. But I do know that it isn't alone your face that your husband loves.

Sincerely yours,

Wyoming
May 20, 1931

Dear Dr. Menninger:

I have read your book *The Human Mind* and I liked it very much. I have also followed your page in the *Journal* with great interest, so I wonder if you can help me. I don't know just what is the matter but I think it is a fear complex. I am afraid of life and living and I just can't seem to "kid" myself out of it. Maybe if I could write the same way I would talk to you I could make you understand, but heaven knows I can't see why I should be afraid of things. I am twenty one years old and have been married for nearly three years. My husband is a man over ten years older than I and he is just wonderful. I love him more than I can say. He is the father I never knew, the big brother I always longed for, the friend I never found, he even takes the place of my mother. I tell him my troubles and know I will find comfort, and I know he will understand. But there is where the greatest fear of all comes in. I have made my husband so absolutely necessary to me that I am constantly worried for fear something will take him away from me.

He is in fair health and ranch work is not usually thought of as dangerous, yet in the back of my mind is always the fear that he will die. Horrible, isn't it? You see I am so terribly alone. My father died when I was a few months old and Mother, a brilliant tho somewhat erratic woman, went back to her career. I was raised by a family rather than a parent, and I think I missed quite a lot. A few months with this aunt, a few with another, a visit to Mother where I was cared for by a hired woman, a little while with my grandmother and then back around the circle again. Mother remarried when I was six, but my step-father didn't care for me and I was terribly afraid of him, so it didn't help toward giving me a permanent home. When I was older I went to boarding schools in the winters and spent the summers with one or more of my relatives. I think I never really cared for anyone until I met my husband. I mean, I never put anyone else before myself.

I hate to say it, but while I thought a lot of my people, I couldn't feel I belonged to anyone or that they belonged to me. I was outside of all their lives. Death visited many times in the last few years. Now I have only two little half sisters and a half brother who live with their father, and an aunt who is a long way away. So my husband takes all their places.

I don't know when I began to be afraid, but I think I've always been a little. I was always afraid to make friends and to chum with people for fear I would be hurt somehow. Subconsciously I never let myself care too much about anything or anybody. If anyone began to mean too much to me, I would try to get over it by thinking of someone else, and usually it worked. I didn't even care a lot for my husband when I married him. It was more for a home than anything else, but being with him constantly made me learn to love him more than I thought it possible. I don't trust other people. I expect them to hurt me some way, but I know he won't and so I am afraid some outside influence will.

And now comes the part that I can't explain but which is the worst phase of it all. These are only the facts—I will leave you to find the true motives, tho I think perhaps it is more or less of a defence against the hurt I am afraid of. Recently I had a tempestuous flirtation with another man. He is a wonderful man and really cares for me, but I *knew* all the time he could never mean to me what my husband does. Yet I tried to make myself care. That is, while one half of me rebelled in horror, the other half tried to care. I only succeeded in hurting my husband, the other man and myself because I had hurt them. Why did I do it? I told my husband the facts, and tried to make him understand, but how could I *make him see what I couldn't understand myself?* He was marvelous about it all. But I know he thinks I must have cared for the other one a little bit to have done what I did.

My husband says perhaps you should know something about my environment prior to my marriage. I have described the way I was raised but not the various types surrounding me. Mother was a very brilliant but also rather erratic woman. Terribly nervous, high strung and impulsive, she kept herself and everyone around her in constant irritation. One of my aunts, the one who is living, is a strong-willed, dominating stern woman, kindly, in her way, but wishing to run others' lives to suit herself. The other aunt was a gentle, timid soul, afraid of being hurt and more afraid of hurting others. My uncle, the only man with whom I came into contact to any extent, is a kind, very good man, but who does not understand others' weaknesses. Because he is not[1] tempted to do things he cannot tolerate

---

1. Menninger has added in the margin "Because he *is!*" and at the top of the letter: "Electra with guilt/death wishes/need for punishment."

those who are. My grandmother was wonderful—and quite normal. I think I was happiest with her, but she died when I was fourteen. The only young companionship I had was a boy cousin, seven years my senior. Does that help you to see why I have this complex?

I do hope you can help me. It is terrible to feel so afraid of everything. Death for myself, holds no terror. In fact it sometimes seems rather to be wanted, but death for E., my husband, keeps me worried all the time.

I have thought that children might be the solution, but they are a physical impossibility, and our financial condition is not secure enough for us to adopt one now. Maybe if I were in a city where I could find work or something to keep me occupied I would be better, but the nearest town is over seven miles away and the nearest neighbor over three miles from here. I forgot to say that I was city bred and that ranching was a new, and not altogether enjoyable thing for me.

Please forgive me for taking up so much of your time, but I wanted to give you a clear picture of everything in order that you might help me to find the reason.

Thanking you more than I can say, in advance. I remain,

Very truly yours,

Jul. 6, 1931

My dear Mrs.:

I have read with a great deal of interest your letter of May 20th addressed to me in care of the *Ladies' Home Journal*.

I have read your letter several times and I think you have made a very true observation when you ask, how could I make my husband understand what I couldn't understand myself? You are quite right, what you have been doing and what you have been feeling have both come from the depths of your own unconscious mind and are quite independent of your conscious intelligence. It is such things as this which convince people most forcefully of the existence of a subconscious or unconscious mind.

Yes there are reasons for what you have done and what you have felt, reasons some of which I can guess but some of which I do not know either and which one could only find out by a very painstaking psychoanalytic delving into the troubled depths of your mind.

Your fears lest your husband die remind me of a story which Goethe tells of a king who was entertaining a wise visitor from another country. While they were talking on the roof of the king's palace, a messenger kept running to the king to announce a new piece of good fortune, the armies had been victorious, the fleets had come in with treasure, an heir had been born, etc. and so on. I can't remember the exact wording of the story but the upshot of it is that the stranger looks troubled and tells the king that it is bad news to have so much good news, that the gods cannot tolerate a human being having so much good fortune. Accordingly, the king takes from his finger his beautiful jeweled ring of great value and tosses it far out into the sea.

The point is that your letter rather suggests that you feel as if you had too much good fortune, as if your happy marriage was too good to be true, accordingly you feel compelled to either imagine or to do something which will to some extent counteract this happiness. It seems very perverse, doesn't it, but it is very human and natural and typical.

So much for a general explanation. I know that what you want is some very practical advice. I do not think any few words of mine are going to make any very considerable difference. I think you can readjust yourself possibly temporarily, but I think your childhood experiences have brought about an instability of your emotions which really deserve rather serious professional consideration.

Frankly, if I were you I should want to get rid of the unconscious sense of guilt which makes you want to punish yourself by fearing dreadful things or doing things which get you into trouble and which your real personality does not want. That would require professional assistance; I think it requires psychoanalytic treatment. Naturally you cannot get this out in Wyoming and I do not know whether it would be possible for you to go east but I think the fact that you have no children might make it a little easier for you to do so than if you were cumbered with several children and other housewifely tasks as so many women in the same predicament are. I strongly recommend it to you however and it is for you to make a decision. I quite agree with you that until you get it straightened out it would not be wise for you to have children.

I have hesitated to recommend a book to you but I think I shall do so trusting to your intelligence to understand that the title has nothing to do with your case. You will find the principles of this sense of guilt discussed at considerable length in a book by Franz Alexander called *The Criminal, the Judge and the Public*[1] recently published by MacMillan. Please understand that I do not regard you as a criminal.

Sincerely yours,

---

1. Franz Alexander and Hugo Staub, *The Criminal, the Judge, and the Public*, trans. Gregory Zilboorg (New York: Macmillan, 1931).

3.

Unconscious Hostility

Norfolk, Va.
Sept. 25, 1930

My dear Doctor Menninger:

After reading your splendid article on "Mental Hygiene in the Home" appearing in the late edition of the *Ladies' Home Journal*, I decided to write immediately, as I am in dire need of assistance, consequently this letter is in the nature of an urgent S.O.S.

Our family consists of my husband, a splendid man—in most respects— forty-three years of age, my small daughter, six years of age, and myself, thirty-four years of age. Both my husband and myself have a fairly good education, he having held, for the past eleven years, a managerial position with a chain store, which is more position than salary; tho we have sufficient funds to live on comfortably by practicing economy, which I, personally, do not mind in the least, finding it fun to take care of my home and doing all my own work, including laundry and sewing, also helping my husband with his office work and occasionally doing substitute office work for others to help take care of expenses. I was a stenographer before our marriage four months ago. We are both actively engaged in church and Sunday school work and my youngster is enrolled with one or two children's societies in the church. I am not very strong, having undergone four major operations within the last few years, nor is S. A. (the youngster), owing to a chronic heart condition, which, of course, means that a number of games and activities which are enjoyed by normal healthy children are forbidden her; my husband is well physically, except for nervous indigestion, due largely I presume to the sedentary life which he leads. We enjoy no recreations such as movies, dancing, etc. as my husband objects to them, nor do we own a car, consequently outings of this nature are out of the question. My husband is a member of one or two fraternal organizations which he

56

attends. We occasionally have friends in for a game of cards during the evening. Both my husband and I are divorced from our first companions, having married utter cads and rotters, and securing our divorces on the grounds of immorality. We were already divorced when we met some eighteen months ago. My husband never had any children. So much for generalities.

As I stated above, I was, before my marriage, a stenographer, and had rather rough sledding to keep things going for Baby and I, as I had no other source of income. Poor Baby, she has missed so much of the joys of life, having, at best, only the most indifferent care while I was working, the big event of her baby life being to watch for MOTHER to come home, and how I loved her, better than my life; no, for she was my life. She stayed for the most part at a Day Nursery where she was taken care of in an automatic, institutional manner, which naturally had a tendency to develop in her a sort of an automatic spirit of obedience (do I make myself clear?) which fortunately she retains, obeying instantly and unquestioningly any command given her. She is unusually intelligent, reliable and truthful, even in the face of certain punishment, passionately loyal to those whom she loves, friendly and innately dainty, clean and refined. These descriptions are, for the most part, the expressions of others and not the ravings of a mother who is foolishly fond of her own offspring.

Now my husband; he is one of the most upright, honest and honorable men I know, a man of high ideals, cultured and simply fine, but, as I have previously stated, exceedingly nervous, at times morbid and morose, and here comes the trouble which is threatening to shipwreck us. Before our marriage he was apparently very fond of S. A. and seemingly took a great pride in her appearance and accomplishments and was much concerned for her welfare. Now all is changed, everything she does is wrong, every childish misunderstanding with a playmate is her fault, no matter what it is about or where it occurs, if in the home of a playmate, she should have acceded to her playmate's wish as she was a guest, if in her own home, how on earth could she have so far forgotten herself as to offend a guest, if she wants a ten cent toy or a five cent ice cream cone she should realize that money does not grow on trees, if she ventures a kiss or a caress or asks a question she is instantly repelled with a cold stare and a holier-than-thou attitude or told that her face is dirty, or her hands might have disease germs on them so PLEASE do not put them around daddy's neck, if a toy is forgotten and left on the floor or in a chair the storm breaks, and recently her afternoons are spent for the most part putting all her toys out of sight so "Daddy won't fuss." When she sits down she is lolling in her chair, when her little bloomers show she is immodest, when her shoes or clothes wear out it was because she was careless with them, because she cannot sweep and dust furniture and wash and dry dishes and so on and on and on, she is lazy and will not help me with the housework and will never amount to anything. She is barely six and not very strong. If she is ill she is playing for my sympathy, if any crumbs fall on the table cloth her table manners are horrible and repulsive, yet my husband will kiss and caress and play with other little children, and in church or when we have guests he is very attentive to S. A. At first I tried to humor and laugh him out of this attitude, but now if I mention the subject he becomes ill and goes to bed with nervous headache and indigestion and I don't know what to do. Baby is becoming reticent and shy and awkward when in his presence. I try to teach her to love him, but how on earth can you teach a child against their intuitions; I tell her daddy only wants her to be nice because he loves her, she says mother that is funny love or mother why doesn't daddy love me like he does J. or M. or mother why doesn't daddy love me like he used to. Really she is rather nice and not much bother; she keeps her room clean and tidy with only weekly sweeping and dusting by me, she takes care of herself, including bathing, dressing, and shampooing her hair, her teeth and hair are always nicely brushed.

At first I tried inventing excuses to leave them alone together, hoping that her sweetness and his sense of responsibility would unite them. It failed to work. I now invent excuses to keep her out of his sight as much as possible. That too is failing to work. If you can help me I shall be eternally grateful to you, if something is not done soon I do not know what the results will be, for the situation has assumed the proportions of a juggernaut ready to devour our home and every day is simply another endurance test for me. I am sure that both my husband and I are mentally ill, and at the rate we are now traveling in the wrong direction I dread to think what the result will be for S. A. in the future. I adore them both and I know they both adore me, but the very love which should be such a beautiful and shining thing is literally killing me. I not only love them, I take pains to let them know it, to tell them so, to do everything humanly possible for their pleasure and comfort, our home is scrupulously clean, meals are well cooked and served, I keep myself as attractive as possible, I make them know in every way I know to let them know they mean the whole world to me; I "baby" my husband more than I do my child, he requires more of it.

I believe it must be jealousy of baby's father that is at the hidden root of the trouble, but my husband would be indignant at such a suggestion, and surely it is not the sporting thing to take it out on a mere baby. What must I do?

This is a long and I am afraid a boresome letter, but it seemed necessary to give you all the facts if you were to be able to help us. I do not know if your answers are to be given through the magazine or by letter, at any rate

I am inclosing a stamped addressed envelope in the hope that you may be able to answer personally in order that I may receive the letter earlier with your suggestion; if not, I shall scan every issue of the magazine until your answer appears, tho I am afraid by that time all my poise and common sense will be smashed to bits and my endurance test at an ignominious end. Thanking you in advance for any advice which you may be able to give me, I am

Yours very truly,

Oct. 14, 1930

Dear Mrs.:

Of the many letters that have come to me in connection with the *Ladies' Home Journal*, I am sure that yours is one of the most interesting and provocative. I have read it several times in an effort to get at precisely what factors in the very complicated case, as you relate it, might be most accessible to change.

Making all allowances for the fact that it is you who are writing the letter, I think the mental health problem most certainly is not in you and not in the child, but in your husband. It sounds to me very definitely that you have a real case of mental ailment in your family, and, of course, I mean him. You say that you think both he and you are mentally sick; you might have concealed it, but I see no reason to think that you are mentally sick because you certainly write a considerate, restrained, and at the same time intelligent letter.

You have succeeded in describing your husband's symptoms without giving any evidence of hostile emotion which mistreatment of your child must certainly arouse in you at times. This shows me that you have taken a very scientific attitude toward it, and it gives me a great deal of confidence in the facts as you relate them. And if these facts are true, as I believe them to be, your husband needs exactly the sort of thing which this department in the *Ladies' Home Journal* is trying to give. He needs enlightenment as to his own mental health.

In the December number of the *Ladies' Home Journal* there is to be a considerable discussion of the theme that many people suffer from the symptoms of mental ill-health without knowing it, the recognition of which would be half the cure. I think if your husband really understood his symptoms in the same light that you and I see them, he would be helped by it. I wonder if you are not at fault in yielding so easily to his adverse reaction to your discussion of the matter. You say he gets the headache and goes to bed, and you do not know what to do. I don't see why the fact that he gets the headache and indigestion and goes to bed is any reason why you should dodge the issue, but it seems to me that it is up to you as the child's mother, and incidentally as the most healthy-minded member of the family, that you place the problem fairly and squarely before him. Tell him exactly what you have told me in your letter. Tell him that he is ruining the home and that it is up to him to find out what is the matter with him. Help him to do so, if he will permit you, but don't let him escape out of it by the evasion of a neurotic headache.

I might point out to you that you are entirely right in your assumption that the hatred toward the child is motivated by hatred which is unconscious. Just why he has this hatred I do not think we know. I do not think we can be sure that [it] is due to jealousy of your former mate. Several things in your account of the matter make me think that your husband is unhealthy in his attitude toward sex. I should think calling a child of six immodest who permitted her bloomers to show was an index of nasty-mindedness which certainly needed some ventilation. I think his fear of disease is another symptom of abnormal psychology, for which he needs a psychiatrist's help. I think his cruelty to your child would shock him if he could see it in the light that I do, and that his aversion to moving pictures and dances is another symptom of mental unhealthiness which frequently passes as commendable propriety or morality.

What should you do? Confront your husband with the facts as you see them, in as fair-minded and honest, as detached and scientific a manner as you can. Take the position that you do not want to ruin him unnecessarily, but that he is knowingly or unknowingly about to destroy a beautiful thing. Tell him that you believe he must be unaware of it as you see it. From what you say in your letter he is a very fine man and an intelligent man; appeal to his fineness to its fullest. Ask him to look at the thing through your eyes for a moment. If you can get him to see what he is doing, no matter how sick it may make him feel, perhaps you can get him to obtain outside help in getting himself straightened out. If you can't, I fear that your husband is lost, mentally. Of course, it is unsafe to make any prophecies, and I have not seen your husband nor heard his story, but from what you say, which is a very well-presented account, I think you have not exaggerated the seriousness of the problem you face.

Sincerely yours,

Oak Park, Ill.
Oct. 26, 1930

My dear Doctor Menninger:

In the November issue of the *Ladies' Home Journal*, I see your offer to help any reader who thinks she has problems you are able to help. I am very anxious to get an answer to some questions without the bias of a personal contact unavoidable in an interview with a psychiatrist, for I seek true, scientific information rather than opinion. It is almost impossible now-a-days to find a man or woman who can give an unprejudiced answer to questions such as mine, or who enjoys a discussion for the simple exchange of ideas without argument. You may feel that the task of reading such a long manuscript should not be involved in your offer, but I hope you will read it all.

Here is a short background of the picture. I am twenty-eight years old, lived in Omaha, Nebraska, until I went to the University of Wisconsin to school. My parents are well educated. My mother is very capable but neurotic, my father not outstanding for anything but his good intentions. I have one sister younger than I. Except for achievement in school, my life was negative in characteristics until evident poor health caused a school nurse to urge me to see a psychiatrist, who told my mother I had been hurt by too much criticism. Following his advice I achieved success in other fields than academic at college, and won Phi Beta Kappa, too. I taught one year, then was married, and after a year of graduate work, I taught in the university at Madison. Now I have been married five years and have a daughter about a year old. My husband is liked by everyone and has generally a very generous and loving disposition. However, he has had a terrible temper from his childhood, is childish in his actions when angered, and uses vicious language and blows. He is an engineer by vocation and has been and will be again a school teacher in a university. We met at Madison. His father deserted his mother.

Since we have been married, my husband has held the idea constantly that we could not make a success of married life together. I have fought this silently, except on three occasions after eruptions of his temper accompanied by remarks that he had not loved me since two weeks after our wedding, and that he wanted to be single. At these times I changed his attitude by keeping very cool, pointing out the weakness in his statements, and by being, as he said, "so damned reasonable." Since our baby's birth, finances have worried him beyond reason, until he even had temporary lapses of memory. Last spring, when the baby was three months old, my obstetrician urged me to have my husband help me to get orgasms which I had not been able to get before the baby was born, though my husband had not known of the lack. He began a series of revolts against me which lasted months, even consulted lawyers planning to take the baby away from [me], put her in a home, and leave for Russia. I went to the doctor for aid, and he, a famous obstetrician, gave me suggestions like a father. Since I returned from a visit to my home this summer, we have been happier most of the time, and I have learned to achieve an orgasm without fail with his willing help. I should add that I did not tell my parents of these troubles because I was married against their wishes. When my husband is himself, he protests that he loves me. I am not a nagging or an extravagant wife.

Now I am anxious to maintain my home, because I want my baby to grow up in a home with two parents and be happy. I want to avoid these storms on my husband's part which show him to be unhappy and which make me most unhappy. I want to help my daughter to become easily adjusted to her place in society.

Recently there have become muddled with the whole thing in my mind several questions which I can't answer, but which involve my understanding of and attitude toward the relationship between men and women, as they have been created by my environment, including my education. My doctor used to tell me that I was too analytical. I guess I can't change in that respect, but I intend to turn this ability, if you would call it that, to some use, when a little more leisure will give me time to study further and put it to use as I have in the past in associations with youth.

These questions came like a bolt out of the blue as the result of a question my curiosity led me to ask the pediatrician to whom I take my baby, a man who is supposed to be an able child psychologist. I asked, "Why do most men, even now-a-days, prefer boy babies to girl babies? Is it a sense of timidity?" He replied, "Men are dominant physically and mentally, and a feeling of biological superiority is necessary to their happiness. The male can always get the female to do as he wants. Modern women in rebellion make unhappy homes." Then I told him that my husband had always replied to the question as to whether we wanted a boy or a girl, that we wanted a fine healthy baby, and six girls or six boys would be equally welcome in our home. "You are only kidding yourselves," the doctor said.

I had no sense of disappointment when my baby was born, just as I have had no sense of inferiority to men, myself. I have always felt we were equals in the purpose for which each was evolved. In my reading I have often come across the statements [that] men have greater physical strength, but women greater stamina and endurance, to serve as I thought, their differing purposes. I have the idea that tradition and repression through superstition were responsible for the apparent inferiority of women; and that better clothing, greater educational advantages, better health as the result of participation in games, and actually greater cultural interest as the result of increased leisure, were destroying the weaknesses which had led to the masculine dominance. From the actions of my married friends I thought that men greeted the growing woman as a partner with whom they were willing to make a 50–50 union of marriage and found her an infinitely more absorbing mate for their lives. I have always regarded woman's physical handicap as a badge of the great privilege of being mothers. And I judge a successful mother to be as deserving of credit as a clever builder of bridges or of skyscrapers. Indeed, I believe the job is a harder one with more involved, because the materials dealt with are human character and personality and the results human misfits or happy citizens. Certainly nothing in my university studies or experience in or out of the classroom ever led me to feel this inferiority the pediatrician spoke of. Though I have not studied biology, I have studied Heredity and Eugenics. I can see that in herds of animals, the leaders are the males; but in insect colonies the leaders are the females. Reading has given me the information that there are and have been civilizations where women are dominant.

After having been under the handicap of a feeling of inferiority during my early years, I don't want to go back to it now. For my standard for judging people has been whether or not they conducted themselves to the best of their training and ability no matter what their color, race, religion, or sex.

Though there has not been any discussion of these points between my husband or myself, nor anything in his words or actions to indicate that he feels as this pediatrician says all men feel, I wonder if this attitude on my part is at the bottom of our trouble, in part. Also could those statements of the pediatrician have been due to some fault in his own training or his failure to "grow with growing America"? Is there any actual basis for his contention that one sex is biologically superior to the other. Isn't rebellion, when it is constructive in its goal, always the means of improving this society in which we live? I probably am borrowing trouble by wondering about these things—but one has lots of time to think while doing dishes.

Instead of being a mother who "resents the fact that she is a woman," I want to feel it is worthwhile to be a woman. The attraction between the sexes will always be balanced by the hostility between them, I suppose. But I feel that there would be more real happiness and achievement for all, if there was education along the lines of mutual respect and a feeling of equality of purpose.

Will you give me your opinions as a scientist, not as a man?

Sincerely,

Dec. 2, 1930

My dear Mrs.:

I find your letter of October 26 addressed to me in care of the *Ladies' Home Journal* exceedingly interesting. I have read it several times in an effort to find the best way in which to answer your questions and help you.

Do you remember your last sentence? It is this, "Will you give me your opinion as a scientist, not as a man?"

I regard this sentence as the key note of your entire letter. You seem to think that in some way or other my being a man interferes with my being a scientist, or at least interferes with my taking an objective view of the problem as to the relations between men and women. In other words, you are accusing me of having a prejudice, or rather of being capable of being prejudiced. It does not seem to occur to you that it is you who have the prejudice and that you therefore project this prejudice upon the other person and accuse him of being the one who is not likely to see it straight.

I am afraid I am not going to make my point very clear to you by beginning in that way and so I shall start over again. Your whole letter to me is belligerent. You start out by telling me that you don't want to see me because "personal contact, unavoidable in an interview with a psychiatrist" biases the discussion. "I seek true scientific information rather than opinion." You see, here again you inform me that if I give my opinion, it will not be scientific.

What I am trying to show you is that you are very much on the defensive. You are almost tremulously excited about this thing, as I can read very well between the lines. Your letter is full of references to "hostility" between the sexes, rebellion, contention, and so forth. One would think that you and I had had a serious quarrel about this matter and that you were rather hot under the collar about it and were going to make your point in no uncertain terms.

Now of course I realize that you do not actually feel that way toward me, and I really do not believe that you feel that way toward your husband. I suspect, however, that you feel that way toward men in general and it is about that that I should like to help you.

You are on the defensive because you do feel inferior, and you feel inferior not because of any actual facts in the case in spite of your attempt to be very scientific and very objective, but because of a wrong attitude toward men and women which I think I understand. You tell me in the second paragraph that your mother was very capable and your father outstanding for nothing except his good intentions. In other words, you grew up in a family where the mother was a superior person and the father just the opposite. This, you see, started you off with the idea of women being superior persons and men being inferior persons. This childhood opinion of men and women you would like to continue. Discovering that you yourself are a woman, one of these superior persons, your own self-esteem adds impetus to your desire to believe that women are at least not inferior. Yet for some unconscious reason or other you are not quite sure of yourself in this matter. Therefore, when your pediatrician suggests that men are biologically superior, it stirs you to the very foundation of your psychology.

Now let us analyze a few of the details of your letter. You say that you asked your pediatrician why men preferred boy babies to girl babies. In the first place, I wonder why you asked him this question. Why did you think he would know? Did you think that he was such a great philosopher or psychologist? Most pediatricians are not. For some reason or other you seemed compelled to ask him about it however.

In the second place, why did you assume that men do prefer boy babies to girl babies? As a matter of fact, they don't. Whatever you may have discovered from talking to your friends, I can assure you from an experience that covers a good many years and involves the minute examination of the attitudes of parents toward their children in many many families, that men distinctly prefer girl babies, as a general rule. It is true that some men prefer boy babies and I will tell you why. Those men who prefer boys are usually men who have never outgrown a considerable amount of self-love. Therefore, they want to create replicas of themselves. It is an expression of their own self-love to a considerable extent. That is not the only reason but that is probably the most important reason. But this is a very complicated matter and cannot be solved in a few words. What interests me is the fact that you assumed that it was so when it actually is not so. And then that you ask a pediatrician about it, and finally that you pay so much attention to what he said. What he said, judging from your letter, is no answer at all to your question. He said that men were dominant, were biologically superior; that doesn't explain why they would prefer to have boy babies. It has nothing to do whatsoever with the children they may have or not have. So you see your whole paragraph is a confused illogical thought, unless we understand why you think it and I think I do understand why you wrote it. You wrote it because of your own sense of inferiority; you were seeking reassurance that the woman is after all equal if not superior to the man; you ask your pediatrician because as a child specialist you thought he ought to appreciate motherhood and expected him to say something about the superiority of women. He surprised and disappointed you, and this shocked you and stirred you up.

I don't know how you are going to take this letter; I think I shall not go further with an analysis of what you have to say because I am afraid you are already so sensitive about it, so much on the defensive that it will be impossible for you to accept what I have been telling you. You will revert to your original statement that I am giving you an opinion rather than scientific information. I think that means that if I agree with you it is scientific information; if I do not agree with you it is an opinion.

I think your whole question is really such a curious, unimportant, academic one. Is the right foot superior to the left or vice versa? Is a person's shirt dominant to his trousers? Is rubber or leather more useful to mankind? Is man or woman biologically superior?

Don't you see the similarity of the type of question? It all depends on what you mean by superiority. The female element came first and the male was added later as a kind of luxury. That we know. Men are bigger and stronger than women, being designed for a different purpose. That, too, we know. The most exceptional achievements of all sorts are better done by man; most routine achievements are better done by women. But these are qualitative comparisons. When you go to making quantitative comparisons you get nowhere. But you do betray the fact that you have inferiority feelings about your own sex for which you are trying to compensate by a logical argument to prove that such an inferiority does not exist in you or in your sex at all.

And so I must agree with your suspicion that a wrong attitude on your part of a general sort may be at the bottom of the difficulties you have with your husband. Mind you, I don't think he is perfect. I don't even think he is superior to you! Nor do I think you superior to him. In many ways I am sure you are not his equal and vice versa. I can see no advantage whatsoever in making comparisons of this sort. But I can see that you are putting yourself to a great deal of pain and distress by your inability to refrain from making such comparisons. I think you must find some compensation for your inferiority feeling in special achievement. Your ability to keep your head as you evidently have done upon certain occasions, in your cheerful and amiable self-confidence.

Finally, in spite of your distrust of psychiatrists' opinions, I think it might help you a very great deal to have a conference with one. I know several of them in Chicago to whom I should be very glad to refer you. I think they might enable you to see yourself and the cause of your inferiority in a way which will help you immeasurably. I think they would help you cut the thorn in your flesh which you keep pressing upon and denying and resisting.

Sincerely yours,

Los Angeles, Calif.
Nov. 17, 1930

Dear Sir:

Having read your article in the *Journal* and your offer to be of assistance to folks in need I am writing you with the hope that you will be able to help me get "straight" with myself once again and to explain to me why it is that I do things that are so foreign to my real self.

Am at a loss as to just how to explain to you but will cite a few little instances of what has already happened. About three years ago I married a man whom I loved greatly and he apparently loved me but from the very first the marriage was doomed to failure owing to jealousy at first on his part and then jealousy on my side too. This jealousy was unfounded on both sides as I was true to him and I feel that he was true to me but at the least little sign we were quarreling and these quarrels led to fist fights on several occasions until after 14 months we decided that rather than have something really serious happen we had better part. This we did and for many months after that I spent the most miserable time anyone can imagine but about six months ago I met a man and we have planned to try the adventure again. This will be the second attempt for us both. Now to arrive at the part that is worrying me, I find that I am resorting to the same methods that brought on the trouble with my husband and I fear to go on. Just for instance. This friend of mine is in business for himself and is in a town nearby here so that we are unable to see each other very often and I have been going down there once a week in the evening and sitting with him in the office for a couple of hours in the evening and at that time if he gets a call on the phone or a woman comes in to see him I just get sick all over. I know that this is all very foolish and that he is playing fair with me yet I cannot seem to control my thoughts or feelings.

Last Sunday I was there to help him with his books and twice he had callers. I made up my mind that I would not act so silly this time but the longer I sat there the hotter I got and I answered him rather short a couple times, then he said that I was hateful. That just about describes how I felt. I really hated him and myself. We then quarreled just as I did with my husband, in fact the performance was a perfect duplicate with all the trimmings. Now the queer part is that ordinarily I am a very peaceful person and would go to any length to keep from making a scene and will take a lot from folks rather than say anything back but when these spells come over me I do not have any control over myself at all. It just seems that I stand off to one side and watch this other person making a perfect fool of herself. Seems as though I am driven by some force stronger than myself to do and say things that I would give anything in world to have left unsaid and undone. I am more than generous and would do anything to help others in need and have gone without things many times in order to be of assistance to others. In public I would stand anything rather than make a scene and am rather shy with strangers until I get to know them yet people all seem to like me and most everyone tells me that I am sweet and refined yet when these spells come over me I am just as near the opposite as it is possible to be. Now the funny part is that these two men are the only ones who have made me act this way and I am wondering if it is because I am losing my grip on things. I am 35 years old and in the last two years have grown as gray as a woman of 50.

I go to bed at night feeling as well and as happy as can be and wake up in the morning with the most depressed feeling and just feel that life is not worth living at all. This may last a day or several days and then leaves me as suddenly as it came. When I feel that way I have a chip on [my] shoulder all the time and would tell the President of the U S A to go jump in the lake.

When I get one of those spells I want to hurt, to tear things to pieces and the funny part is that I don't mind in the least being hurt myself, in fact if they hit me it gives me a thrill. I am really ashamed to admit it but that is a fact. Now all this is so foreign to me and anyone to look at me or to be with me ordinarily would not believe me if I told them. Before my marriage it was almost impossible for me to cry but now I cry at the least little thing and just indulge in regular orgies of weeping and pray to die and it makes no difference whether I am alone or with someone else. I have a very good position that I have held for over four years and have had others before this and my work is as good as ever.

To be real frank with you I am fearful that unless I can get a better grip on myself I am going to some day do something that is going to ruin other lives besides my own for when I am in the throes of temper such as I have tried to explain the only thing I can think of is to hurt, to even kill and you know some day I will just happen to have something handy that will do the job up right and then where will I be? I say to myself that all this is very foolish and that I'll never do it again and then right out of a clear sky something will come up and I am off again. Am I crazy or what is the matter with me?

Please believe that I do sincerely wish to overcome this fault if it is possible, and anything that you may do or advise will be greatly appreciated.

Yours very truly,

Dec. 15, 1930

My dear Miss:

I have read with a great deal of interest your letter of November 17 addressed to me in care of the *Ladies' Home Journal*. I am glad you wrote me because I think it is very necessary that someone put you straight, as you call it, and I think perhaps we can show you how that should be done.

I think your lover made a proper diagnosis of your case when he said that you were hateful. He probably meant it just as a word, but it is a correct diagnosis. I think you are full of hate. I think your whole letter shows this. You say that you would tell the President of the United States to jump in the lake, you have a chip on your shoulder, you want to hurt someone, tear something to pieces, you want to be hurt yourself, you want to kill, and so forth and so on.

There is so much of this hate evident in your life that it almost over-whelms the love. Of course all love is apt to have a little hate mixed in with it but you have so much hate mixed in with the love that I think it would be more accurate to say that you had a little love mixed in with the hate. This little love attracts a lover to you, particularly a lover of a certain type. I should say that your lover might possibly be a man somewhat like yourself who also wanted to hurt and be hurt. But of course I don't know enough about him to have any very definite opinion.

Now I don't think that it is possible for a woman of the sort you describe yourself to be to achieve a happy marriage until she gets over that. And to get over it is a tough job so you had better prepare for a battle. I think you can do it but you will have to work. The only way I know of that it can be done is thru a complete clarifying of the depths of the mind, the subconscious, or unconscious part of the mind. Because it is here that the real struggle between your love and hate is going on. The outside world is just a field of action for your subconscious to express itself. That is the reason you have these peculiar experiences in which you do things that you really don't want to do and don't understand why you are doing them.

Now you are lucky in that you live in Los Angeles which is a big city and therefore has good psychiatrists and psychoanalysts. I would suggest that you go and see one of them. I am not sure just who in Los Angeles does practice psychoanalysis but there are numerous people who can tell you of a good psychiatrist and I think you should by all means consult someone.

Sincerely yours,

Long Island, N.Y.
Jan. 27, 1931

Dear Dr. Menninger:

I have found your articles very interesting and would also like to turn to you for a solution of my trouble. I am extremely negligent and although I simply abominate this bad habit I can't seem to escape from it, in fact the more I try the worse it seems to get.

I read every article in books, papers and magazines on self-control, mind training and the like, but as far as it gets me is to realize that while reading them I have forgotten to put on the potatoes, or while in the midst of cleaning the living room I will sit down to plan in mind how I would like to rearrange it, and waste about an hour this way and the living room never gets a change. I will go out and buy material for a dress or curtains or anything else and don't get to making it up for weeks or even months, or until it is absolutely needed, in fact I never seem to get to do anything until the last minute, and then get all upset because it is not done the way I would like it to be done.

From what I have told or written I suppose you will think I must be an awfully lazy and disorderly person, but the strange fact is that although I will do things at the last minute my home is always clean and orderly and that is because however long I may take to do a thing I must have it done just so.

I have also tried planning my days and work on paper, but it is just so much times wasted, because I never will follow it while there is a magazine in sight, or books or drawers to rummage in, and chairs to sit in and daydream.

I am thirty years old, married five years, and have a little boy four years old, who is about the only one I will not neglect, in fact he has been always cared for with the most exact schedule in feeding and other habits, and he is a dear and happy boy that everyone likes.

I don't know whether the fact that I had a very unhappy and sickly childhood has anything to do with my lack of self-control. My mother was very stern and severely strict, and as a child all she instilled in me was a terrible fear of her. She went out to work and from the time I was eleven till fifteen years old I did all the housework and cooking besides my school and caring for my younger sister, and my greatest fear was mother's homecoming every evening from work. Also I was an anemic from the time I can remember till I was nineteen when a very good doctor took me in his care and cured me so that I have not needed medical care ever since, but it seems he only cured me in body but not in mind.

Whether my childhood matters or not, the main thing now is is it possible for me to learn to control my daydreaming and negligence, to learn to write letters on time and not wait until people complain, to be able to come home from a shopping trip on time instead of poking around in the store until it is too late to get dinner ready without an awful rush, not to promise people things I will do for them and never do it until it is too late.

These things may seem trivial for another person, perhaps, but it is something that is making a wreck of my nerves and still I can't seem to be able to help myself, so I would like to know if you, Dr. Menninger, could suggest anything to snap me out of this dilemma.

Yours truly,

Feb. 23, 1931

My dear Mrs.:

I have read carefully your letter of January 27th addressed to me in care of the *Ladies' Home Journal.*

It is quite evident from what you so vividly describe that there are some serious inhibitions between your conscious wish and the carrying out of those wishes. It sounds to me just a little from what you say about your mother as if you were unconsciously battling with conflicting notions about housework which her attitude is partly responsible for. Because she made you do it and terrified you and made you hate her, probably whether you realized it or not, you dislike housework and would like to throw it all out the window and be done with it.

On the other hand, for various reasons, because you love your husband and because you love a pretty home you consciously aspire to be a good housekeeper. Now I think there is a conflict between your wish to be a good housekeeper and your wish to defy your mother's insistence upon your doing housekeeping. I wonder if I make myself clear. The result is this curious spasmodic postponement, resolution, sudden last-minute-clean-up, etc. Yes, I think your childhood matters a good deal; I think it is rather definitely responsible for it.

You could get over these tendencies if you wanted to spend the time, money, and energy to do so by being psychoanalyzed. I don't think you can do it by just resolving not to. You might accomplish something by considering it from the standpoint I have suggested in realizing the conflicting nature of your psychology. Since you live in New York however I don't see why you don't go and at least consult with a good psychoanalyst. It might help you a great deal.

Sincerely yours,

Philadelphia, Pa.
Mar. 17, 1931

Dr. Menninger:

About two and one-half years ago I had my first child—an infection developed twice, my temperature reached 107½. At those times I knew that I was looking in on death but my one thought was how can I ever be sane again after this?

Now it seems to me that I am not the same person I was before I had my baby. Before, I had an almost perfect disposition, capable of taking the bad spots along with the good and about the last to give up hope in moments of despair. After my baby came and I was somewhat settled it seemed that I was completely changed. I was blue, despondent and suffered untold mental agony and am sure I would have taken myself out of this world had I not felt so keenly my responsibility toward my baby and also that it was the coward's way out. I determined to fight my way back to mental health but my advantages have been few while my disadvantages have been great.

Finances do not permit me to travel or rest from responsibilities. And now I'm beginning to feel it's a hopeless task, while my despondency does not reach such depths as before I find I'm developing an uncontrollable temper, a rage that makes me want to spank, strike and hurt my child when he displeases me, and I find myself clenching my hands and gritting my teeth innumerable times during the day in order to control myself and be able to deal fairly with him.

I don't want to discolor the lives of my husband and child and I'm afraid that's what is happening.

And too I am becoming afraid of myself, afraid of the future and most of all afraid I shall never know happiness again.

I don't believe this would apply to the average person, may I suggest a personal reply—and thank you.

Apr. 3, 1931

My dear Mrs.:

I have read with care your letter of March 17 addressed to me in care of the *Ladies' Home Journal.*

It is quite evident, I think, that what has happened in your case is this. I think the fever which you had upset your psychological balance just enough to release some of the buried hates which everyone has and which in your case were probably pretty well controlled prior to your illness. Once they were unloosened they began to vent themselves on yourself and on your child, as you so beautifully describe in your letters. You wanted to shake and punish your child and you wanted to kill yourself. If you could in some way or other transfer these hostilities, which are of course largely unconscious and therefore cannot very well be attacked at their source without prolonged scientific therapy which you possibly cannot afford at the present time, to some other object it would probably relieve you a good deal. I mean, for example, if it is at all possible for you to take up some competitive sports or games, particularly golf or tennis, or even only to get interested in bridge or some other game which will allow you to compete vigorously with someone else, I think you will be surprised at how relieved you will feel. This may seem to you a very trivial suggestion in regard to so serious a feeling as that from which you suffer but it is the best thing I can offer under the circumstances. I am going to discuss the matter at considerable length in the forthcoming issue of the *Ladies' Home Journal.* You would be surprised to know how many people suffer from very much the same sort of thing, that is, the direction of unconscious hostilities against people whom we really love.

Some people get sufficient relief from these hostilities from ordinary business competition and such things as that but evidently you are not getting sufficient relief or else you are unable to transfer your hostilities in those directions. That is why I made the additional suggestion. You did not tell me a great deal about yourself, as you may remember, and therefore I cannot be more definite as to just how you can accomplish this. Perhaps your ingenuity will do the rest.

Sincerely yours,

Newport, Tenn.
May 1, 1931

My dear Dr. Menninger:

I am writing you in the hope that you may help me overcome a most miserable condition.

From childhood I have been extremely timid and sensitive. During my early 'teens I developed a severe case of acne. My physician did not seem to think the condition very unusual, and nature was left, more or less, to take its course. As the years have elapsed and the condition has continued, I have consulted other physicians with the result that the physical condition is much better. However, the mental state caused by this condition throughout the years has become almost unbearable.

I have suffered such constant agonies of self-consciousness that it seems that my face has possession of my mind. Whatever I try to do this over-powering consciousness seems to have first place in my mind.

During the first years of the condition, it was impressed upon my mind that I looked terrible. Being of a sensitive nature, I immediately formed the idea that I was repulsive. I began to shrink from association with others. School became torture. I was actually so face-conscious that I could not concentrate my mind upon my studies unless I was alone.

The state gradually grew worse, this consciousness gaining a steady headway in its supremacy over interests that tried to enter my mind.

Today, as a result of this condition and an intangible fear of everything, life itself, I am a failure. Upon my personal appearance, this mental ill has had an alarming effect. My face becomes swollen and I actually have a fever. A brown discoloration spreads over my face and seems to be becoming permanent.

Perhaps I may explain my condition more clearly by asking you what effect such a state of mind would have upon an individual, lasting over a period of ten years. The only enjoyment I have is when I am asleep, for it is then that I am unconscious.

I blame myself for being such a weakling, not having strength to fight this off at the start, instead of allowing it to take hold of me as it has. I realize that with a healthy mental attitude and confidence the effect of the physical ailment would have been negligible.

Yet, facing present facts, can you offer me any hope of overcoming this illness?

A reply would probably be valueless to any other reader, so I am asking that you make it personal, if you will.

Thanking you, I am
Yours very truly,

May 23, 1931

My dear Miss:

The interesting thing about your letter of May 1 addressed to me in care of the *Ladies' Home Journal* is the great intelligence that you bring to bear upon this problem which so greatly disturbs your emotions. You are intelligent enough to recognize, as most people with such afflictions do not, that in some way or other your mental attitude is involved in the affliction.

I wonder if it is asking too much of your credulity to grasp the possibility, which is only a possibility and only a theory and nothing that I can prove but still something which I suspect, namely, that unconsciously your severe acne was a kind of self-indulged affliction. Of course I recognize that acne is a physical disease and I recognize that we ordinarily think that mental conditions are brought about by physical disease instead of physical disease by mental conditions, but there is much in your letter to make me think that unconsciously some way or other you have made your face a kind of object for your own attacks. You say you were extremely timid and sensitive in your early childhood and it seems quite remarkable, not to say beyond the probability of coincidence if your childhood was unusually timid and unusually sensitive, this particularly blighting and distressing affliction should occur. We know from experience that it sometimes happens that people bring upon themselves something which they appear most to fear.

The reason I write the question is that something psychologically produced must be psychologically removed. It is my impression from your letter that you would be a very good case for psychotherapy and I would strongly advise you to consult with a psychiatrist about the matter at an early opportunity. Ask your family physician in regard to a good psychiatrist or psychoanalyst for you to consult.

Sincerely yours,

4.

Narcissism and Infantilism

California
Oct. 15, 1930

Dear Dr. Menninger:

I wish to take advantage of your offer through the *Ladies' Home Journal* to help with problems of mental maladjustment.

I am interested and care very much for my husband's sister. Seeing her fairly wither before my eyes and not being able to help (all members of the family have done all they could), I am writing you.

She was a very beautiful girl at twenty. Her parents were able to give her advantages the average middle class girl receives. Her beauty, however, brought her admiration from all classes of men and she eventually became, as we term it, spoiled. She became engaged to a young man, representing himself to be of well-to-do parents and a title in the background a generation back. The girl really lost her well-balanced viewpoint and allowed "good family" etc., to become an obsession. The man, sensing the girl's interest in titles, etc., fed her interests of course.

They were married in a year's time or less—a month later the girl, finding the man an ordinary young man with his mother making a living as a very fine seamstress, began to be disillusioned. A baby came before any adjusting could be done. The young husband had tried to live up to his colorful pictures, but in a year, money spent, he found himself looking for work—he had misrepresented his prospects.

The girl, accustomed to admiration and lovely clothes and no responsibilities, spent more and more time with her parents.

The husband, without a position, found himself with too much liberty and acquired a social disease which he passed on to the girl. Of course, the year or two following were terrible. The man found a position and girl's family stood by.

Because of the child, the girl had decided to stay with her husband, although her family had agreed to help her in case she wished a divorce. This is the problem:

Although she continues to live with her husband, she is most unhappy, makes his life miserable and seems at a breaking point. He makes a small salary but the girl's family helps by giving clothes, etc. However, the girl is not able to have "things" as she had expected and seems obsessed that she can't have beautiful clothes, social life, etc. All arguments, all efforts to help her adjust herself seem of no avail. She just can't seem to see anything but that she can't have what she wishes.

The child, now six and a beautiful child, does not make any difference in the girl's unhappy "lot." Of course, the youngster is suffering from such an environment, but the girl, though seeing it, does not make any effort to adjust herself. Her health is very poor (finest specialist took care of social disease) and mentally she is a pitiful person. Her interest is in herself wholly. We have tried to interest her in outside things. The lack of enough money to do as she wishes is her excuse for not doing things. She sits and broods and cries most of the time. The husband makes $160.00 a month and the girl's parents practically clothe the child and mother. The money is not much, but many manage with even less an amount. I happen to know. Her ill health, from examination, does not come from past experience, but nervousness. She is thin and fast losing her beauty.

Is there some way to make her look at things differently—we have tried Unity, etc., but with no success. When speaking of the child in an effort to make her view life differently, she continues to pity the child, etc.

Thanking you in advance for any suggestion, I am

Very truly yours,

Oct. 31, 1930

My dear Mrs.:

I have read with a great deal of interest your letter of October 15 addressed to me in care of the *Ladies' Home Journal.*

You have an unusual gift of writing of which you may or may not be aware and your letter is so beautifully written and at the same time describes so tragic and so dramatic a problem that I should like very much indeed to use your letter in a forthcoming number of the *Ladies' Home Journal* if you would permit me to do so. I will modify it somewhat if you like so that no one would suspect that it was you writing. For example, I might change the writer from being a woman to a man, perhaps this girl's father. Of course, I would not print your name. I will not print it at all if you say so, however. Now let me proceed to my reply to it.

I think you have summed it all up quite well where you say in your letter that "her interest is wholly in herself!" That, of course, is quite obvious. It is obvious in all her relationships, in all the things you relate about her. It is quite obvious, for instance, that she married her husband not because she loved him but because she thought she was acquiring something illustrious and something which would increase her own prestige. He was a new trinket for her collection, that is all. And he turned out to be exactly what a wiser person would have seen at first; namely, a trinket. And now you ask what can be done about it. Almost nothing can be done for a person who is so in love with herself that she continues to indulge this love in spite of the fact that it brings more unhappiness than happiness. I am afraid that is the case here. Perhaps not, tho. If she will cooperate with you at all, I would strongly advise you to take her to a psychiatrist immediately and let him undertake an analysis of her problem with her. I hesitate to make this recommendation because so much depends on your getting in the hands of the right man and I do not know just where your city is and where the closest psychiatrist would be. If you will write me whether you are closer to Los Angeles or to San Francisco or whether or not it would be possible for you to go I will try to make a suggestion in the way of the best man to consult.

I cannot help but be impressed, however, with the fact that this girl seems to want to perpetuate her troubles. I do not see why she did not take advantage of the opportunity her family offered her to get a divorce. You say it was for the sake of the child but obviously it is much worse for the child to be exposed to such a miserable atmosphere of unhappiness than to be off somewhere with her mother alone, providing her mother could be happy. My position is that a child is much better off with one happy parent than with two unhappy parents. And may I ask why does her family continue to indulge her in the matter of clothes and money? Apparently this help they are giving her is not making her any happier and it is more than possible that it helps to make her [feel] inferior and encourages her to continue in her unhappy mood. I would suggest that they save their money and devote it to a scientific attack on the psychological problem which has brought her to such a jam.

I hope you will pardon my saying that I regard your letter as being a very fine example of healthy-mindedness on the part of a sympathetic relative. Your analysis of the case is very fair and unemotional and at the same time sympathetic, and shows a genuine concern for your husband's sister which I am sure he must feel very grateful to you for.

Sincerely yours,

San Diego, Calif.
Nov. 1, 1930

Dear Sir:

I suppose I am what you would call a neurotic mother. At any rate, there is something terribly wrong with me. Nothing I do seems to have any meaning and I wonder why I am living at all. Am 24 years old and have been married six years and have a little boy three years old. Up until about 8 months ago was perfectly satisfied with everything and was as good a wife and mother as I knew how to be. We had moved to Los Angeles and had been there a year when my husband lost his job and I had to leave him and come here to stay with my folks and also to have my second baby boy who is now 7 mos. old, as we had no money.

If we had never been separated I know we would be perfectly happy now but I began to depend on my mother to take care of my children and neglected my responsibilities so much that I just about forgot what it was to be a good mother. Perhaps if we had gone back to Los Angeles to live, away from my folks, I would have taken a fresh interest in life.

It began to look as if my husband never would find work and I grew resentful towards him to think that he couldn't support us or be with us. Would have even gone out with other men if the opportunity had presented itself. My thoughts became morbid and I thought of committing suicide. Then he obtained work here and came back to find me in this terrible state of mind and with all my love for him gone.

My husband has always been in love with me and always will be I guess—at least he says so—so of course he was terribly hurt to see how I had changed toward him. We have rented a little cottage and have been here a couple of months but I can't seem to become interested in anything. Of course I go through the motions of housekeeping and taking care of the children but my mind seems to be in a sort of stupor. He has been awfully kind and patient with me but the fact that I am perfectly sure of his love seems to hinder rather than help me. If I could only revive my love for him then I know that everything else would work out of its own accord. I ought to tell you that some time before my marriage I had been in love but though my parents disapproved I lost this boy and also my girl chum at the same time. I became very bitter and foolishly resolved never to make any more friends and really got married to get away from my unhappy home life although I learned to love my husband. Since I was a girl I have always been shy and self-conscious and have never been able to overcome an inferiority complex. My husband's work keeps him away from home from about ten in the morning till eleven or twelve o'clock at night. Sometimes he can come home in the afternoons for two or three hours but not every day—so we have practically no home life, and it leaves me to myself too much for my own good.

I know my case sounds pretty hopeless but would appreciate it if you could help me in any way.

Hoping for an early reply,

Sincerely,

Nov. 26, 1930

My dear Mrs.:

Your letter addressed to me in care of the *Ladies' Home Journal* doesn't sound at all hopeless to me, in spite of what you say.

I think your case is a fairly clear one. You were unhappy at home, you say. You loved a boy and he ran off with your best friend. That gave you two good reasons for being resentful against people. Then along came your husband. You were grateful to him for rescuing you out of a bad situation. You learned to love him, as you say. And I think you really did love him and that you still do love him. But when these hard times came and he had to look for a job and it looked as if he were letting you down, at least financially, you revived a whole lot of your old grudge. Only this time you made him the goat instead of the other fellow, instead of your own folks. You went home and lived with your folks, with whom you appear to have some difficulty. That still further stirred you up. Then you began acting very childishly, acting again as if you really were a child and were living at your own home and could act like a child and that your folks would look after things for you. In technical language we call that regressing, that is going back and acting as if one were a child again. Now that you have your husband back I can see it very clearly, you don't want to grow up, you want to go on being childish and depending on someone else and pouting and saying you aren't treated right and so forth. Inferiority complexes nearly always mean a certain amount of self-pity and martyrdom. We think we aren't getting a square deal and people are not treating us as nicely as they do someone else and so forth. All of this is quite childish and petty.

I am further confirmed in this opinion by the fact that you say that the very knowledge of your husband's enduring love for you seems to hinder rather than help you to love him. You see you would like to continue to have a reason to fuss with him, condemn him and be angry with him. His goodness and honesty and love for you hurt your conscience.

The best way to get over the whole thing is just to get over it. I mean look at yourself for what you really are, a grown-up lady acting like a baby, as the popular song puts it. Cut it out. Grow up. Help your husband who is undoubtedly worried and working hard trying to make good. Meet him as cheerfully as you can and whether you feel like it or not at first, go to a lot of trouble and fix up pretty meals and a pretty table and fix yourself up as pretty as you can, make the whole home a place where your husband really gets restored in spirit. Smile and be sweet to him if it is nearly killing you (which it won't). You will see some revolutionary changes in yourself and in your husband. If you don't you will soon be feeling several times more dismal than you do at present and you will have a very good reason for feeling so.

Sincerely yours,

Indiana
Nov. 9, 1930

Dear Sir,

On account of deep distress, I am appealing to you, for my problem seems difficult to solve alone, yet there is no acquaintance to whom I would consider giving this confidence.

My husband tells me frankly he no longer loves me. We have been married three years, and have two wonderful children, a boy two years and a little baby girl. During this time we have had business misfortunes, so that the strictest economy has had to be observed, even though his salary is good.

With the advent of this second child while the first was still a baby, my hands have been pretty busy. The summer was excessively hot, and my husband detests heat. In trying to keep them cared for, and quiet for his return after work (which is very trying mentally), I perhaps was not always the carefree play fellow of former days.

Now he says if I'd had any sense, I'd have seen him slipping and stopped him, but as it is now the breach is too wide, and, well, I'm sort of a housekeeper nurse—not a wife. He is an excellent provider, courteous—just no lover.

Unfortunately, we are not held by memory of sexual satisfaction. The engaged three years [*sic*], and feeling a perfect understanding about each other's mental and social or family endowments, we had that disappointment to discover.

I'm afraid I have been a spineless ninny to have let him do as he has done, and feel now that I have babied him when he needed spanking, but his nerves seemed so ragged after an auto smash up in the early spring that I overlooked much on that account. Then he seemed not to want to love our little girl, even though he always wanted a family. Perhaps because she took a great deal of time that he felt should be spent with him. But when they're tiny and helpless, mustn't it be both parents' loving duty?

So with two children, all my own work, a dog, cat, four guinea pigs and about forty rabbits to take care of (his hobbies), I'm continually criticized for tasks not accomplished to meticulous perfection.

And yet, I'm crazy about him—but I can't stand living this way, and a divorce is unthinkable. Please tell me some approach to his heart. Any affectionate advances are curtly repulsed with "I'm too much of a gentleman to take what I can't give." In the last week or so, since the baby has started to walk, he has begun to love her, and is teaching our boy to say "Love Daddy best." Ouch!

Our religious training made us practically recluses, and when his work brought him here a year and a half ago, away from all our old friends, we have not made new ones—the usual channels not being open to us. A story of "just us" with not enough outside distraction, or enough money for the thrill of an occasional lark or new clothes.

Please don't misunderstand. He is *not* stingy. I have a washer, electric sweeper, and last week he ordered a radio, which has broken much of the restraint. But they are only things, after all, when what I want is my mate.

Hopefully,

Dec. 1, 1930

My dear Mrs.:

Out of many letters which I get addressed to me in care of the *Ladies' Home Journal,* yours is one of the few which interests me a very great deal because I think it presents such a very important problem in people whose intelligence is evidently much above the average, of a sort for which I think mental hygiene certainly should be able to do something. Just what I am not sure.

Of course I haven't heard your husband's account of things, but only yours; nevertheless, I think you condemn yourself in your own letter. How? Let me point out a few things. You have permitted him to impregnate you twice in three years. You are more concerned about the fact that heat bothers him than about the fact that you had to live through the same heat. You speak of trying to keep the children quiet for his return after work. You speak of how trying his work is. You say that you failed to be a carefree playfellow. You say that he tells you you should have seen him slipping and stopped him. You say that you have had no sexual pleasure. You tell me about his nervous upset. You say that a dog and cat, guinea pig and rabbits are his hobbies but that you take care of them. You say that you permit him to criticize you for not accomplishing tasks about the house correctly. You let him teach your son to say "love Daddy best."

And then you end this all by saying that it isn't things you want but "my mate."

Now, if you have given a correct account of this, your husband has never been your mate but your tyrant and he has been a tyrant only because you have seemed to want it. I doubt very much if he wants to be your tyrant. If he does you have certainly played into his hands. If he doesn't I think you have made him a tyrant, like a great spoiled boy, and now I imagine he is tired of being a boy. He either feels guilty or bored at being treated as if he were either a cruel taskmaster or a weak tired little boy coming to his mother's knee. I am blaming you because I haven't heard his side of the thing and I don't know what he really thinks. I only know what you have told. You see when I put all these things together how clear it is.

Now in my experience it is quite impossible for one person out of a couple to straighten out a thing like this. I think both you and your husband ought to consult someone together who has had experience in adjusting problems of this sort. Just how far are you from Chicago? If you are close enough, I would suggest that you consult someone there. Let him talk to both of you and then to each one of you and then to both of you again. I am sure that your husband would be a great deal happier because I am sure it distresses him more than you imagine and I am sure that you can be happier because you would see what you are really doing wrong and it is probably not the thing that you think you are doing wrong. I would like to see you get it straightened out because it is quite obvious that both you and your husband are superior people and you have these little children to think about as well as your own happiness. And I really think it could be done. But I think it is going to take some rather radical change.

Sincerely yours,

Nacagdoches, Tex.
Mar. 18, 1931

My dear Dr. Menninger:

Surely your article in the *Ladies' Home Journal* was heaven sent—it seems that I must turn to someone if I am to remain sane, and keep my husband that way. I have wanted so long to consult someone about myself but I know that if I were face to face with you or any other doctor that I could not tell you all this—that perhaps I shall want to destroy even this letter in the morning but I shan't.

I read the article in your magazine and how I pray for some of that same "self-adoration." I don't know but I think that I must have an inferiority complex that will match in size some of their egotism. I shall try so hard to write things that will help you to understand. I have tried so hard to analyze myself and explain to myself why I feel as I do.

First, I was left an orphan at the age of ten. I had adored my father and I always disliked my guardian, who was my brother-in-law, very much. That, I believe I understand, was my childish way of resenting my father being taken from me. It wasn't until after I was grown and married that I realized how wonderful he had been to me but he has never forgiven me nor never will and that hurts me terribly.

I was a very proud child and young woman—with ideals too high— they never could have been lived up to. But when I would do a foolish thing—perhaps not nearly so bad as everyone else did—it would almost kill me. Also, my sister and her husband made little things that I had done seem such terrible things. But up to the time I was twenty years old, eight short years ago—no one could have been finer—sweeter—or better. I began teaching school at eighteen and made every cent that I spent until I was married at the age of twenty-three.

When I was twenty-two, I was refused a school in my own home town and it almost killed me. Whether it was over a small town jealousy between families or something that they thought I had done or what, I don't know. But it was so cruelly undeserved that I felt that I could never go home again. I do go but even to this day, I don't go downtown very much there. Oh, I know that they don't know, that they have perhaps forgotten.

After that I did do more foolish things but I can truthfully say, nothing wrong. When I was married, it was at first secretly but I didn't live with my husband for those six months before the wedding was announced because my sister hated secret marriages—then I spent one night with him before we announced our wedding one week later.

Oh there's no use—no use—taking your time with this long recital—it's my only chance or I wouldn't.

I was terribly in love with my husband—and he loved me too—passionately at first and then, it seemed that he thought passion was alright for him but as for me—I must be passive—sometimes at first it seemed that I should die for the very lack of love. But now after five years I have learned and it is very very seldom indeed if ever—I go to him for love. His kisses are mere pecks—but it is alright. That is, unless I am drinking, yes I have added that to my accomplishments since I have been married. Then, I have let other men kiss me—make love to me. Yes, even wanted them to. But I hated it all so—was ashamed when I was sober again. Even hate drinking—and then I'll do it again. Poor weak despicable character that I am—no one can hold a person who does those things in more contempt than I.

There is only one thing in God's name that keeps me alive—my baby girl—the dearest, sweetest, most beautiful child in the world. If it were not for her I wouldn't live—but I *must*!

I have been fighting and trying so hard lately—and then it all falls about my ears—I have seriously considered leaving the gas on and holding my child in my arms while we go to sleep. Yes it's cowardly—it's weak—but I'm so tired. A few months ago my husband lost his position. He came down here, I sold all our furniture and everything and joined him here. Again, we "started over." It's got so that I am unable to talk even to another woman of my acquaintance—just dumb—plain dumb—was asked to play bridge with three other women and I sat there all afternoon—*dumb*! I couldn't talk—everything I said sounded silly and I let women I know to be my intellectual inferiors snub me—and I sit there *dumb*! It seems that I am freezing up on the inside and I'm a nervous wreck. I am so desirous of being liked and other people's good opinion that I'm positively impossible.

I know all these things about myself—there is nothing you or anyone can do is there? But oh for just enough self-adoration to make me sit up and be a worthy mother for my baby girl—so precious—and with me for a mother she doesn't have a chance in the world.

I haven't even told a half—but I've tried to tell it all unbiased so that you could judge me fairly—but nothing you can say will hurt me for I know it all too well. I've been hurt until it seems that I'm numb. Oh yes, [my husband] says that I am too sensitive—may be I'm that too. Oh if I only couldn't see so plainly.

But I can't go on writing forever—is there any way I *can* gain enough self confidence back—any way I *can* grow a thick skin of the rhinoceros so that I'm not *"too sensitive"*—any way—I can get back to *"Normal"* again? I'm always wanting things too perfect perhaps—that's what I try to tell myself—try to make myself believe. But I know better. I know I'm just all wrong—every way—there's no use pretending.

I'm glad that I'm not where I can see the scorn in your face for the poor creature that I am—and the funny thing about it is that if you were to meet me I don't believe that you would know I have ever harbored such thoughts in my mind. I have tried so hard to keep up a front to the world—and I do some way—I can't much longer.

If I only knew what to tell you that would help you to understand and help me. I'll do anything you say—*anything* to help.

Sincerely,

Apr. 9, 1931

My dear Mrs.:

I have read carefully your letter of March 18 addressed to me in care of the *Ladies' Home Journal.*

It is difficult for me to answer this letter with you so far away because it is clear that what you need is not a letter but a conference with some psychiatrist who can sit with you face to face and talk things over. I shall do my best by correspondence and hope and trust that you will not misunderstand me.

Did you not think it a little incongruous that you should say on the first page of your letter that you prayed and wished for the self-adoration which other people have and then on the third page of your letter you say that no one could have been finer, sweeter, or better than you? In other words, you first say that you wish you could love yourself more and explain this by saying that you don't think anything of yourself at all and then you go on to praise yourself rather extravagantly. The rest of the letter reveals chiefly that you are extremely sensitive and that your sensitiveness, your self-love, has been grievously wounded by various things that have happened in your life. You have not met with the reception that you thought you should by people and by circumstances and you have reacted by rather vigorous efforts at making a go of it some way or other, drinking and flirting, and so forth, as you say. These things don't give you the satisfaction that you thought they would and so you find yourself increasingly distressed.

It is a little hard to tell you in so many words that the fact of the matter is that your letter shows that instead of suffering from a lack of self-love, you have really had a good deal of self-love to make up, I think, for the fact that you did not feel that other people loved you enough, particularly the people in your early life. This is a very common picture. You must not get the idea that all people who love themselves are conceited. Many of them are merely sensitive and highly concerned about their reputation and their impression upon other people and so forth. I think you are quite right that the love of your little girl keeps you going. The love of your husband will also keep you going if you can develop it and the love of other people. You are not to be censored for self-love; I tried to make that clear in my article. Self-love is something which handicaps people and which keeps other people from liking us as much as they really want. It is something that we are better off without, including you. But it is not something that we ought to be ashamed of or hostile toward ourselves on account of.

I think this different view of things may help you somewhat; I think it will also help you to do a little reading on the subject. I suggest in particular the book *Outwitting Our Nerves* by Josephine Jackson.[1] Then at your earliest opportunity I think psychoanalysis would give you a great deal of help and make your own situation a great deal happier and the rest of your life a great deal more fruitful and comfortable. I presume under the circumstances this is impossible at the present time but keep working toward that end and some day it will be possible. In the meantime I think your life will be considerably more bearable because of your changed attitude and your different point of view.

Sincerely yours,

Miami, Fla.
Mar. 21, 1931

Dear Sir:

After reading the first section of your *The Human Mind* I was strongly tempted to write you, presenting my own peculiar problems. This smacked a bit of the "Advice to the Lovelorn" columns in the daily papers; and, besides, it was likely that it would be not only presumptuous but perhaps an intrusion upon your time and practice. In glancing through the March issue of the *Ladies' Home Journal* I noticed the department you are conducting and the little note at the head of the article gave me the necessary permission to indulge the temptation.

I have not yet had an opportunity to finish *The Human Mind* but have promised myself that pleasure when leisure is available to do it justice. The occasional whimsicalities, the saneness, the tolerance and the strength apparent in that portion of the book read appealed.

After these preliminaries, let me introduce myself. I am a college graduate, out of school nearly four years, unmarried, an only child, and, as the final bit of damning evidence, a private secretary.

There seem to be several angles to the problem—me—and perhaps I had better explain my biological origin and the question it has raised in my own mind and which I bring to you for solution. It is likely that the thing that bothers me in this respect is an inferiority complex based on the fear that perhaps there is something lacking in my psychic (or psychological—I am not quite sure of the correctness of the application of the two words, psychic being so often used in the sense of mind-reading) make-up. Physically and mentally I am apparently "all here." I have never had a serious illness, and except for one "bad" eye seem to have no organic

---

1. Josephine Jackson with Helen M. Salisbury, *Outwitting Our Nerves: A Primer of Psychotherapy* (New York: Century, 1921).

or chronic ailments. Disgustingly healthy. But, in the nebulous mysterious realm of the personality—I wonder. You see, I am the child of first or "blood cousins." There has evidently been no social disease or mental disease in the family, or according to the laws of inheritance as I have heard them propounded, I would be marked by physical deformity or mental incapacity. Is there a possibility that such a child would be lacking in emotional equipment? The thing that has brought about this questioning is the fact that, although I see my friends fall in love and marry, I seem unable to experience this emotion; although I am sorry to confess that I have been guilty of trying. Wanting to and not being able to is rather a tragic experience—for everyone concerned.

Another angle, and one that is, in a sense, tied in with the first, is brought about by conditions at home. My family are in more or less comfortable circumstances, but both Mother and Dad are distinctly unsocial. There are a few family friends. There is practically no opportunity for me to meet people other than those with whom I come in contact at the office. I do not have the leisure to keep up friendships with the girls I knew before I went away to school. They are married and of course are not at leisure when I am. Those few friends I do have must be quite charitable, as my family makes a great many demands on my time. We have a perfect scene every once in a while because I insist upon having a few of my Saturday afternoons and Sundays to myself. I am accused of being selfish and unwilling to give others pleasure because I prefer to remain in my room reading or writing letters when callers come—to see the family. Mother is even jealous of my girl friends and sometimes sulks and won't even seem to see them when they come into the room unless they make a point of speaking to her first. Because it starts an argument I have practically ceased dating inasmuch as I have no one here that I am particularly interested in. It sort of takes the pleasure out of an evening when it is preceded by disapproving silence, and either a grim silence the next morning when one is relating the evening's events, or if one remains silent, the query, "Well, weren't you out last night? Can't you tell anyone anything?" Shall I leave home? I am afraid that if I don't I shall become a real "case," or, perhaps also, a confirmed old maid—a situation for which I have no appetite. I cannot entertain friends at home, and that doesn't help either. I have no social contacts with the men connected with the company for the obvious reason that I am secretary to the president. The company is a public utility, the largest single organization in the State. Of course, my work is interesting. My employer is about as nearly a perfect "boss" as could be found. He makes no unreasonable demands of any sort and is altogether a gentleman. But, as you can imagine, the work calls for no initiative on my part, merely that I be a serene, intelligent, efficient parrot.

My family have given me a very good education and I don't want to cause them grief or dissatisfaction, but I feel I must have an opportunity to do some sort of creative work and freedom to meet people and make my own friends. I can appreciate my mother being solicitous about the company I keep, but I feel that I have high enough ideals and good enough sense to be allowed quite a bit of freedom. I don't like to be quarreling all the time about the clothes I may choose to wear, the books I read, and the thousand and one little criticisms. Sometimes I feel that I'm being absorbed and that by and by there'll be nothing left but the blotter!

I shall very much appreciate you thinking these matters over. If there are any other questions you would like to ask I shall be very glad to reply to them to the best possible effect for our mutual purpose.

Most sincerely,

Apr. 25, 1931

My dear Miss:

I appreciate very much indeed the kind things you say in your letter of March 21 in regard to my book, *The Human Mind,* and also in regard to my department in the *Ladies' Home Journal.*

So far as your hereditary disadvantages are concerned, I should say that the fact that your parents were cousins is of no consequence whatever.

In regard to the tyranny which you feel that they exert over you, I must remind you that it takes two to make a bargain. They cannot possibly tyrannize over you unless you submit to it. I read between the lines of your letter that more than you realize, you are the victim of a certain amount of repression and self-tyranny which is undoubtedly a handicap to you. For this reason, I think, I can without qualification recommend that at your early opportunity you consider the possibilities of psychoanalysis. I think psychoanalysis would free you from a great deal of bondage of which you are more or less unconscious but which causes you, I am sure, to be far less efficient and far less comfortable and happy than you might otherwise be. I never advise anyone in regard to so critical a matter as to whether or not they should leave home. If they cannot make that decision themselves, the fact that I said it was a good or bad thing would make no real difference. On the other hand, the thing for them to see and the thing for you to see is the fact that you have not been able to make that decision indicates a certain emotional conflict in your mind which it would help you a great deal to have solved. That solution must come from you and not from without. I, therefore, hope very much indeed that you will consider very seriously what I have told you in regard to the matter of a psychoanalysis sometime for the relief of what you call an inferiority complex and further difficulties which your letter indicates.

Sincerely yours,

Tucson, Ariz.
Mar. 30, 1931

Dear Sir:

I am a hypochondriac and I don't know what to do about it. It all began after a hideous and all-but-fatal attack of typhoid when I was 28. The horror of those chills and of the rapid pulse and the fever and the nervous sensations made an indelible impression on me from which I have been unable to free myself. That my condition is due to an infantile regression to the autistic level of sexual development is clear to me, but how can I overcome it? I have identified myself with my husband and children so that when illness threatens them I go thru the same tortures as when it threatens me. I don't want my two little girls to grow to be like me.

Probably I should never have had children. I have never been rugged since that typhoid experience. They have both been frail and it has been one continual fight to save them. They have been ill so much that they have hardly ever been in school. The older one has spent two years in bed under treatment for tuberculosis of the bronchial glands. That is why we are in Arizona.

As a child I was independent and executive and unafraid—qualities that irritated my immediate family immeasurably. They joined forces to make me conform to their pattern. My reaction was rebellion for all the years of my youth. In later years I gradually lost my self-confidence and acquired a sense of inferiority and self-consciousness from which I recovered only when I began to study the causes. My very happy marriage did more than anything to restore what I had lost.

Probably the acquisition of new interests would do much for me. The chief obstacle is lack of leisure. I am a college graduate, as is also my husband. I like to write far better than I like to do the things I have to do—I refer to housework which I should rather enjoy, I think, if there weren't so overwhelmingly much of it. I blithely hit the high spots and worry about nothing except impending illness. I believe there is hope for me. All I want is instruction. I honestly don't know how to tackle my problem.

The *Ladies' Home Journal* has offered a fine service to groping ones like me. I shall value your advice.

Sincerely yours,

Apr. 30, 1931

My dear Mrs.:

It is a great pleasure to reply to a letter so intelligent as that of yours of March 30 addressed to me in care of the *Ladies' Home Journal.*

The fact that you have had a good education, that you are interested in psychological theories and that you have studied, as I can tell you have from your letter, something about the workings of the human mind and the basis of human personality [*sic*]. I think you are quite right in saying that there is hope for you. I think, however, that you need more than instruction. At least I doubt whether the acquisition of information is going to make very much change in you. I might point out to you, for example, that the anxiety you suffer when your children become ill is probably not an expression of identification as you call it, but more likely a projection of some hostility with a sense of guilt lest they be gratified. I know this will seem incredible to you and that is one reason I mention it. Just telling you new facts about yourself is not going to help you get rid of these things.

What you need, and should have if there is anyway to do so, is psychoanalytic treatment. People such as you, who have lost their poise and self-confidence and are increasingly inhibited by so many things, ought by all means to have the advantage of psychoanalysis because it is for them a great boon. It liberates them from the combination of repression thru which their unconscious is constantly thrusting disguised satisfactions which carry with them more pain than pleasure.

Perhaps I can make it more clear if I put it in another way. I think from your reading and study you have already gotten a pretty fair notion of what is wrong with you. But learning about this does not clear you from the satisfaction which you have in what you call, correctly I imagine, your infantilism. You can only get away from those thru the personal relationship which one develops in the course of an analysis with the analyst. Then you will be free to transfer these from the analyst to other objectives. Then you will be able to know what you want to do and able to do it.

Sincerely yours,

Philadelphia, Pa.
June 3, 1931

My dear Doctor Menninger,

After reading your article in the April *Home Journal* I decided to take advantage of your offer to answer personal questions dealing with mental-health problems.

I am a girl of twenty-five years of age not very homely and considered neat in my dress, but very lonely, and there is no obvious reason for this loneliness as I live with my Mother, Father and two brothers and I also have a few so-called friends. My girl friends stay for a little while then drop me like hot butter. The boys that I like don't even see me and I don't like the ones that like me.

You say that people of my type do not see and are not willing to relinquish a satisfaction that self-invested love is giving them. Personally I cannot see or feel satisfaction of any nature. I may be selfish, but when I am with others I'm perfectly willing to do as they wish (being only too thankful for their company). I have a sharp tongue, am very disagreeable and utterly dissatisfied with life.

Mother says I have always been very independent and that I have no time for affectionate expression, for some reason I can not show my feelings altho I long for someone to understand me. People like me for a while, then it's all over, why? I honestly like them and put myself out to do things for them.

As far as I can see there is no conscious love of self, but a self-pity with self-contempt and honest distaste for my own company but I stay alone rather than inflict myself on others. They tell me I am too sensitive, I may be, but cannot overlook slights and small meannesses. I try so hard to be fair and a good sport.

> What shall I be at fifty
> Should nature keep me alive,
> When I find life so dreary
> When I'm but twenty-five.

From a book I read years ago and just how I feel.

Very much ashamed but desperate.

July 3, 1931

My dear Miss:

I have read with interest your letter of June 3rd addressed to me in care of the *Ladies' Home Journal.*

You are candid and honest enough with yourself to face the fact that you have a sharp tongue and are disagreeable and give others the impression that you love yourself. You must be honest enough in your analysis, therefore, to go one step further and see that the self-contempt and self-pity and self-disapproval which you announce are merely used as disguises which permit you to continue to love yourself inside and seem to hate yourself outside. I know this will be difficult for you to understand and I do not expect you to do so at first reading.

Think it over, however, and do a little reading on the subject and I think you will begin to visualize it. Perhaps you have seen a book I wrote called *The Human Mind*. If not I think you might get a little understanding into your own motives by reading it.

May I point out for example that your whole letter is summed up when you say that you long for someone to understand you? What's the matter with your trying to understand someone else? By understanding other people you will come to understand yourself but by merely wishing for someone to understand you you will never be gratified nor will you ever understand either them or yourself.

When you first read this letter you may be angry and you may be quite sure I am wrong. When you have thought it over a few times I think it may help you to make the beginning to accomplish the things which you so definitely want to accomplish consciously.

Sincerely yours,

5.

Isolated Personalities

Whitewater, Wis.
Oct. 20, 1930

Dear Sir:

I'm interested in your articles on "Mental Hygiene" published in the *Ladies' Home Journal.* I shall be so very grateful if you can help me. Here is my problem:

Psychologists would say I am an introvert, because I am shy, sensitive, emotional (but keep my emotions suppressed so that people think I am cold and proud). But knowing all that, I can't find a remedy. For five years I attended and graduated from the Wisconsin Conservatory of Music— graduating in 1928. At that time I was so interested in my work, in the people in Milwaukee, and in various beaux, that I was happy. But following my graduation I had to settle down to teaching in a small town with no young people and no ways of recreation. There is a Teachers' College here, and I enrolled there for work in the mornings because my teaching keeps me busy only in the afternoons, but I was older than the rest of the students and I was sensitive of that fact and failed to make any friends. The townspeople are all 60 years of age and over so I really haven't anything in common with them.

I never go to the movies, to the Lecture Course, or any other public place, because I am too sensitive about going alone. I refuse to go with older married people because I think they are saying I can't get a beau to take me, and I can't.

My mother lives here with me, but she is a semi-invalid, and can't be left alone very long at a time. My brother is attending the University of Wisconsin and comes home every weekend. I have asked him several times not to come home, because he upsets me so terribly that it takes nearly all week to get over it. If I didn't stay with my mother he couldn't attend the

University, but he doesn't appreciate that at all. Whenever he comes home he tells of the good times he has had, and I can't stand it because when he is here, he never takes me or my mother anywhere. He takes someone else and we stay at home the same as we have done all week, and week after week.

The University Band gave a concert last spring, and the Director invited me to come to Madison to hear it. I was so proud of the invitation, and planned for a month to go. That weekend my brother came home and I told him I was going. He absolutely refused to allow it, and drove off without me. This last weekend was Homecoming at the University. My brother invited a girl from Whitewater and her father and mother to spend the weekend with him in Madison. Then he came home and asked me if I had listened to the game over the radio. I went all to pieces and became actually ill. He said "No wonder you haven't any friends—the way you act." I know that, but what can I do about it?

I'm so unhappy that I don't enjoy my teaching any more, and I never play the piano any more. If I get worse as rapidly as I have in the last 4 or 5 months, I shall go insane or else kill myself.

I can't adjust myself to living in a small town, and I can't leave here. What shall I do?

Thanking you, I am, truly yours,

Nov. 5, 1930

My dear Miss:

Your letter of October 20 sent to me in care of the *Ladies' Home Journal* almost stumps me. There are so many problems that I scarcely know where to begin.

In the first place, you say that you are shy, sensitive and repressed, and wonder what to do about it.

Well of course that is one big problem. I don't know whether there is anything to do about it, and I could not tell without discussing matters with you at considerable length. It may be a characteristic personality trend, and it may on the other hand be the result of circumstances which are a little too big for you. The rest of your letter makes me think that that is the case.

What to do about the emotional stifling and the crippling of social opportunities which one encounters when one moves from a large city to a small town is puzzling a good many heads other than yours and mine today. How can one redeem the small town? Whitewater is not exactly a small town, however, is it? I was under the impression that it is a city of ten or fifteen thousand. Even if it is only five thousand I think it might be livable. You could surely find companionable people. Why not take the initiative and do a little entertaining? If I were a girl I presume I would prefer to have some men friends but if you can't find them, get some girl friends. Your feminine instinct will guide you in this matter if you don't let your pride stand in your way. Where do you spend your summer vacations? That is quite an opportunity to afford you some amusement if not a good deal more.

I don't think you ought to turn down older married people who want to take you places. Why not confess the truth to them, namely, that you do long for a beau and don't have one. They might help you. And even if they don't, why not be interested in them for their own sakes. I know you are not looking for a meal ticket, you are looking for someone to be interested in you.

Now we come to this affair about your brother. I can't quite understand how he can have so much power over you as to tyrannize over you and abuse you and make you suffer and scold you, and ridicule you as you describe. I don't see why you have to put up with this. You hint at the fact that you are in some way or other making it possible for him to go to the University, financially. You say he doesn't appreciate it. Why don't you make him appreciate it by withdrawing that support. Don't threaten to do so; do so. In some way or other you ought to stand on your own feet in this matter. Your brother would respect you more; he might even begin to love you as he apparently does not at present. Do you enjoy permitting him to have this power over you? If you do not, take it away from him. He is not your lord and master and you do not have to be his slave unless you permit yourself to be.

It would be much better to attack the thing in this fashion than to allow your emotional reactions to engulf you. I wish you would write me again about the matter. If you can't get the thing straightened out alone you must get some help. We will find a way to do this. Write me again, please.

Sincerely yours,

Kansas
Oct. 27, 1930

Doctor Sir:[1]

I read your letter on "Mental Hygiene in the Home" in the last issue of the *Ladies' Home Journal.*

---

1. Menninger sent this letter to Leo Bartemeier, his friend and colleague in Detroit, with the comment, "Amazing connection of guilt propitiation and stammering." Bartemeier replied, "Let [her] keep stammering! This is fascinating!"

I am 23 years of age and I cannot say that I have made much of a success of life; so I ask "Why be unhappy?" First I have a mother and father who could not possibly be better to me. Dad has a small business here and I am trying to help him with it but I cannot seem to get interested in it or anything else. Yet I know I should be.

I thot perhaps you could help me to readjust myself someway and so I shall try to give you an outline of my past history.

Since I was two years of age I have had a hesitancy, or stammering really, in my speech. I suppose I have always let it be more of a handicap than I should; but I am very sensitive about it and always have been. When I first learned to talk, at about 9 mo. of age, I was not troubled at all. The stammering followed an illness when I was about 2 years old.

I graduated from high school with high honors and then took a complete commercial course. However I could not seem to do office work on account of my stammering.

All doctors to whom I have gone at different times say there is nothing wrong physically; altho I am run down and need building up. I have a hearty appetite as a rule but do not gain any.

Now what is troubling me is this: I think it was in my freshman or sophomore year in high school, all the churches combined in a revival meeting and of course I attended some. I suppose that is what started me off. At any rate I got into my head the idea that I should be a missionary to some foreign country; China perhaps. I worried all day and half of the nights but managed to fight it off for a while but have since had several sieges of it—on an average of about one a year. I would just argue with myself first one way and then another.

Then in my junior year, my parents arranged for a man to come to our city who taught stammerers to speak correctly. There were three others in the class, a boy of 8 or 9 who was greatly benefited; a girl about 12 or 13 who has since practically overcome her difficulty; then a boy a year or so older than I but who had much more difficulty than I in getting anything said.

Well you see I had the idea in my head that if I ever learned to talk I would have to be a missionary, that that was why the Lord sent this affliction on me etc. and as I very decidedly did not wish to be one I guess I didn't try very hard to learn to talk.

About 1½ years ago we moved here and last winter in January they held meetings here. During December I had worked hard here in the store and was pretty worn out but I thot I could go and behave myself so I did a few times; but it only served to start my mind running on the missionary line again. This spell lasted a little over a month, then I went to Texas to visit an Aunt for a couple of months and thoroughly enjoyed myself there.

Then one day Mother happened onto an article in the Wichita *Eagle*, written by a teacher of singing, explaining his method of instruction which not only made singing easy but he also cured stammerers by the same principles, "correct breathing and diction." He teaches one to carry the tones to the sounding board in the head instead of cutting or choking them off in the throat. His method is quite different from the other teacher I tried; in fact I can see where he fell down now with his instruction.

At first I was not in favor of trying this method but one day I was so miserable because I couldn't talk and be like other girls and it just came over me that if I could only learn to talk correctly I could teach others who had the same trouble. After that I was very anxious to begin on my lessons. So the first of July, I went to Wichita and stayed 6 weeks, taking a lesson every day except Sundays. I was so interested and so determined to get it when I found out I really could that it was continually on my mind and I suppose I just overdid it. After five weeks I came home over the weekend and Mother and Dad were so pleased with the progress I was making and I was the happiest I think I have ever been. Then I went back for another 10 days as my instructor said that by then he could start me on some songs and make my work more interesting.

Well, about Thursday of that week I woke up in the middle of the nite with that same old missionary idea running thru my head and I couldn't throw it off. I haven't been able to do so since and that was in August. It always seems to be there in my mind no matter what I do—just a kind of hazy fear that some time I might have to do it. Mother and Dad have both explained to me that people aren't called to life service that way—that I could not stand the work—have not the training and no way of getting it—that I do not have the personality etc. But that doesn't seem to help. I just keep wondering if perhaps the reason I am not progressing now with my lessons is because I won't give in and do that; and that some day it might be that I could do it and then I would have to. But how could one be happy trying to do something one does not want to do? How do people know when they are called to life service for the church?

I have nearly driven Mother and Dad both crazy as well as myself on this last fit as mother calls it; so if you can throw any light on the subject we shall all be very very grateful to you.

The last time I went to Wichita my teacher suggested that I take lessons every other week until next fall, then begin teaching singing and speaking. He said he did not suggest it except to those who had had the most difficulty in learning it as he knew they would be the best able to teach and help others. Sometimes it seems as if everything were working out to that end or would if I could get peace of mind long enough again to work on it as I did at first.

Perhaps I was selfish because while I was getting along so nicely I rather let slip the idea of teaching music and I think now sometimes that this might have been brot on just to bring me back to that idea. I feel now that if I could get this crazy notion out of my head that I would love to work hard at my lessons, then teach singing here as there are no regular teachers of music here that I know of.

Mother said that I just overworked while I was staying out there and nearly had a nervous breakdown and that of course my mind would dwell on the weakest point. But whatever it is I can't get rid of it and certainly I am not happy nor making anyone else happy.

Have I too much religion or not enough?

Well I have tried to tell you all the details except this: When I was small Mother said I used to read her missionary magazines and say I wanted to be a missionary so I could travel to all these countries and see things. But I don't remember much about that. I just think now that because I have a home and so much that I should give it up and go to some foreign country.

I used to be a great hand to read and as one doctor told me—am somewhat of a daydreamer I guess. But when I have those spells, the only way I can forget them is to read and I have nearly worn my eyes out the last month or so.

If there is anything you wish to ask please let me know and I shall be glad to answer any questions.

Sincerely yours,

Nov. 20, 1930

My dear Miss:

Among all the letters that I have received in care of the *Ladies' Home Journal* I think yours of October 27 interests me among the most. I will tell you why.

The new discoveries in psychiatry, psychology and psychoanalysis indicate very clearly that stammering is usually brought about psychologically, and that it has nothing to do with the way the voice is controlled by the muscles of the throat and so forth. We know that in most cases of stammering, the reason is a very definite one but that it is hidden in the subconscious mind, or more correctly speaking, in the unconscious part of our mind. Treatment for stammering, therefore, consists in eradicating this deeply buried thorn.

Now we have also realized, as we have studied more and more cases, that this urge to be a missionary which so many young people have, in addition to all the well-known advantages and disadvantages and reasons pro and con which we all know about, also has certain unconscious motives. These unconscious motives are really unconscious. I mean they are quite unknown to the person who has them, to the person who has this urge to go into missionary work. But it is not often that the people who have them are as intelligent as you are; they usually do not realize that they are as you say "crazy ideas."

Now the interesting thing in your case is that you have both of these symptoms, and I can assure you that they are both symptoms, and that you realize that in some way or other the two are connected. You don't know why or how. Neither do I.

I do know, however, that you can not only find out how they are connected but why you have both of them. You can get rid of the whole problem that faces you. Until you do your life is going to be tied down by your neurosis, for that is what you have. You have a neurosis of a type we call compulsive and obsessive neurosis. Personally I have no confidence whatever in the kind of teaching you have been having. I do not mean that your teacher is not sincere but I do not think that he understands at all why you stammer. You see I think that if the unconscious difficulty did not exist in your mind, you could stop stammering in fifteen minutes. I don't mean by that that you can get rid of it in fifteen minutes, however; I think it will take a very long, hard, patient pull. You will have to go to a psychoanalyst and have the thing carefully and painstakingly worked out for you. It will take a good many months but in the long run it will certainly be worth it.

As to where you could go, I would naturally think first of my friend Mr. John Stone at the Menninger Clinic in Topeka.[1] You see I am not in Topeka any more, I am in Chicago, but the Menninger Clinic, with which I am associated, is an institution which treats nervous diseases of all sorts and is very fortunate in having Mr. Stone with them to do psychoanalysis. If you can afford to go further East and would prefer to do so, I should be glad to recommend someone in Chicago or even in New York. You can let me know about it.

Sincerely yours,

Washington
Jan. 29, 1931

Dear Doctor,

Since you have made other people happy, I need your aid too as I am unhappy.

---

1. John Stone was one of the original investors in the Menninger Clinic and its longtime business manager. Menninger was in Chicago undergoing his first serious analysis; it was conducted by a fellow member of the Chicago Psychoanalytic Institute, Franz Alexander.

I am a girl of eighteen years. I am very nervous. In fact so nervous that I seldom talk to anyone and some people think I am sort of crazy.

They don't understand my situation and how I feel about it because I hope it isn't that bad.

What I have just told you about makes me unhappy and I have lost practically all of my friends, both boys and girls, by being "bashful." Even my sisters don't get along with me.

This is one of my greatest troubles but it is not all of it.

I get blue when I cannot get things that I want very badly or do things which I like to do. Maybe I am rather selfish or hard to please but I cannot be optimistic even though I try. I am grateful for what I get and I have a good home but if I cannot have what I want I feel unhappy.

I don't have hardly a happy moment.

Can I ever be happy? And if so, how?

Sincerely yours,
Blondy

Feb. 23, 1931

My dear Miss:

I have your letter of January 29th sent to me in care of the *Ladies' Home Journal* and signed "Blondy." I don't know just why you sign yourself in that way but I suppose you think I am going to print your letter in the *Ladies' Home Journal*.

I am not going to do so. I get hundreds of letters just like yours. They are all more or less the same sort. I wish you could sit here and read them and pretty soon I think you would begin to feel rather uncomfortable. You would see that they all sound the same way. "I want to be happy. I am not happy. Other people don't notice me. People don't get along with me. People don't treat me the way I wish they would," etc. and so on.

I think you would ask me "why don't some of those girls talk about the way they do instead of the way other people do to them" [*sic*]. That's the whole point, I think, Miss V. Your letter is so full of "I" and "me" and how you want people to treat you that I don't think you realize that you are getting from the world just about what you give. If you are not interested in other people, if you don't like other people, if you are not going to talk to other people and try to give them a little pleasure, or a little amusement, or a little something to think about, or a smile, or a little love, if you are not going to give other people these things they are not going to give it to you and that's all there is about it.

Now, we know from a great deal of medical experience that there are people who shut themselves away from others and try to get along without any social contacts. They are not healthy-minded and that is the reason some people think as you say they do that you are sort of crazy. That is not a healthy-minded thing to do. So, instead of trying to be optimistic as you say you do, etc., try to make yourself helpful or interesting to someone else and the rest of your problems will begin to disappear.

I recently saw a little booklet called "How Not to Be a Wallflower," published by Haldeman-Julius, book No. 488. Some of it is trash but some of it is rather good. It wouldn't hurt you to read it. A good deal more valuable thing to read, however, would be a book called *The Quest for Happiness* by Bertrand Russell.[1] Get the latter and read it and think over what I have just told you and try to follow these suggestions.

Sincerely yours,

1. Menninger means *The Conquest of Happiness* (New York: Liveright, 1930).

6.

Philandering Husbands

Newark, N.J.
Nov. 1930

Dear Sir:

I read your article in the November issue of the *Ladies' Home Journal* and I am going to tell you my troubles to see if you can help me. I am 26 years old and married. Before my marriage I was just a poor country girl, coming from a large family, and never had any chance of seeing much of the world. So when I met my "ideal" of course we planned and he promised me so many things and I thot as they all do it would be heaven. I was married when I was 21 years old and we were happy for awhile but then my husband lost his job at the time our first baby was born and I worried. Thirteen months later we had another baby. Four months later we lost our eldest child and that was quite hard to bear. Then when our 2nd baby was 14 months old we had twin boys. I have always done all the work, including washings, and at night I was exhausted and would retire early. Meanwhile my husband has been working very hard and has been successful. I now find he is so far my superior that I feel very self-conscious when in his presence or with any of his friends. He is very popular and very well liked by the ladies. I am inclined to be jealous and lately I discovered he had a girl's picture and a ring and several names and addresses of girls. He says we are mismatched but I believe if I am given some good advice and by hard work on my part everything will be rightened. You see I have been dull and tired in the past as I never had any chance to get out and have a good time. All my friends and relatives are living in Penn. I am not a high school graduate but I was a junior when I quit and had the highest marks of my class.

So if by reading this you can suggest or advise anything for me to do I surely would appreciate it as I know it's only me that thinks life is miserable.

I will be anxiously waiting to hear from you
and thanking you

I am
Truly yours,

Nov. 26, 1930

My dear Mrs.:

I have your recent letter addressed to me in care of the *Ladies' Home Journal*.

What gives me encouragement in writing you is your determination. It is the sentence in your letter where you say, "I believe if I am given some good advice, by hard work on my part everything will be right."

If you have that attitude, I think it will be. You see you are very young and you have been married just about the number of years at which troubles of this sort begin to happen. And you have analyzed it pretty well. I think you have been so overwhelmed by the hard realities and necessities of life, that you have forgotten the reasons for which you were living with your husband. You were living with him for the increasing of his happiness and the increasing of your own by your mutual treatment of one another. Now if you have had to work so hard that your house and your work were more important to you than your husband, you can be pretty certain that sooner or later his work will be more important to him than you are. Well as soon as that happens, women become merely a diversion with them and there are a lot of women who will be more diverting and amusing and entertaining than you are. What you have to do then, is to reassemble your husband's interest in you as his beloved and also as his greatest source of happiness. I think you could do that because I believe you love him and I believe you see your mistake and I think you are going to be sensible about these other women that he likes. Whatever you do, I think I wouldn't at first be too disagreeable about these other women. Tell him that it hurts your feelings of course that he likes someone else but that you can quite understand it and are going to try to make him like you better than he does them. Then set out and do it. Make yourself just as attractive as you can. I often tell women that I believe the thing men like most in them is a sunshiny smile and cheerfulness. Most men take life rather seriously and gloomily and it makes them feel a great deal better to see the woman whom they look to for happiness and pleasure and joy be smiling and gay. It may be rather difficult for you to be smiling and gay when your heart is as heavy as I am sure it must be; nevertheless I think you are up against it. You must do it. Your education, your knowledge, your wisdom, all these things are unimportant, your husband doesn't care if you don't know as much as he does or as much as some of these other girls do. That is nothing to him. In fact it probably rather pleases him to think that he is your superior in these ways. You mustn't care about that. The way in which you can be superior to him is in your cheerfulness and in your gaiety and the evidences of your love for him. Don't try to be too coy. Meet him at the door every night and all that sort of thing and I am sure that the situation will straighten out.

I wish you would let me know some time when my prophecy comes true.

Sincerely yours,

New York, N.Y.
Jan. 22, 1931

My dear Doctor Menninger:

I have read with much interest the answers to questions about mental hygiene that appear in the *Ladies' Home Journal*. My case may not come under that caption but I have been wondering whether it did or not. Hence this letter. I am a woman fifty-four years old. Was pretty I am told but now I only weigh a hundred and fifteen pounds. The weight plus five pounds that I had when I was married—I've never been really thin as my height is only five feet three. My hair, unfortunately, refuses to gray and is still very black. I am in robust health and active in sports—a good shot and a fair fisher with a fly. Play a fair game of golf and have ridden a horse since I was eight years old. I married a man when I was twenty-one, two years my senior.

He also was in sports interested and for thirty years we had a wonderful time doing things together. We had three children. Two boys and a girl. There never was any worry about finances.

When last January came this husband and friend combined and asked me for a divorce.

I told him that I was not a dog in the manger and said yes. I had to perjure myself to give it to him. Six days after the decree he married his secretary. A girl of twenty-four—six years younger than his daughter.

She knew nothing of housekeeping or how to entertain. All of which he was accustomed to. His children refused to recognize her and clung to me. All of which made him unhappy. The town in which we lived refused to accept her and this naturally cut him off from his friends.

Now to the point upon which I want advice. He came to me last week. Told me that he had made a mistake. Asked me if I would take him back. That he had lied to the Roman Catholic Church in which he was married about his baptism. This being the case he could get divorced at once. He did not seem to consider the state. Said I was still his wife in the eyes of God. For the children's sake I must do it.

He had tickets for a West Indies cruise. Insisted that I go with him and "let the opinion go to hell because I was still his wife."

This attitude cannot be normal. But just this morning a wire came to meet him at the dock.

Can you advise me?

Feb. 9, 1931

My dear Mrs.:

I have just read with a great deal of interest your letter of January 22 addressed to me in care of the *Ladies' Home Journal*. I think of all the letters I have received since I have been on the staff of the *Journal* yours is one of the most interesting.

By all means go back to your husband. Marry him and go on the West Indies cruise or go on the cruise first, which ever happens to be most convenient. Don't hesitate.

You say this attitude cannot be normal. I think it is exactly normal. I think this interest in his secretary and this divorce and all the rest of it was a kind of neurotic flight, a "Strange Interlude," and if I were you I would take him back as if nothing had ever happened and love him just as much as ever and make him as happy as possible. I think this is about as beautiful an ending to a thing of this sort as I have ever heard of because usually they discover only too late that they want to come back and there are too many obstacles.

Let me call your attention to the fact that he unconsciously expected to come back all the time. That is the reason I am sure that he fixed his wedding so that it could be declared invalid by the Church.

I have a notion to send you a telegram but this letter will be out in a few days and I hope you will set upon it immediately. You have my best wishes and congratulations.

Sincerely yours,

Oakland, Calif.
Feb. 13, 1931

Dear Dr. Menninger:

What chance is there for me to bring back lost mental health and contentment, under the following circumstances?

My husband is forty-one years of age, I am forty-three, just entering a serious phase of life. We have in our home my husband's eighty-two-year-old mother who depends on me to see her through, and our seventeen-year-old son.

We have been married eighteen years. I have always enjoyed my life and every phase of our marriage, and thought my husband did, too. We seemed to care more for one another with every passing year. Last year I had the shock of discovering that he had been intimate with a woman in the same office for several years. I never even dreamed of such a situation, and once or twice when warning bells sounded in my brain, I hushed them as base suspicions. He states that I have been the best wife a man ever had, and he wishes no changes, even going so far as to threaten to kill himself. Is my idea distorted when it seems to me that it would have been better if he had let me and the boy go years ago, when I could still have been sure of making a living? I was an experienced office worker.

Now I cannot go. The truth would kill his mother, and it would be spiritual disaster to my boy at this age. In all other respects my husband is almost perfect, kind, generous and affectionate. But how can I forget the long deceit, lies, and betrayal, with not the slightest apparent compunction? How can I forget that he is still with this girl every day? If you could help me, I would be so grateful.

Sincerely,

P.S. We don't talk about it at all.

Mar. 12, 1931

My dear Mrs.:

I have read with great interest your letter of February 13 addressed to me in care of the *Ladies' Home Journal.*

I can fully understand the distress you feel, but at the same time does it not occur to you that you are taking this matter much too seriously? Don't think that I am wishing to condone your husband nor to make light of his offense. But I think the important thing is that your husband has loved you and still loves you, that you have loved him and I think still love him. I think if you were to persuade yourself that you did not love him because of an offense of this sort that it would indicate that you had invested your love in a false ideal. Your husband is not a Sir Galahad; if you imagined that he was it was your illusion, an illusion which you should have thrown off long ago. Unfortunately it is true that in our present civilization girls are brought up to suppose that men are Galahads and to be disillusioned by some such shocking way as this.

What you call his deceit, his lies, and his betrayal might also be interpreted as his very decent endeavor to keep from wounding you. He is trying to keep from you things which have happened to him which he knew it would hurt you to know about. I think it is a mistake to attribute to him a deliberate intention to hurt you when it is quite obviously just the reverse.

In other words, to me, a perfectly neutral person, the problem you present is one in which your husband deserves even more, and attracts my sympathy just as much as or even more than you. The poor fellow is evidently torn terribly between his love for you and his attraction for this girl. It does not make matters easier for him to have you condemn her or to have you condemn him either for his love for the girl or for his attempt to hide it from you. His attraction for the girl is something which he does not understand any more than you do. What he knows is that it has happened to him. The only way to fully understand it would be to undertake an elaborate psychoanalytic investigation of his whole personality. I don't know whether he has either the inclination or the means to do this. I do know that many others who have done so have discovered that the psychological mechanisms leading up to this love for two women at the same time are very complicated and often times very distressing.

If your love for him is of a very deep sort, which I believe it is, it will love him not because of this other woman, but in spite of her. It will certainly not be demolished by the realization, however humiliating and disappointing and saddening and disillusioning, that your husband is not perfect or that he is not exactly what you had supposed him to be. In the essentials for which you loved him, he still is the same man you once loved. For that reason I think you ought by all means to be loyal to him, to love him and to stay with him. I think you would be making a great mistake to leave him unless your resentment on account of this matter is so great that you actually hate him. In that case I pity you but I think for the happiness of you all it might be just as well that you left. I do not believe that to be the case or I would not say this. As a matter of fact I practically never advise couples to separate. If circumstances are such that it is impossible for them to live together, they know it without any such advice from me. It is sometimes necessary for me to point out, however, that they have theoretical or imaginary reasons for separating in the face of very practical and powerful reasons for not separating. I think such is the case with you.

I would not tell my husband any lies about the matter; I would not tell him other than that I was very grieved and sorry but on the other hand I would not be bitter or disagreeable or reproachful. That will certainly not be the way to win him back to yourself. I am not sure that you ever can win him back to yourself entirely but it is possible and it is certainly worth making the effort to accomplish. Something about you evidently did not hold his love. You should not reproach yourself for this any more than you should reproach him for what he has done. The thing to do is to examine yourself so far as you possibly can and examine him to find out what it is that he needs which you are not giving him. This may lead to some very astonishing discoveries. In the meantime, it will lead to a heightening of your own nobility for which he, and yourself, cannot but have respect.

Sincerely yours,

Quincy, Ill.
Feb. 25, 1931

Dear Dr. Menninger:

It is necessary that I give you some details before I can give you my problem. I have been married, very happily for fourteen years. After eight years of married life we had a little girl who we lost at birth. Later we had another who is now four. And both of us adore our baby.

Two years ago it was necessary for me to give a home to my father and young brother. My father has since become ill and is unable to work. My brother won't work. I did everything to help him but it seems that he just won't do anything. My husband was able to give him several jobs but he took advantage of it and made hard with the rest of the help.

My husband is a very hard working and an ambitious man. He has had several promotions promised him but the one that meant most to him failed to materialize due to the business depression. But it has been a bitter disappointment. It probably means that he will never get the chance again.

During these two years that my father has been here I have had a steady run of relatives. We haven't any spare room so it has made it uncomfortable as well as extremely expensive.

We tried to get my three sisters and brother to help support my father and they won't. They become angry and I couldn't turn my father out but I did my brother. But here is what has happened. My husband went somewhere else for shall I say sympathy, or is understanding better?

I didn't intentionally neglect him but with a child and two other adults in the house and I do every bit of my own work, I didn't have much time to spend with my husband. And he had always been used to my going everywhere with him and I did after the baby came as I had a reliable woman to keep her. He has not failed to provide as always but he says it seems that I was willing to turn our home over to my relation.

To sum it all up he has never failed me in any way except he has been unfaithful. And I'm honest when I say that I don't blame him much. I would have been tempted too if the shoe had been on the other foot.

Here is my problem, does he still love me, he says it's all over and outside of the pain it has given me, he is glad that I know the truth. And he will make it up to us. And he will always be good to my father. And I do love him and I can't stand to think maybe I'll lose him or have lost him. Do you think just loving him a lot will make up for what I did to him?

Sincerely yours,

Mar. 24, 1931

My dear Mrs.:

I do not know when I have had a letter connected with my work with the *Ladies' Home Journal* that has given me more satisfaction than yours of February 25. You will probably wonder why.

The reason is that you obviously have a rather serious problem, and in spite of this both you and your husband have faced it with so much good sense, so much honesty and authority and so much good mental hygiene that about all that is necessary for me to do is to write and commend you both.

I think you were exactly right that your relatives almost ruined your home. Some relatives have a tendency to do this and the worst of it is sometimes they prey upon our own emotions so that we let them do it. Sometimes it is necessary to steel ourselves against the demands of our kin because of course our own home, your husband and your children, are more important than any relatives, no matter how close. Your duty to your husband and children takes precedence over your duty to all the rest of the world, your father included.

I think you are quite sensible when you say that you can't blame your husband for being disgusted with the situation and for permitting himself an indulgence in unfaithfulness of a sexual sort. I can see from your letter that you do not exaggerate the importance of this. You are quite right in that. It is quite obvious from your letter, from your husband's frankness and honesty to you that he does love you very much and that his excursion into other fields was not as satisfactory to him as it might have been, and was not a serious damage or serious reflection upon his love for you. I think he has shown a very deep respect for your feelings in not having wanted to wound you about it and also a high degree of conscientiousness in telling you frankly what he had done. I do not think that you ought to feel that he should "make it up" to you as you say. I think this episode may make your love for one another a great deal firmer than ever before. Whatever you do I think you ought to recognize that you have both been at fault and that you both see things in a different light and that you are starting again to love each other in a way which is more likely than ever to succeed in bringing about a happy home. I think you are both to be congratulated in having one another.

Sincerely yours,

Illinois
Apr. 20, 1931

My dear Dr. Menninger:-

My problem perhaps is an all too common one and yet it impairs my mental health and surely must have an evil effect on the home atmosphere. We have been married for nine years, our splendid son is almost eight.

When we were married it was my great pleasure to assist my husband in his office, on his obstetrical cases, in his hospital surgery. When he decided to enter a special field, I returned to my own profession for two years that he might be relieved of the burden of supporting me and our little son. Now he is established in a fair-sized town with a most inspiring practice.

For one entire year he has had all his sex life with his office girl. Recently she has suffered her mouth to be used. Apparently she is a very nice, sweet girl in the early thirties. I am thirty-eight and still cling to the quaint belief that there should be absolute fidelity between married mates. I think a man should live with the one with whom he has his sex life.

Upon suggestion of divorce he is upset and declares he would not continue to practice here should I insist on carrying out this plan. He was faithful to me for eight years and I adore him. I am not cold sexually.

We approached marriage from different planes. I always kept all that I had to give for this marvelous love that I felt was to be mine.

His experience was that every girl was willing to go the limit.

I love him with that terrible loyalty that is the curse of some of us.

Even after a year of despair I look in his dear face and think it cannot be possible. I suppose there are the inhibitions left from my nursery days. What can I do to rid myself of these unmodern ideals. To create within me a more wholesome attitude. I am so often consumed with bitter, base jealousy.

To me intercourse was an uplifting spiritual union that washed away all misunderstandings and let us emerge into the fresh pure air of the mountain top.

To give over to another the sweet intermezzos of marriage after our years of association and close co-operation is unthinkable.

The routine of the home runs smoothly enuf on the surface but I cannot adjust myself to this only great sorrow I have known. I supposed, oddly enuf, that the love between man and woman was one of the things one carried with one into eternity.

May 23, 1931

My dear Mrs.:

The problem you present in your letter of April 20 addressed to me in care of the *Ladies' Home Journal* is one which I find most difficult to answer and at the same time one about which I have more letters than perhaps any other one thing.

We cannot, of course, change the facts. The facts are that you had one ideal and your husband had another, that your husband conformed for a time to your ideal and then broke over and went back to the plan of living which seemed most satisfactory to him. This wounds you deeply.

You do not make it clear in your letter whether or not he has discontinued his relations with this girl since you have discovered it and protested about it. Neither do you make it quite clear to me why he has discontinued having any sexual relations with you, altho you say that he has. I wonder if this is because you have refused him when you found out that he was not faithful to you. In that case I think you make a mistake because if you expect him to make a certain compromise with his ideals, you must make a corresponding compromise with yours and meet him halfway. In other words, you must at least forgive him or overlook what he has done in the past.

I can fully understand your feeling about this which I think represents the attitude of the majority of American people, men as well as women. I do not say that I think it is the best attitude, but I think it is the prevalent one, and I think you are quite justified in having it. I do not think, however, that you are justified in letting your whole married happiness stand or fall on it. In other words, while I think you are entitled to disapprove and regret what you husband does, and even reproach him for it, I do not think you are entitled to make yourself unhappy about it. After all, there are very much more serious things that your husband might do and if he loves you, I think this should not matter so much as it otherwise does. Furthermore, I think a tolerant and unbitter attitude on your part may have very remarkable results with him. I should not be surprised if he would give up entirely his extra-marital interests, because I think it is quite clear from your letter that he really loves you very much and if for some reason or other his sexual interests have been temporarily switched away from you, you have very good reason for believing that they will be ultimately switched back again.

If one of my little children came in and broke a beautiful picture or vase of which I was very fond, perhaps my most valued treasure of art, I should feel very badly but I should love my child just the same. Something beautiful would have been broken which could never be replaced; it would not have been broken had the child regarded it with the same tenderness and care with which I regard it. Nevertheless, because of it I shall not cease to love my child just the same, to be as happy with that child as possible. I do not mean to say that you should look upon your husband as a child, but I do mean to say that you should look upon this particular indulgence perhaps as a parent might look upon the misdoings of a child. This I think makes it not only easier to bear but it makes it more likely that you will have some control over your husband and exercise greater influence and attractiveness for your husband.

I should appreciate it very much if you would tell me frankly what you think and what the effect of this program is after you have tried it for a while.

Sincerely yours,

Phoenix, Ariz.
July 24, 1931

Dear Doctor,

I've been reading your articles on "Mental Hygiene" in the *Journal* and thought you might be able to help me.

To state circumstances briefly: I have been married 14 years, am nearly forty years old, and have four children, the youngest a baby 10 months old. My husband is five months older than myself. When we were first married he was a struggling clerk. I am a school-teacher. We have had some pretty tough financial pulls and both have sacrificed but gradually we have bettered our condition. We live in the country, my husband has always had poor health; he is generally not strong; specifically, arrested tuberculosis and a weakened condition of the heart which doctors say is not serious, yet it worries him. He is a successful politician at present, has been serving in office three years (he is now on his second term). Our children are healthy normal youngsters. As for myself, my health is superb, lacking perfection in "nerves" only. Which sounds bad enough, but is not really. I have kept up my reading, taken an interest in community affairs, etc. In short we are just the average family. My husband and I are both church members, he being always more active than I. In fact, it was his interest in church that first attracted me, for above all I wanted a Christian home, a man I could depend on to keep his marriage vows and be a worthy example to his sons. If ever a marriage started auspiciously it was ours. Love, loyalty, willingness to do our share, and an unusual amount of knowledge in complications that often arise. We had our problems solved before they occurred! Ours was a real partnership. Because I was the stronger I took on duties not often assumed by the woman, such as building fires in winter. As he needs so much more rest, I've done nearly all the waiting on children at night. But he has always been appreciative of all my efforts and sacrifices and in turn has been kind, generous and courteous as well as helpful in many ways. I have my own car. He is thoughtful and remembers all anniversaries and special days. Our friends refer to us [as] the one couple who never bicker and it always seemed to me that ours was as near perfect a union as possible.

But—18 months ago a woman started working for him. She was rather notorious though I give him credit for not knowing it. Immediately there was gossip. It was positively funny to me. I believed as much in his honor as I believed in God—and he knew it. And even when he began acting differently I thot nothing of it. I attributed his silent moods to his feeling ill. Then like a bolt out of the blue I quite accidentally discovered something in his car. I was so dumbfounded I immediately went to him. The explanation he gave was an insult to my intelligence but I swallowed it, trying to believe, and yet I began to think of former things that had happened before which I had not noticed. Oh, how I tried to believe in him and prayed for faith. So many things happened that summer and there was so much talk but I kept my doubts down. Almost at times I persuaded myself there had been nothing to it, particularly as he began to change in his attitude toward her and his conduct was above suspicion. And then when the baby was just about a month old he was with her again. Oh I knew, and I knew too that the other time in the spring was true and goodness knows how much else. All day I pondered on how to talk to him and I finally decided I would make no accusations but would give him an opening to come clean, letting him see I was willing to regard everything as past. Only, I was fully determined not to let him know *how* I knew for I knew there would always be a doubt and I did not want to put him completely on his guard in future occurrences; also I wanted to be able to assure myself in the future of his decency. When anyone has not played fair, no matter how unquestionable his conduct, we cannot help but feel that the same thing could happen again. But, when I brought the matter up he insisted I was the only one who mattered, he had done nothing wrong; that I was everything he desired in a wife and that I had given him no reason to seek companionship outside. What could I do? I was not ready to tell him I knew he was lying for if I did it would mean a definite break and I felt I must keep the home for the children's sake. It seemed as if my heart was broken but I tried to be my old self. On the surface everything went on as before and I felt that he was really sorry and loved me more than ever. He let her go from his office and I know he became so disgusted with her that he surely must be ashamed and had learned his lesson. I even began to feel what I had thot was impossible, the same old trust in him. A few weeks ago he was out supposedly to a meeting—and while I cannot be sure anything happened, I know he *meant* it to. It has killed all hope, and at times it seems my love. I don't want to keep on loving him because those things hurt so. I can't talk to him for he would admit nothing. I simply cannot leave him and deprive the children of their daddy whom they adore for he is really a good dad to them. We have such good family times together and he and I go out together a lot. He takes me everywhere he can, seldom goes out alone. He always acts like a lover—and I go on pretending everything is fine, tell him what a dear good husband he is, etc. Sometimes I think I shall go mad. I feel he is taking advantage of my faith to have his fun. And I also know I would be more miserable if I left him (as long as things are not considerably worse) than if I stay. I suppose it is fortunate I can have my different moods. At times I can be real gay and cheerful and I always try never to act blue or depressed when he is around. Sometimes I feel that he can go to the devil if he wishes. I'll do my part and live so that I need not be ashamed. Again it breaks my heart when I think of the first twelve years of perfect happiness, our plans for our earthly life together, our hopes of an eternity spent together. And all the time now I am trying to tear out my love—I don't *want* to love him anymore when it *hurts* so. And yet to live with a man feeling that way about him, makes me feel like a common woman of the street. I know he doesn't know how I feel for he couldn't act as he does toward me. He must really care in a way for me, for he could not always be so patient, sweet and loverly [sic] if he didn't, yet he doesn't care enough to be decent. I don't know exactly what kind of help I want from you. I can't go to him and tell him how I feel and what I *know* for I am not ready for a definite break. I tell myself things could be so much worse for what some wives put up with is so great beside my own trouble—yet it is poor consolation when there is not necessity for affairs being so bad. If I could blame myself at all, I'd feel better for I could do something about it then by correcting my own shortcomings. But according to him, he desires no change in me. He says he's completely satisfied with me in every way. He appears proud of me and as I said takes me everywhere with him, his only "stag" affairs being his lodge.

Please don't tell me I'm jealous and suspicious. I am not jealous—no one ever accused me of it. I honestly feel no envy of anyone unless it is the happy young couples who have the happiness I once knew. Suspicious? Yes, but not in the beginning, only when unmistakable evidence presented itself. I realize I only can work out my problem but the way is so slow, perhaps one who is wiser than I can show me a few shortcuts. I know now why older women cry at weddings. Whenever a young girl I know takes that step I want to cry myself. It is heartbreaking to realize how lightly men take their marriage vows—I am so cynical now. Seems to me if that wonderful Christian man I married could slip, they all could and will. There are even times when I understand why women kill themselves. If it weren't that my children need me, I'd want to die too. Mental hygiene in the home! How long can a broken-hearted homemaker keep up pretense of serenity and happiness?

Aug. 19, 1931

My dear Mrs.:

I have read carefully your letter addressed to me in care of the *Ladies' Home Journal*.

As you can well imagine, I get a great many letters, the circumstances of which are the same as yours. I know how I should like to answer them but I do not think my readers would understand what I mean. I would like to say that I think you are making a mountain out of a molehill, or at least I think you are emphasizing something into an importance which it really does not possess, viewed from an impartial standpoint. Now I am sure you will think this is heartless and indifferent on my part or perhaps you will think I am standing up for your husband because he and I are both men.

The fact of the matter is that the whole understanding of sexual behavior and the taking of a proper attitude toward it is made exceedingly difficult because of certain attitudes which have been passed on from generation to generation for the past 2000 years until it is very difficult to distinguish fact from prejudice. I should like to make this clear to you because I think it would save you an enormous amount of suffering but I realize before I state the almost hopeless difficulty of making this plain. You tell me you have a charming, loving, attentive husband who has had sexual intercourse a few times with another woman and who has deceived you about it and out of hurt pride, anger, disappointment, disillusionment and spite you are ready to kill yourself, divorce him or what not and keep yourself in mental agony all the time. I honestly don't think it is worth it.

I would suggest that you read Mrs. Bertrand Russell's book, *The Right to Happiness*, Briffault's *Sin and Sex*, and Margaret Mead's *The Coming of Age in Samoa*,[1] and I think you will have a little different feeling about the whole business. By doing so I think you can change your attitude in such a way that instead of so much hostility toward your husband you will have a greater attraction for him. This in itself may be the beginning of a better adjustment for him to his sexual life. It is quite apparent that he is maladjusted to sex as well as you; he takes it out by doing certain things and you take it out in feeling a certain way.

Sincerely yours,

1. Dora Russell, *The Right to Be Happy* (New York: Harper and Brothers, 1927); Robert Briffault, *Sin and Sex* (New York: Macaulay, 1931); Margaret Mead, *Coming of Age in Samoa: A Psychological Study of Primitive Youth for Western Civilisation* (1928; rpt. New York: Morrow, 1961).

7.

Abusive Husbands

Maplewood, N.J.
Oct. 16, 1930

My Dear Doctor Menninger,

I am a wife with a bad problem on my hands, and I am worrying so about it, that I decided to write you to see if you think there may be any hope of a solution.

I am married to a miser, that is, as I see this case, it is a case of true pathological miserliness. My husband, a lawyer with an office in N.Y., and I were married thirty-two years last July. He has always been mean and small about money, allowing me $5.00 a week for years. When the children came, and there were four of us instead of two, he allowed $10.00 a week, and this continued until fifteen years ago when he decided—for what reason I never knew—to give me exactly nothing. This went on for six weeks. He seemed to have gone crazy. I went to our butcher and charged provisions. The butcher had to collect the bill. I would ask him for money for the children. No answer. I bought a suit for our boy—$2.98—sent it C.O.D. He sent it back. I had no money in the bank, but I cashed a check for $5.00 in town as I was absolutely desperate. The check came back, of course, and our tradesman came up and I told him Mr. D. [her husband] would make good on it, but he never would.

Well, this condition went on for six weeks and I became sick. I am a conscientious woman and living this way completely unnerved me. I couldn't understand a person, unless he had gone suddenly crazy, allowing his fellow townsmen and brother Masons (these men are all members of the Masonic Lodge) to be compelled to sue for small amounts.

My doctor at that time sent me to his lawyer. This lawyer was wonderful in every way, and procured for me $200.00 monthly.

Mr. D. and I are not living together as husband and wife, nor have we been for sixteen years. This came about by my saying to him, as the lawyer told me to, that until he treated me as a wife should be treated, I would not be a wife to him. That was the end. He has never in any way made any attempt to change conditions. I don't think he wants to live with me. I made one very desperate effort after I procured the allowance to right things. I went to him and told him for the sake of the children we must try to make a go of the situation. I told him if he would stay at home New Year's Eve, I would plan a party at home, and we would make it a reconciliation party. He always spent all of the holidays, beginning with New Year's, away from home. Where, I never knew. He would never tell. Just said he wouldn't be home and would leave no address; or he would go without saying he was going to be away. I talked to him this particular night for about two hours, thought I had completely convinced and reformed him! He never said a word. He never does. Just listens to all you have to say and does exactly as he wants to in the end. I know now that it takes two to make a reconciliation, and I have never made but one more attempt since. It met with the same success—or lack of it. But about the party. One of our friends telephoned me the day before, and I could tell from the way he was talking that he was trying to spare my feelings. He finally told me that Mr. D. told him he wasn't going to be at the party, that he had made other arrangements. I called him up and he admitted it. Told me he would get one of his friends to look after me. I told him I didn't want his friends, I wanted my own husband. Well, he hung up on me, and I was so excited I thought I never would get over the disappointment, as I think I realized, vaguely, what it all meant, tho' I didn't want to admit it to myself. I realized the hopelessness of the entire situation—his lack of desire.

We found out afterwards that he kept an engagement with a woman in Brooklyn. He got a friend to take me to a New Year's party, saying he would call for me at eleven o'clock. He came in at sometime after midnight so drunk that we could do nothing with him and I went home alone at four o'clock and left him sitting with two women, his arms around both of them. Mr. D., up to sixteen years ago, was a heavy drinker. Then he stopped suddenly, and has never, to my knowledge, taken anything since. He is, and always has been, very abusive. He refers to me as that "female in the bathroom," "that Irish woman in the kitchen," threatens me, and I am very much afraid of him, altho' I pretend not to be.

You may wonder in this enlightened day why I continue to live with him. Well in the first place I think women will do everything to hold a home together where there are children. My son was my reason before he was married. He was going with a lovely, wholesome young girl. I talked over the matter of a separation with my son, but he asked me not to just then. Now I do not want to do anything to jeopardize my young daughter's happiness. She will be twenty-one next month. She has a lovely group of young people she is going with and she fears that she may be disgraced, and so I live on.

We did try to get evidence once. My lawyer, in order to get better terms, tried to find out something of his movements. I think he became suspicious. He never is away any more. Comes home every night, goes up to his room; sits and listens to the radio or just "sits" for hours. He is distinctly anti-social. Altho' he belongs to many clubs, he has no friend. No man ever enters our home, except once in two or three years when a group of college men meet here.

He has lately begun to show acute symptoms again, i.e., his resistance to parting with money has become so pronounced that I realize an explosion is impending and I am in a very nervous state. Last month he cut down my allowance $25.00. This is always the beginning of his systematic way of economizing at our expense. My daughter spent exactly one hour last week trying to get $4.00 to pay a cleaning woman, and she was exhausted. This happens all the time. He is supposed to allow her $1.00 a week, but she seldom gets it. She will tease sometimes for an hour for that money without success.

I have been working. I thought to make things better this way, but when he found it out he stopped paying the maid $12.00 weekly, then he stopped the money for the weekly cleaning woman, and I find that the money I earn I have to use this way. He says he has his will made out to our daughter, as well as his insurance, and I feel I must work in order to provide for myself, but if I must use the money for the house as I have been doing now for some time again, I am not making any headway in any way. He maintains his boyhood home in Connecticut, that is, he pays the expenses of running this house. This has been a matter of much dissatisfaction and we have had many scenes on account of this. He will have the kitchen and other rooms in this Conn. house painted, and refuses absolutely to paint our kitchen here. I have to do this myself. Conditions are so bad at present that I realize they cannot go on, and I was about to take the matter up with a lawyer again, when I read your book *The Human Mind*, and realized that Mr. D. undoubtedly is a "hooked fish,"[1] and I wonder if you can offer any

---

1. In the first paragraph of *The Human Mind* Menninger uses the metaphor of a trout hooked on a line for the way a "human being struggles with his environment and with the hooks that catch him" (p. 3). See the quotation of this passage in the Introduction to the present volume.

suggestion to help me. There is no need to tell you that I am not happy. I have no family to whom I can go, and I worry so much about this situation that sometimes I think I am going crazy. Mr. D. is absolutely heartless. If we get sick we are out of luck unless I have the money to pay the doctor, as he will pay no doctor bills. E., our daughter, had a boil in her nose. The last doctor we had had to sue him for a small bill and we couldn't go back, so she went to her father and asked him for money to go to the doctor. He said it wasn't necessary, altho' her nose was swollen all out of shape from the boil. She reminded him that he had had the same thing and had been to the doctor, but he said his was different and more painful. Just as he said to me once. I was crying one night when I was young because he would never take me anywhere. I told him I was lonesome being alone so much and I longed for a good time the same as he did. He told me I was a woman and that a woman's place was at home with the children, but that a man *had* to have recreation.

We live miserably at times. He is so bent on saving that he won't start the furnace fire till Thanksgiving and lets it go out the last day of Feb'y. Sometimes when he has been going to be away he would go down in the cellar and turn off the current—he has an electrically driven coal furnace—and hide the charcoal so we couldn't start it. It is a Chinese puzzle to start the furnace and if he lets it go out I have never been successful in getting it started again.

He throws away *nothing*. He has old rags, soiled underwear, toothpicks, buttons, tacks, newspapers, boxes—everything that has ever come into his possession, stored in his room. His two chiffoniers are loaded halfway to the mirror with junk. I cleaned this junk all out about ten years ago; refurnished his room, bought him a new four poster bed, did over his chiffoniers, mirrors, etc. Had the room in a lovely condition. But it is awful once again. He has some filthy habits and is a most repulsive human being. The children won't go anywhere with him because he is such a slovenly looking man. Of course I hate him and when he comes in at night, tho' we have no communication except about money, and then only to fight, I lose heart as well as appetite, tho' I am very happy when I am away from him in the summer for one month. It gets harder each year to go back, and I am afraid the time is coming when I won't be able to go back. I want very much after my daughter marries to separate from him, but I thought it might be wiser to take this up with a psychiatrist and see if he could be helped. While I hate him, I still wouldn't do anything to hurt him if it could be avoided, and I recognize that he is in need of help. I have told him his attitude to money was not normal and tried to reason with him, but I guess you know how futile this was. Mr. D. is 63 next Dec. 9th. I am nine years younger.

He has a very peculiar effect on me. I am ambitious, progressive, alert, and love people, like to mingle with them, love company and the young folks. Mr. D. is a pervert. He wants to go back to his childhood and take refuge from reality that way. He complains *all the time*. Business is always bad, he is never making any money, he is always having to borrow from the bank. He complains to the children because I can't listen to him any more. Thirty-two years of that is enough for the rest of my life. I am beginning to wonder if this influence is bad where my daughter is concerned. She said to me the other day "Mother I'm beginning to feel badly every time I think I am spending Dad's money, and feel as if I should go to work, he says we are so poor." You know, "Vice too often seen . . ." What has particularly got him going just now is that I would not send E. to work in a department store this fall, where she worked this summer, but sent her to art school instead which costs him $190.00 a year. She has a distinct flair for designing and it will bring her in more money later than department store work. He was willing to send our boy to college, but not the girl. He doesn't believe in education for women. He is in a very ugly mood and I know something is coming, tho' he has no need to worry. He has a good business. Is very clever. His father died three years ago and left him between $25,000 and $30,000 and he has been tighter than ever since then. My daughter said many times, "Mother, Dad gets worse by the minute."

Before I was on an allowance—which takes care of all household expenses, clothes for myself and children, recreation, doctors, dentists, entertainment for the young people who come here, wedding presents, as he will buy none, laundry, gas and electric, food, oculists, etc. I needed to go to Orange one night. The fare was 25¢ for the round trip provided you bought the ticket at the station. If the station was closed the tariff was 15¢ each way. I asked him for 30¢ for my expenses and he would only give me 25¢. I told him the station was closed and it would be 30¢. He remained obdurate. Said the fare was only 25¢ and if they chose to close the station he couldn't help that. I was awfully nervous all evening at the entertainment as I knew I didn't have the money to get home and was figuring out all through the entertainment how I would manage to put it to one of my friends that I needed money to get home. Now this is a characteristic attitude and a characteristic incident, and he is as immovable as Gibraltar. He is stubborn and contrary beyond all belief.

Doctor Menninger, have you any suggestions that may help a very trying situation. One thing I'm never afraid of, and that is a nervous breakdown. I love problems, that is healthy ones, but I'm absolutely at a standstill where this one is concerned. I dread his scenes. His mouth opens so wide when he is in one of his rages, that I always think of a cavern. You can't imagine what an awful looking creature he is when he is in one of his rages. I don't know this minute whether they are simulated or genuine, but either way they are awful to witness.

I desire to thank you for any help you may be able to offer, and any expense attached to disentangling this situation I will gladly assume.

Sincerely,

Oct. 25, 1930

My dear Mrs.:

I think that your letter of October 16 addressed to me in care of the *Ladies' Home Journal* is one of the most remarkable letters that I have ever read, and I have read a great many. As much as I should like to print it in the *Journal*, I dare say you would not like for me to do so, so I am going to answer it personally.

If my book, *The Human Mind*, prevents you—as you say it did—in carrying out your idea of taking this whole matter up with your lawyer again, I am very sorry that my book fell into your hands. For the life of me, I cannot understand why you have put up with the misery which you describe.

You must pardon me if I look at this from the standpoint of your mental hygiene rather than his. For the symptoms you describe seem to me to be so numerous and of such a nature that they are past all hope or remedy. However, I am interested in your make-up. Your letter is so intelligent; your diction is so good; your insight and understanding seem to be so great that I cannot understand how you can be so illogical. You say that you have continued to live with him in order that you will not jeopardize your daughter's happiness. Do you seriously mean that your daughter would be unhappy if you did not continue to submit to that sort of thing? Do you really mean that your children are going to be made miserable if you bring it about that you shall at last have the modicum of comfort and peace? I have puzzled over this paragraph of your letter quite a while. I have concluded that you have raised your children to believe that a bitter and miserable marriage was better than a happy divorce. I believe that many people do think this—personally I do not think so at all.

You state in your letter that as a matter of fact you are married in name only (incidentally, as you may or may not know, it is very common for misers to be sexually impotent, to lose their sexual desire). I doubt if there has been as much adultery as you suspect; I think this will also explain to you why the man you describe has remained at home so much recently.

You ask if this may not be a psychopathic case, and if your husband may not, after all, be suffering from some kind of disease toward which we should take a psychiatric attitude. It is entirely too late to do so, from the standpoint of the family involved. For the sake of your own happiness and the happiness of your children, I think what you need is a lawyer's advice rather than a doctor's. From what you say, I think it is highly advisable to continue your original plan of taking the matter up with an attorney to get you your just deserts. I say this with no harsh feelings towards your husband, whom, of course, I do not know; but there are certainly many psychiatric cases whose behavior is such that society has to protect itself against them. At the same time, some of these cases cannot be regarded as insane, according to the interpretation of the laws of most states. Therefore, they cannot be confined by legal process. There are ways, however, of protecting ourselves against them, and this you are certainly entitled to do.

Please write me again and tell me what you do; I feel certain that no one who has written this Department has a greater possibility of improving their happiness by a few simple steps than have you. I should be glad to think that you had achieved it.

Sincerely yours,

Brooklyn, N.Y.
Oct. 16, 1930

Dear Doctor:

I never have read the *Ladies' Home Journal* but happened to be in a friend's home and picked up this magazine. I came across your article which interested me a great deal as I am in a very unfortunate predicament now.

I am about to become a mother, and don't know what to do about my husband. He at times is very good, yet at other times becomes so irrational as to strike me and use the vilest language. I have left him on many occasions during our one year of married life, but returned to him each time on his promise that he would be different.

I have had a miscarriage three months after my marriage due to his striking me and throwing me to the floor. While I lay in the hospital he came to me and cried and said he was terribly sorry for what had happened, that he must have been out of his head, and that it would never happen again.

I was so terribly run down in health that when I was discharged from the hospital I went to live with my mother. He came to live there with me, and at the beginning seemed to be alright, and then he began behaving in a most terrible manner such as striking and abusing me for no good reason at all, and if my parents interfered he would stop at nothing to abuse them, even as much as wanting to strike my seventy-year-old dad. I had to leave my parents' home because of this, and because I became pregnant, so I opened up home again with him, saying this would be the last chance I would give him. I lived in these rooms for two months during which time he behaved alright and then one night came home from business and struck me when my back was turned, as I was in the midst of preparing his supper. I became very frightened, and told him if he did not change I would be compelled to leave him again, that life with him was unbearable. That night he was in a terrible state. He even showed me an unloaded gun and said some day he would kill me. The next day he was still at his most peculiar behavior, and even went so far as terribly abusing me and shouting "I'll kick you in the stomach and give you another miscarriage." He also cut the furniture. I had to call a policeman as he was becoming worse and worse.

When he is in one of these conditions he frightens me very much, as his voice and his facial expression change completely. Always after one of these terrible outbursts I ask him whether he knows just how terrible he acts, and he seems to know everything. This has me puzzled.

I am now living with my married sister and he continues to call me on the phone. He wants to make up again, which I dread doing very much, as I know it is of no use. He also continues to confess his love for me. Sometimes I think he does not know what it is all about. He is not very clever.

What do you think is ailing him? I think he is not just right. Is there a way of finding out whether he is sane?

Your kind reply will be most appreciated from one who is puzzled and bewildered.

Yours truly,

Oct. 31, 1930

My dear Mrs.:

I have your letter of October 16 in which you say that your husband has beaten you, kicked you, threatened to kill you and so forth. You also say that time after time you have told him you would leave him if he did it again, but you have also indicated that you did not keep your promise. By this time your husband probably thinks you don't intend to keep your promise. I don't think you should permit yourself to get into that predicament. You already have a serious problem on your hands in your husband, as well as in the fact that you are pregnant and have children to take care of and to support. And I can understand exactly why you do it, you keep hoping against hope that he is going to be different. But as you say yourself in this letter, it doesn't look as if that were likely to be the case, at least not without help.

Probably your husband has times when he can be reasoned with. You say he calls you up and promises to be good and wants to come back.

Now I should certainly take advantage of those moments if I were you, to see if something could not be done with him. Many times I have seen this thing straightened out in this way. The wife has agreed to come back providing the husband would go with her for a mental examination at a psychiatric clinic. Let them examine him and let them have a social worker keep in touch with you and the family. This will protect you and will also help him to control himself. It sounds to me as if he were indulging in temper tantrums, like a grown up baby, and your way of dealing with him has apparently encouraged him in it instead of discouraging him. Now a social worker will back you up in your firm resolves and will also help him to toe the line, which apparently he sometimes very much wishes to do.

There are many good psychiatric clinics in New York, one of the best of them being the new Medical Center's Psychiatric Institute, way uptown in Manhattan. There is probably a psychiatric clinic in Brooklyn but I don't know just where it is and there are some downtown in New York.

Sincerely yours,

Lakewood, Ohio
Oct. 23, 1930

Dear Dr. Menninger:

I've read *The Human Mind* and have been following your work in the *Journal*, and have made up my mind that you are the one to help this family, if help there can be.

I am the problem. I am one to my husband and a worse one to myself. Married ten years ago at 19, to a man 18 years older, I've made a dreadful mess of things. I've failed my husband all along the line, and failed myself as well. You see, he has a rather violent temper, the first I'd ever encountered, and comes of a line of Puritan ancestors. He is honest and straight as a die. Cautious, too—the kind of man who never pays a bill, even by check, without demanding a written receipt.

Quite soon after our marriage he flew into a rage over a small money affair—some I'd spent as he thought extravagantly. And from that day to this it has seemed to me I've never been straight with him about any financial matter. We have four children who are reasonably well dressed, and I dress nicely myself, altho I haven't a lot nor very elaborate clothes. But I've ruined his credit in this town by charging the most moderate of amounts and concealing the bills until they called up the office to know why they weren't paid. No matter how reasonable the purchases, how really necessary, I could never submit those bills. I have snatched them from the mantel as he drove in the yard sometimes, unable to face the row.

Then we arranged that purchases should be sent C.O.D. and sometimes, almost always, it will take me half an evening to get up the nerve to ask for a check for things that are coming next day. My palms will be wet and my throat dry.

For a period I kept his checkbook, made out checks which he signed, and balanced it. A year ago I made a $100 mistake, and when I found it out could *not* tell him. And he made out a check for a large house payment, which I knew we couldn't cover—and I didn't mail it. For three months I held that thing until past time when the next payment was due. And told him the notice hadn't come in. Then I did mail it, and it overdrew the balance, of course.

On one or two occasions, in an emergency, I had signed checks for him. From time to time, then, when I needed money I would write one myself, which, altho not even an approximation of his signature, the bank honored. He finally sternly forbade that, and I didn't do it until a period of stress came, when I needed an unusual amount so I did it again, knowing that when the statement came in I'd be found out. And knowing that I decided it would be as well to be hung for a sheep as a lamb, and took as much as I wanted. Finally, since I couldn't eat nor sleep from worry, I blurted out the story, and you may imagine E.'s anger. He nearly killed me and I don't believe I'd have cared. Next day he went down and talked with an official of his bank warning them against me. Why, I sat down that night and thought "This can't be *me*. I'm not this person banks must be warned against" and yet of course, I am.

E. says I must be insane. He shouts at me "Why did you do it?" And when I can only say I don't know—and I don't—he gets dreadfully angry.

I can't be all bad. The maids, of whom there are several, who have worked here and married, come to me first when the baby is expected, bring it to show me when it is born, and things like that. My present maid has been here almost three years and dearly loves me. Surely those who live right here day after day should feel the badness? I've been told that I'm a delightful companion, and the same husband who has suffered so at my hands loves to go about with me or just to talk with me at home and deeply loves me. He'd have divorced me long since if he hadn't. I'm quite sensible about a great many things—but money isn't one of them.

I'm so discouraged, I don't know what to do. Even while I'm bitterly repenting some folly such as I've told you about another one is in the making and I'll let it happen.

What is it that makes some people all right and some all wrong? If you can diagnose this trouble so I can change things don't hesitate about a few bold words. E. has used plenty, and I am used to looking at it impersonally by now. Several lives are bound up in this and they all bid fair to be ruined.

Could you send some sort of help in the enclosed stamped envelope?

Gratefully,

If I.Q.'s mean anything mine is high and so are all the children's. Exceptionally so. E. is a graduate engineer.

Nov. 5, 1930

My dear Mrs.:

Your letter of October 23 is one of the most remarkable letters that I have received in care of the *Ladies' Home Journal* and I can assure you that means one out of a great many. I have read it very carefully several times and I very sincerely hope that I can say the right thing in reply. I agree with you that you have a very serious problem in your home, and I may say at the outset that I do not agree with you that it is all a question of you. For that reason I am writing this letter to you so that you may show it to your husband which I earnestly hope you will do.

Obviously you do some things you shouldn't do. There is no question about that. You should not deceive your husband, you should not overdraw your checking account, you should not injure your husband's credit. You should not forge his name to checks. You say he shouts at you, "Why do you do it?" All you can say is that you do not know. Now I wonder if it is true?

Isn't the truth of the matter this, that you do it because you need the money or the thing which the money gets for you and you are afraid of your husband's reactions to being asked for the money? And then because you are afraid of this, and yet very much desire and need the things, you decide to postpone the inevitable storm and make the purchase anyway. This gives you an immediate satisfaction and postpones the punishment.

Now there is something very wrong about that, of course. What it indicates to me is a tendency to evasion which is even more serious than the actual evasion. You have no right in the world to be afraid of your own husband. And you have no right to be afraid of an honest attitude toward money. I think the first one is your fault and I think the second may be your husband's fault. But let us settle with you first. For some reason or other, and I am inclined to think it is the result of your husband's explosions, you seem to have an enormous sense of inferiority and an enormous sense of guilt. You say you are a problem when it is quite obvious that your husband is more of a problem than you are. You say you have messed up the home when from all you say it has been his fault at least as much as yours. You say he nearly killed you and then you go on to say you don't blame him for having done so. This is a free country but even in a free country a husband does not have the right to kill his wife or even nearly kill her as you say, no matter what her sins have been. But you seemed to think that it was perfectly all right; you say so. You seem to think that your husband is justified in losing his temper and shooting off his mouth, and shrieking, and threatening you and otherwise acting like a wild man simply because there has been a misunderstanding about money.

Now I don't think your husband would do this unless you stood for it. It seems to me that what you do is to let yourself in for some grief because of your fear of your husband, and thereby intensifying the emotional reaction which he has, and because of the guilty feelings that you have offering no check to his anger [sic]. I don't believe I make myself very clear. I mean that you know that your husband has the peculiarity of being overly strict about money. And rather than work the thing out with him on an intelligent basis, you evade the issue and do something that you know will make him angry. Then because you feel guilty about it, you don't stand up for yourself in the face of this anger. You give him cause for his anger and then you yield to him in grand style and let him get madder than ever for that very reason. If you resented his anger, if you stood your ground and defended yourself, if you told the truth instead of saying, "I did this because I was afraid you would raise such a racket about it that I couldn't face you with it," I don't believe you would let yourself in for so much trouble.

I think this because I am sure your husband is an intelligent man, and probably realizes that he is a bit abnormal on this matter of strictness. If he doesn't realize it, God help him. Men who fly into rages over money affairs, men who demand receipts even when they have paid by check, men who think it is more important to be honest than to be kind, are suffering from a psychological mechanism, a complex if you like, which hurts them far worse than it hurts anyone else. I can't take the time and space to tell you just how they injure themselves, but they do. Sooner or later most of them develop either stomach trouble or high blood pressure. Perhaps if your husband is going to read this letter I should not have told him this as it will probably worry him. I hope it worries him enough to try to get rid of it, however, because it undoubtedly handicaps him greatly. The enormous wastefulness of energy that outbursts of temper such as you describe must cost him are paid for very dearly. As an engineer, as a man with a keen mind, as a man who is well acquainted with the laws of conservation of energy, he must know this. And he must realize that his attacks upon you are like a two-edged sword that really hurt him as much as they hurt you. If he doesn't know this, someone in whom he has confidence and who is acquainted with this branch of science should help him to see it and help him to control himself better. I think both of you would be very much benefited by going to a psychiatrist and there is a very good one in Cleveland to whom I can warmly recommend you. It is Dr. George Reeve. There are several other good psychiatrists in Cleveland but I happen to know Dr. Reeve particularly well and know his work is excellent.

There is one final thing which occurs to me and that is that a man with as good a mind as your husband and a woman with as good a mind as yourself ought surely to be able to get together and work out a financial budgeting system whereby these things could not possibly happen. You say nothing in your letter as to how your husband gives you money or as to how you have arranged your domestic expenditures. Perhaps he has already done this. If you haven't I strongly advise it. If you have, and it is really altogether your transgressions which cause the explosions, I think it is partly a matter of your correcting your attitude as I have suggested and partly a matter of your husband coming to realize that his explosions do you no good but rather make you worse on the one hand and injure himself on the other.

I have been very frank; I don't know you nor your husband and know nothing of your problem except what you have written. You may have unintentionally misrepresented it. I do not see how you could have made the case out much worse for yourself, and I have a notion that you have perhaps even spared your husband in this letter. Be that as it may, I am trusting that you are both intelligent enough to take this letter in the spirit it is written, namely, a spirit to be helpful to you. I have no other conceivable motive and I should like very much indeed to have you both write me and tell me what you think about the situation in the light I have suggested.

Sincerely yours,

Wisconsin
Jan. 25, 1931

Dear Sir:

Your article on "Mental Hygiene" in the home interests me more than I can tell you, especially your article in the Febr. number. The case you described compares with ours—our Dad does not live with us now—he is 40 yrs. old and like the other story, he was a business man, worked himself to death, and consequently burning the candle at both ends, soon broke down. Unknown to me for six months—he was hiring detectives at $25 a day to sit in cars and watch the house as he said I had lovers coming to see me, there were nine of them—his best friends and one our family doctor. He took $16,000 out of the business for this detecting work and he positively believes there were men coming here to see me. I have plenty to do to take care of my family of four children—the youngest is only four now and this story dates back two years tomorrow. Even after I found out about these detectives he continued having me watched—insisting it was necessary. The way I found out about this detecting part of it was this—one day a man called me on the phone and insisted I meet him at a confectionery to settle something that concerned my husband, myself, and a third party and if I didn't see him, it would cost my husband everything he had. (This was a threat by one of my supposed lovers to put us out of business if my husband didn't take back what he was saying.) Needless to say I did not meet this man but called my husband up and told him to come home—he did. I shall never forget it. He admitted his hiring detectives and grabbed me and almost killed me—only a girl who helps me with the children came in in time. I'm sure he would have killed me. He had bought a gun and said after had he known what I called him home for he would have knocked me cold. Well, there was but one thing to do—I was convinced he had lost his mind as he had been working *so hard* and he had been so moody—sitting staring into space and quiet like—so I was advised by our family doctor to have him examined. (We had always gotten along so well and please do not think we had had trouble because we hadn't—he was wonderful to me and the children and we just lived for our family.) The doctors declared him insane and he was sent to have Dr. [William] Lorenz at Madison pass his opinion on him. He said it was a most difficult case, that he thot if I let him come home and stay here with us that he would snap out of it. He came home—but moody and sullen and peering into my eyes—first one and then the other and always wanting to know if I was out that day. I was afraid of him and decided to ask about the business, our insurance policies and etc. and knew of course that he would object to telling me and he got huffy and left the house and told people I finally got rid of him, that I wanted to get rid of him and had even tried to put him in an insane asylum and he'd never go home and didn't. He had been going to *fortune* tellers too and reading detective stories.

Then when he left home, he refused to support us—flatly refused so I had to take it to court and try that way to get something to live on. I sued for separate maintenance, feeling in time if he got well we could always re-establish our home, but when the case came up he filed suit for absolute divorce and got it on the grounds of cruel and inhuman treatment. The judge waylaid me right for having him examined and said I was cruel and unattending to him as he was a sick overworked man—but how else could I protect the children and myself? I feel so terribly hurt about this. I never was cruel or inattentive to him in the fourteen years we were married and I feel so positive that what I did was for the best and to get pounced on like I did, it's terrible. The judge said there was no evidence to show that Mr. had any reason for hiring detectives and that Mr. was exonerated from those accusations but that he felt it his duty to give Mr. an absolute divorce on cruelty because if I had kept him home—he'd have been alright. Yes—maybe—but perhaps I wouldn't be here to write this too. Isn't it strange that after the affair—the day he beat me, he started right in to gain in weight—he told people he felt better—the *"bubble broke."* He hadn't been eating well and now he is so fat—has gained about 30 lbs. and works for a concern and seems to be getting along. Do you think he might do us harm sometime tho and just what *do* you think of the case doctor? I can't figure it out and, I feel so lonely—the kiddies do too for him and I wonder if you think that some day he might get well and realize it was his imagination. It's terrible to have anyone unjustly accuse you.

I shall look for your answer, as I am always anxious to know what the different doctors think, mental cases must be hard to diagnose.

Thanking you I am
Most Sincerely,

Apr. 13, 1931

My dear Mrs.:

I think your letter of January 25 addressed to me in care of the *Ladies' Home Journal* is one of the most amazing documents that I have ever seen. I cannot believe that in this enlightened day and age a judge would be so blind and, I might say, so stupid as to call a woman cruel and inattentive for having done what the doctors advised her to do with regard to her husband's mental condition.

But if what you say is true the judge, let us hope, was perhaps conscientiously mistaken or ignorant of mental disease. I am sure Dr. Lorenz, who is one of our most able psychiatrists, must regret exceedingly the outcome of the case, the distressing situation into which it has thrown you. The attitude exemplified in your letter is certainly most reasonable and fair and lacking in revenge. I think you take a very sensible view of it. I, too, am sure that what you did was intended for the best and it sounds as if it were.

Worst of all, I am sure, is the sadness you feel because you are lonely as well as wrongly accused and, as you say, the children miss their father and need him. I think under the circumstances you ought by all means to go to Madison and have a long talk with Dr. Lorenz and see if he cannot get your husband to come and see him and explain matters to him. Perhaps Dr. Lorenz could confer with the judge. Sometimes cases like this recover their mental health and it is entirely possible that Dr. Lorenz might be able to effect a reunion by helping your husband to completely recover and at the same time renew the happiness you seem to have lost.

Sincerely yours,

Houston, Tex.
July 18, 1931

Dear Mr. Menninger;

I have read your articles in the *Journal* and found them interesting. Probably you have a solution to my problem. Anyway you can advise me from a man's point of view. Any number of my women friends have come forward after seeing my predicament, and I have plainly noted the compassion in their eyes, but they have never dared to offer a solution. This is probably for the best.

I am thirty-nine years old, have been married nineteen years, have two splendid girls in high school and two boys in their graves. I have undoubtedly lost whatever attractiveness I ever had, but I am in no way dirty or repulsive. We have two little homes, one Bay and one town house. Both are pleasant, cheerful places and are always kept so. I am an easygoing, comfortable sort of a person. My worst enemy couldn't say I was a nagger. I have a good education and have held several responsible positions both before and after marriage.

My problem follows; I would appreciate honest-to-goodness, straight from the shoulder advice:

In many ways I am married to a perfectly splendid man. He is fifty-three years old, in good health, and has held for many years a good position that takes both skill and intelligence. He is from a good substantial American family. He seems genuinely fond of me when just he, the children, and I are by ourselves. He is tender and considerate, his salary is as much mine as his, and he voluntarily never spends an hour away from home without the girls or me, but here comes the rub and it is such a severe one to me, I feel as if if something is not done about it I will die or my reason will be unseated.

We have a great deal of company and they are all splendid, well-bred folks. My husband invariably takes upon himself to bawl me out before them. I use the language of the street because nothing else expresses it so forcibly. His scoldings are administered for the most trivial matters. It does not amount to just a slight nervous irritation but to actual abuse administered in the loudest of tones and the most crude language. If this happened only occasionally I might look over it but it occurs again and again. I am beginning to dread guests. I feel that they come only for a thrill, out of curiosity or sheer compassion for me. Maybe I am becoming super sensitive but it seems everywhere I go I encounter only looks of deep pity. Our girls are fond of both of us and maintain a strict neutrality but they have been humiliated to the bone by their father's actions to me before their crowd. It is simply ruining them socially. We are such "nice" folks people cannot turn us down, but they are beginning to make excuses and who could blame them! It's as if they sat on an edge of a volcano. My husband too is becoming universally disliked and this is such a pity too as he really has many lovable things about him. I have tried to show him this in a tactful way and appeal to him through the children, but all to no avail. Sometimes when he sees how horribly I am hurt he will promise to do better but he is right up and at it. It isn't because he doesn't want these guests. He is hospitality itself, is fond of these people, and has ample means to entertain them. Once or twice I have lost my temper and answered him in anger. The tirade was increased three-fold. Ordinarily I accept it in deep silence. Here of late it hurts so badly, I excuse myself, go to my room, and am attacked with a species of dry sobs that I cannot control for hours. He seems to take a fiendish delight in these outbursts, very much as a bad boy tortures an animal that he has at disadvantage and cannot get away. He enjoys so much "turning the knife" before his female relatives. His sisters are very fond of me and highly disapprove. I have tried to get them to express this disapproval to their brother, thinking it would help, but they reply, "No we would not interfere for worlds." I sometimes think, if I had a father or brother, but maybe it's best that I haven't! I have had all sorts of feminine advice from divorce to striking him publicly as soon as these tirades get well underway. I would sooner do the second than the first, but know it would only be that much more gasoline. I made a rather nice-looking bride. It was just the same then as now. Otherwise I might feel my appearance was to blame.

Sincerely,

Aug. 22, 1931

My dear Mrs.:

I have read your letter addressed to me in care of the *Ladies' Home Journal.*

Since you have been following my articles in the *Ladies' Home Journal,* you will remember that in every relationship of two people there is mingled love and hate. Now you have noticed that in your husband's case the love is strongly predominant at all times except when company is present, when he seems to take every opportunity of humiliating and distressing you in the presence of others, particularly his women relatives.

It seems probable that in early childhood your husband was humiliated, perhaps in no very obvious way, by a woman—perhaps a relative—and that he takes this means, unconsciously of course, of retaliating. You could not get him to see this but a third party might be able to, and so I recommend strongly that you get him to go to a psychiatrist who could help him to understand his motives.

You are right in thinking that answering back and striking him would only add fuel to the flame. Under the circumstances, until you can persuade your husband to take treatment, I would suggest that you refrain from having much company since these scenes are so distressing to you, the guests, and your children.

Sincerely yours,

8.

Disappointing Husbands

San Diego, Calif.
Oct. 24, 1930

Dear Sir:

As I have heard and read a good deal about you, I was very glad to read in your article in the *Ladies' Home Journal* that you would be willing to advise anyone who needed it. For some time I have been miserable and dissatisfied in spite of good health, a good husband and the creature comforts of life, if not the luxuries. I am hoping that you might help me overcome this mood for I have been unable to do so myself.

Two years ago I married a very good man who also had a good mentality. He was ambitious and hard-working so I believed he would some day become a success in business. My husband has always been liked where he worked although this did not reach an intimate stage because of his rather shy disposition. Mr. P., my husband, has worked hard to get a certain position in his place of business, but when someone was chosen to fill this position, another man with about the same qualifications but a favorite of the boss was chosen.

This failure to advance has discouraged me as well as my husband, and made me feel that I have married a mediocre person who will always have someone else get ahead of him. I have suggested to my husband that he stop trying or expecting to get a better position and be content to be a common laborer, then he will get fewer disappointments because he is not aiming so far.

Now I feel rather bitter towards life to think that I have married a man who will never get ahead. I still care for my husband and appreciate his hard work but I am tired of poverty and feel cheated to think there are not even hopes of anything different. This attitude of mind makes me irritable toward my husband and leaves us both unhappy. This letter sounds like the reflection of an ugly disposition, but because I feel exactly like that I am writing to you and hoping you might give me a better viewpoint.

Thanking you in advance, I remain

Yours sincerely,

Dec. 2, 1930

My dear Mrs. P.:

I read with care your letter of October 24 addressed to me in care of the *Ladies' Home Journal.*

What are the facts according to your own statement? First you married an ambitious, hardworking man who was well-liked. Secondly, he has given you the comforts of life, if not the luxuries. Thirdly, he recently worked hard to get a certain position which was, however, given to someone else who was personally preferred; fourth, this discouraged both him and you. Fifth, you suggested to him that he had better stop trying or hoping for a better position and take a job as a common laborer. Sixth, you are tired of poverty and feel cheated to have been given such a husband.

I am reciting these facts which you have given me because it will look and sound different to you coming from someone else. I think it will become perfectly obvious to you if you study over it, that you have been heartlessly cruel toward your husband. Instead of encouraging him, you have discouraged him; instead of boosting him a little when he met with a reverse which every man has to meet with in the battle of life, you gave him a further kick when he got home. Instead of loving him, it sounds to me as if you almost hated him. And why should you hate him? Because he didn't bring you the luxuries of life. I am quoting almost your own words.

Yes, I think you are dead wrong. I think you have the wrong attitude toward your husband entirely. I think it may be this disparagement of him, this unconscious depreciation of him, this doubt of his ability, and so forth which has been partly responsible for his not having more self-confidence and getting further ahead than he has. But your husband hasn't made a failure; he has failed in one particular as every man must do. Not once but many times if he ever amounts to anything. As a wife your duty is to do just the opposite from what you have done. You ought to love him more than ever. You ought to back him up, encourage him, reassure him, tell him that he has the stuff in him and next time he will be more successful, and so forth. This is the only way in the world for you to accomplish the thing which you say you want to accomplish. But the way you are treating your husband is the surest way in the world to achieve the things you say you cannot stand. I am a little surprised that your womanly intuition does not show you this.

Did you ever hear about Nathaniel Hawthorne's wife? Hawthorne was fired from his job and came home heartbroken and discouraged and in tears. His wife was sunshiny and happy and he was so afraid it would break her heart and make her cry that he didn't want to tell her. But finally he did. She burst into laughter and clapped her hands and he was amazed. But Darling, he said, how can you act that way, how can you be happy? Sweetheart, she said, now you will have time to write your book.[1] And he sat down and wrote one of the most famous novels ever written, and certainly some of the finest literature ever created in the United States. I think that Mrs. Hawthorne went to work and supported the family while he was at home. However that may have been, the point is that she encouraged him when he was so discouraged so that he was able to turn out a great piece of work, and turn defeat into success.

What you must do is to help your husband turn this little minor defeat into a greater success. But what it looks to me as if you were about to do is to turn his little defeat into a disaster for both of you. I think there is still time to change, but get busy.

Sincerely yours,

Council, Idaho
Dec. 4, 1930

Dear Doctor Menninger:

Reference is made to the enclosed clipping published in the *Ladies' Home Journal* for December 1930. I would like to add a few comments which you probably couldn't say in your article.

Isn't B. F. D. exercising just as much deep-lying emotion as his wife in his insistence that his lodge must come first, before the wishes of his wife? He has insisted that his lodge come first for a great many years and his wife has taken her only means of defense against that insistence. She has suffered in unhappiness because of his greater desire for his lodge than for her. Isn't he also in need of a reorganization of his thinking?

This letter was discussed at our last Club meeting and most of the women seemed to feel as I have written above. We all of us seemed to have had this common experience that B. F. D's wife has had, namely: that we (the wives) take a back seat when it comes to a man and his lodge. We none of us knew why it was, nor seemed to have an understanding of a man's way of thinking.

---

1. Newton Arvin in his biography, *Hawthorne* (Boston: Little, Brown, 1929), relates that when in the summer of 1849 Hawthorne told his wife, Sophia, that he had lost his surveyorship at the customhouse, she replied, " 'Oh then' . . . 'you can write your book!' " (156).

If you could give me some understanding of the masculine state of mind on this subject I would appreciate it very much. Last winter I lived in town with my husband and found that even a dinner party could be called off an hour before the guests arrived if my husband's lodge called a special meeting. Guests have come to our home, and been left listening to the radio while my husband went to lodge till midnight. The winter ahead of me, again in town, is one I am facing with dread. My husband is gone for weeks at a time and is only home in the winter. That is my time to get acquainted with him, but he seems to prefer three or four nights out of the week to be spent at lodge.

Very truly yours,

Dec. 28, 1930

My dear Mrs.:

I have your letter of December 4 addressed to me in care of the *Ladies' Home Journal*, in which you bring up the question in regard to a letter from Mr. B. F. D. printed in the December issue.

I shall try to comply with your request to give you a better understanding of the masculine state of mind on the subject of lodges. I think you possibly wrote me in a somewhat sarcastic mood and I don't know that I can blame you in view of the experience that you have with your own husband. But I shall not answer it in any sarcastic mood because I think it is really a very important problem. You sound a little sad about it and a little bitter and I don't know that I blame you at all. But perhaps with a little better understanding of just what is happening you can understand the problem more easily in your own home.

You ask me if I do not think that Mr. B. F. D. was also exhibiting some manifestations of a deep lying emotion because he insisted upon going to lodge. I quite agree with you. But in most cases it is a very harmless manifestation. I think it is very much better that a husband should want to go to his lodge occasionally than he should want to get drunk, for example, or half a dozen other manifestations of behavior which both of us could think of. The point I was trying to make in answering Mr. B. F. D's letter was that his wife's reaction to it was a very unhappy one, expressed in a very unhappy way and expressed apparently without understanding just why she was expressing it altho to an outsider it was pretty clear.

Now I should take issue with something you imply in the first paragraph of your letter which will serve as an introduction to what I shall say in answer to the last paragraph. You say that Mr. B. F. D. is insisting that his lodge must come first before the wishes of his wife. I don't think that Mr. B. F. D. insists upon this. I am quite sure that many of the wishes of his wife are fully gratified by Mr. B. F. D. I am sure that he loves her as he says and does many things which please her. He also does this one thing which displeases her and he insists upon doing it altho it distressed her.

Now I think it is quite impossible for any two people to do absolutely nothing except such things as please the other one of the partnership. This kind of ideal relationship would be quite Utopian. There is no perfect match in the world. There are no two people who absolutely please each other after the first intoxication has worn off. And as I have already said I don't think going to lodge is such a bad piece of behavior, and therefore I don't think that his wife's wish that he should not go is justified. I think it would be a very serious mistake for him to do as you suggest in your letter, namely, to give up going to lodge just because his wife doesn't want him to. To do so would be to sacrifice a satisfaction out of deference to an unreasonable wish of his wife's. It would be only one step in a successive surrender of privilege which would soon lead him to nourish a great deal of hostility toward her. At the present time he loves her and he is perplexed by her prejudices. If, on the other hand, he gave in at this point, he would be doing what she wished but he would not love her so much because he would have begun to hate her for the thwarting of his secondary interests in life. She is already his first interest and she should not expect to be his second, third, fourth and fifth interests as well. It is because some wives are so greedy in this respect that they lose their husbands. They are so anxious to have everything that they ultimately don't have anything. Don't you remember the story about the fisherman and his wife in which the grateful flounder made so many presents because the wife kept insisting for more and more. Ultimately, you remember, she lost everything.

Now the last paragraph of your letter sheds a little light on why you feel so strongly on the matter. It is quite obvious that in your own case your husband has carried the lodge business to an extreme. It is even possible from what you say that your husband does put his lodge first and you second and in that case I don't blame you for being resentful about it. You say he prefers lodge three or four nights a week to being home. Perhaps this is because without his knowing it and without your knowing it he is somewhat afraid of you. Perhaps you are not doing all you can to make yourself loved by him. You can't make a man love you but you can make yourself irresistible so that he can't help loving you. Then the attraction of the lodge will be less.

I have not yet told you what I thought the attraction of the lodge was. The attraction lies in a number of things which it offers that the home does not. One of these is conviviality; another is the association with other men. In many cases a man gets a satisfaction out of his lodge because it does not demand anything of him. Perhaps you demand too much of your husband.

It is a curious thing that this demanding too much works in the opposite direction; it drives a man to do even worse than he might spontaneously do. Then there is another reason why a lodge attracts some men. It gives them an opportunity to be the high potentate and the most exalted leader and one thing and another and feel very important for a little while. They are bowed down to and respected and saluted and so forth by other men and they have a lot of fun in this little play just like boys do in playing king and robber chief, and so forth. To some extent this is a very good thing for men to indulge in in their lodges; it is much better that they play a little at the lodge and then be grown up men in the daytime than that they should reverse the process.

Think these things over and I believe you will see the whole matter in a different light and perhaps [at] the next meeting of your club you can give the women some new suggestions in this very painful point about the lodge. Not only that but perhaps you will be able to change your husband's home environment and your own attitude just enough to change the ratio of his lodge attendance and his staying at home evenings.

Sincerely yours,

New Mexico
Mar. 4, 1931

Dear Dr. Menninger:

It seems rather odd to put such a formal, businesslike opening to a letter and then tell you things I cannot tell intimate friends. The charm of the unknown, unbiased mind I suppose. Here goes, at any rate.

I married when I was 21—that's old enough for one to know one's own mind if they have supported themselves for eight years, as I had, but it's not old enough to know the man's when tinged with love's rosy gleam. My husband was—and is—a charming individual—and utterly irresponsible in financial matters. Taken out of my home background, and bearing two children seventeen months apart, crippled my earning power, and seeing one's children undernourished is a rather powerful incentive to get back to work and give them the right kind of food and clothing even at the expense of being with them less. Two years ago I came back to my old haunts with the children—have my old position as teacher back, have finished my two-year normal degree and am working toward my A.B. I've worked hard in my teaching and in my school work—extension and correspondence in the winter and summer school in the summer. I've been recently given a new raise in salary which gives me the limit procurable in this county for grade teachers; have my little house and children, a steady income ($1500 per year), I like my work immensely—and I'm not happy. The husband, frankly glad not to be worried with mine or the children's support, goes blithely on his way. Writes an occasional letter that is 2 or 3 times a year, saying that he will send something to buy the kiddies winter clothing, etc., next week, and it's not fooling either of us, because he knows he has no intention of doing it and so do I. I don't want him back—love's young dream rather wilted when I had gone without food four days and given the children oatmeal—the only edible in the house, and he came home from his business trip (he travels) with a new Buick roadster. What's wrong with me? I like my work, like my educational work, love my children and by all signs and omens should be at least comparatively content.

There's a constant urge in me to "do something" and I don't know what. It's not social—I don't care about parties, despise bridge and teas—have no use for clubs—so I take up another class in extension from the University I attend in summer, teach night school, play with the children, my own and others, get wound up in extracurricular activities and have a tiny sneaking feeling that it's distractive activity all the time with all these things except my children. Again—as a child says, "Why aren't I happy!" Am I crying for the moon? If so what moon?

I've rambled on until I feel as tho' you'd recognize me even on a dark street, so with an apology for using so much of your time, and an honest desire for a bit of constructive thought—believe me.

Yours hopefully,

Mar. 31, 1931

My dear Mrs.:

I have read with interest your letter of March 4 addressed to me in care of the *Ladies' Home Journal.*

Yes, I think you are crying for the moon, as you say. "What moon," you ask. That I think is the secret of your unhappiness. I do not think you know just what you want. I don't know either unfortunately or I would tell you but I have the impression that your unhappiness can be ascribed to the fact that the circumstances of your early life forced you into assuming an aggressive independent role which is not biologically characteristic of women. You evidently married a man who is just as willing to renounce the masculine role as you are to accept it and naturally, altho you were very compatible emotionally, you couldn't adjust yourselves with that inverted kind of relationship to a world in which the man should be making the living and supporting the family and the women should be building up the home.

As things have turned out it is necessary for you to do both, and many women can be happy doing either one or the other and quite a few women can be happy doing both. I grant you that it is not a very solid happiness because of course the natural outlet for the expression of love and sexual satisfaction is denied and in their place there is a compulsory activity in other lines which is diverting, interesting and socially valuable but unfortunately not always entirely satisfying.

It is probably cold comfort for me to tell you that you will just have to make the best of it but that is about all I can say. Theoretically psychoanalytic treatment might accomplish something for you but as I look at your case as a whole I think I would not particularly advise it. I think, in short, you are making a fairly good social adjustment and that as time goes on and you get a little more sure of yourself and your children become increasingly interesting to you you will find your lot less hard and less disappointing than you now feel it. In other words, time will partially heal part of your wounds and the others I think you can take care of yourself.

Sincerely yours,

Sandusky, Ohio
Mar. 12, 1931

My dear Dr. Menninger;

Ten years ago when I was 23 I married a very intelligent man of 37. We are both journalists and we are still very deeply in love after a decade of marriage. Yet our entire married life has been most stormy and I believe our troubles are almost entirely mental.

First I will tell you briefly about my husband. He was the eldest child in a prominent Kentucky family and came of good Scotch Irish stock. But his home environment during youth was not of the best. His father drank and there were three other children in the family, one an incurable invalid. Most of the parents' care was lavished upon this child; the others got little expression of love from the parents. My husband began to drink at an early age and when I met him had been drinking steadily for more than ten years.

During the period of our courtship he did not drink as he knew how much I objected to it but after we had become engaged I found that he was married—had been married while intoxicated and had never lived with his wife. I should perhaps have given him up then but we were very deeply in love and I thought he had quite reformed. So he ultimately divorced this woman, who had been a wife in name only, and we were married.

In less than a year he began drinking heavily—not continuously but rather periodically. He is a perfect beast at such times and also cruel. He declares that the cruelty is due to my attitude about drinking. I seldom say anything about it but I know that I must show the disgust I feel after days and weeks of this sort of thing.

We have three lovely little daughters and my husband adores them. He says he wants to stop drinking but he apparently cannot do so permanently. He has been a patient in private and state sanitariums—not drink "cures"— at various times. He is seldom cross to the children but has tried to kill me on several occasions and I have gradually grown to be afraid of him. He knows this.

Now I am not blameless. For one thing the difference in our ages made me quite unable to understand the gravity of our situation during the earlier years of our marriage. My father died when I was eleven and I had no brothers. I had infantile paralysis as a child and was—and still am to a certain degree—an abnormally sensitive person. I am nervous and high-tempered. But I can control myself very well under reasonably normal conditions—even when my husband drinks I can do very well for the first few days. A long drawn out spree with the consequent worry over a lost job undermines my nerve.

There have been about fifteen jobs, maybe more, during the ten years, so my fears are well grounded. Three times I have packed up my babies and come home when things reached what I considered the unbearable stage. My fears are both mental and physical and I can't seem to overcome them.

Right now I am back working at the newspaper job I held before my marriage. My husband is trying his hand at a selling job and looking for a newspaper job to replace the $90 a week job he lost last fall. I have been supporting him for four months and will continue to do so until he gets a job but here is my problem. Will it be worthwhile to try to establish another home with him?

Our furniture, bought on the installment plan, and the second lot so purchased, is not yet quite paid for. We may or may not be able to keep it. If not it means starting all over from the bottom again. We have no savings, no insurance, and my husband is now 47 years old. I am 33.

Is there any possible hope of getting him to stop drinking, or failing that, any way you can suggest for me to handle the problem so that I can keep our home together?

I feel that the children need a father and when he is himself he is a very good father—of more help to them than I am as a mother.

What can I do? Is drink a mental sickness or am I to blame entirely? I feel that I must be greatly in the wrong somewhere and it seems so unnecessary for two supposedly intelligent persons to wreck five lives over the drink question. We never have a serious disagreement over anything else and I am not a prohibitionist although I do not drink myself and never serve liquor in our home.

Have you any suggestions to make? What do other people do under such conditions? I want to be as fair as I can to my husband and to my children.

You will consider this letter confidential, I know, and I enclose a stamped envelope and hope you will have time for a reply. Thanking you very much, I am,

Apr. 3, 1931

My dear Mrs.:

I have read with care your letter addressed to me in care of the *Ladies' Home Journal*.

Your last question is, "What do other people do under such conditions?" The answer to that question is that they do just what you do. They worry and grieve and sigh and go on trying to bear the almost unbearable. Your problem is one of the most difficult and puzzling problems of all because the victims of alcoholism are as a rule such lovable people, between attacks. Personally I regard alcoholism as a manifestation of a neurosis, as I have explained in some detail in my book, *The Human Mind.* It is an expression of an inability to face reality on its own terms. Usually this reality is very intimately connected with the problem of sex and for that reason marriage usually causes an exaggeration of drinking tendencies.

Theoretically there is a cure for alcoholism, at least for some cases of alcoholism, in which the victim is earnestly desirous of obtaining that cure. Usually this earnest co-operation is pretty difficult to get. Moreover the treatment is exceedingly difficult to administer because it is a tedious, long, drawn-out, expensive business and most alcoholic patients have done just as your husband has done. That is, they have lost their jobs and have spent all their money.

Psychoanalysis is the treatment to which I have reference. I think a properly conducted psychoanalysis by a competently trained man effects a remarkable benefit in some of these cases. You might as well face the facts, however, that it is an expensive business at the best and difficult to obtain under any circumstances. There is a very good man in Cleveland, altho it might be wise to send your husband further away from you and the children. I am not sure that it might not be better for him to go to Chicago or even further West. You will know best about that. There is no reason why he cannot go on with his work at the same time.

The man in Cleveland to whom I have reference is Dr. George Reeve. The man in Chicago is Dr. Thomas M. French.

Sincerely yours,

Cedar Rapids, Iowa
Mar. 19, 1931

Dear Dr. Menninger:

I need help with my problem. I will give you a bit of background.

Father a Methodist minister whose main urge in life was to be famous or to have famous children. I am the eldest in the family of seven and the only one who was able to measure up to our father's standard of excellence in school. I was naturally a little quicker than the other children I came in contact with so I always led my class without much effort. Mother, too busy bearing and rearing children to bother much with any of us if we were not causing trouble. I did not like her, and though she is a good woman and I respect her I do not admire her now. She does not reason and she cannot understand anyone who does. My father was always sharpening my wits in verbal tilts and compelling me to see the cause and effect and the logic of things in an academic rather than a practical way.

I worked my way through college, graduated with honors, having been prominent in all campus activities, having had plenty of dates—chosen as representative college woman and all that stuff. Taught school and made a success because the youngsters like me very much. Married at the age of twenty-six.

My husband. Orphaned at eighteen months and taken into a family of adults by a maiden daughter who kept him in spite of the protests of the other members of the family. As a child he knew that he was not wanted. The maiden daughter whom he called his foster mother was the domineering type so the child never made a decision for himself. He went to high school and spent two years at college, his only occupation being working on the family farm where he was needed. He had just returned from the army when I met him. He was thirty years old. There weren't any other eligible young men in town so I enjoyed his company. We seemed very congenial. He took me hunting, which I loved, went with me to all sorts of lectures and listened with a show of interest when I talked about poetry and philosophy.

I did not especially want to get married. I do not know why I did. Probably curiosity about sex and a maternal feeling for the sad little boy, and a wish to make him happy. I thought that with my encouragement he would become happy and accomplish much—like the storybook husband.

Have been married ten years. Hard, lean years, financially. No children though we both wanted them. I have had to be the backbone of the family. When my husband is discouraged he lies down on the job and refuses to face the facts. He shunts all the financial matters off onto me and will not listen when I try to talk things over with him.

I say, "But we absolutely can't afford to make payments on a new car."

He answers, "Alright then, I'll run this damned old wreck into the junk pile and walk to work."

He complains so unceasingly that I finally agree to getting the new car just to shut him up. But he begins to complain about the new one. It is not perfect, "Do you hear that knock? Just a damned pile of junk! Where do you think that rattle is? etc., etc."

I try never to seem to take the responsibility, make him think that he is going ahead, but I always have to augment the income. My husband is also neurasthenic. He is really afraid all the time that he has some physical ailment or is going to have a cancer or something.

He talks about it constantly. He dislikes to be in the company of anyone who makes him feel inferior in material things so as our friends prosper we must drop them. Nothing that we have suits him. He is always complaining about our house, our furniture, our radio, and his clothes. Lately he has taken to criticizing my appearance.

But he has his lovable qualities. He is very affectionate and is constantly telling me how much he loves me and asking me to promise that I will never leave him. He remembers Valentine's Day and anniversaries. When things go well life is not at all bad but just let something happen! To avoid a more serious accident I ran our car into the curb and bent the wheels. He knew the circumstances and that I would pay the repair bill with money that I had earned but after his first flare-up of anger he refused to speak to me for several days. He would sit with his head hanging down and would not eat. He felt terribly that the car had been hurt.

We have nothing in common; I soon found out that the interest he showed in things that I liked was merely an interest in me. I gravitate toward the intellectual people of the city. I can come from a visit or a lecture feeling exalted and almost happy but in two minutes the complaining and cursing of my husband will wipe out all the glow and make me feel like I have been doused with dirty water.

I have tried to say, "I made an error in judgment and I must be a good sport and take the consequences. I can live my own life within myself and grow. I cannot be responsible for what might happen to the little morale my husband has if I should hurt his self-esteem by leaving him."

That has worked, on the surface. I have made a place for myself in the community. I have created a garden that I love. And now that I thought things were going to move smoothly something else has come in. Just yesterday I faced the fact that something is wrong with me. I sat down and checked myself over and found, as nearly as it is possible to find in one's self: 1. That I have developed an inertia that I can't understand. I can hardly make myself go to the telephone to call up any one. I keep putting it off. I can hardly bring myself to pay bills on time. Letters that do not look interesting on the outside I will put away unopened because I do not want to read them. I used to delight in writing to my friends, now I can hardly bring myself to do so. Once started at a task I seem to move along almost as efficiently as formerly. 2. I sit and daydream like I used to when I was younger about accomplishing a miracle of writing or something that releases me from worry about money and home ties.

Sunday evening my husband flatly refused to go to spend the evening with people we had promised. I was very angry because I knew that under the circumstances their feelings would be hurt. I went without him and tried to furnish a convincing alibi for him. When I came home I was resolved to leave him. I planned out a method of procedure but the thing that was lacking was money. In the morning I checked over my plan basing its fruition upon the possibility of getting a check for a story in the morning mail. As I planned to be gone I realized that I was thinking with relief that I would not have to think about where the money to pay the interest on the mortgage was coming from, and that I would not have to go on with the plans for a Garden Club activity. (I was not afraid of failure because I have done the same thing with great success the past two years.) I just did not want to make the effort. The money did not come. I walked into the house from the mail box saying aloud to myself, "Then I guess I will shoot myself. That will be nice." I thought it would be very nice but I did not do it. I lay down and went to sleep.

I have never worried about myself but I do not like this new person who is taking my place. I do not know what she will do. She is certainly uninteresting. It all sounds very stupid when written down. I know that I am not a very nice person.

I wish that fate would intervene and remove my husband from me by making him fall in love with someone else who would look after him or that he would smash into a telephone post and be gone. That is despicable because he has the same right to moral standards and life that I have.

Something makes me think mean and talk mean, sometimes, but will not let me act mean. In actions I am loyal and faithful and loving, but inside of me I am not. I have not been brooding. I just feel that I have reached the place where I must face something or go under but I do not know what.

Do you have any idea?

Very sincerely yours,

P.S. Please do not tell me that I am self-centered. I know that. Do not tell me to think of others and to lose myself in doing so. I can't. I have spent much time with the young people of the city in Nature guiding. I love them and to work with them but the activity does not make me lose myself.

Apr. 14, 1931

My dear Mrs.:

I have read with a great deal of interest your letter of March 19 addressed to me in care of the *Ladies' Home Journal.*

I receive many letters somewhat like yours but yours differs in several ways. In the first place, the important difference is that you have an unusual degree of understanding. Many other women with the same problem write me much the same facts but do not understand it. You apparently do.

Therefore, I shall treat your case somewhat differently from what I might another. I think it must be quite clear to you that you wrote to me with at least a subconscious notion that I would take the responsibility of advising you to leave your husband. That, naturally, I cannot do. It seems to me that since you have no children that the decision in that direction would be a great deal easier for you than for those women who have borne children into an unhappy marriage and have that to consider. I must confess, however, that I don't exactly understand what you mean by saying that you wish that fate would make your husband fall in love with someone else. Why must he be in love with someone? He is quite obviously much in love with himself and has depended upon you as a mother. On the other hand, it is, as you say: you chose him for the purpose of having someone to mother and now you are tired of your job. You do, therefore, have a certain responsibility but whether that responsibility demands that you continue to make yourself, and probably him also, as miserable as you appear to be doing, is another question.

I think the question for you to decide is whether or not the satisfaction that you are yielding him in the present situation, compared to what he might be able to get if you forced him to stand on his own legs, is equal to the improvement in your own situation that you would derive by separating from him. This kind of a question, obviously, I cannot help you with. The answer to this, of course, no one can give but yourself, but I think you can get considerable help in it by a conference with the right kind of a psychiatrist, but I feel from your letter that you have just about decided things already yourself. I should be very interested in hearing from you again a little later and knowing what you have done and are doing about the matter.

Sincerely yours,

Birmingham, Ala.
Apr. 11, 1931

Dear Doctor:

I am going to state my case to you. It's a long one. I have been married going on ten years.

Before I married my husband, I went with a young man for years, in fact, we were raised in the same neighborhood since we were little kids. We loved one another very much but my parents objected to him for many reasons.

Well, to please my parents, I didn't marry him. A year or so after I married, he married and moved from here. I tried to put him out of my mind. For a while I succeeded. Last fall he returned and I realized I loved him more than ever and learned that he still loves me. He was separated from his wife and after talking to him I convinced him to go back to her and to his children. That sounds like I don't love him, but I wasn't thinking of his wife I was thinking of his children for you see I have two. If it wasn't for them I would know what to do.

Now to go to my husband. When we first married he was everything you would want him to be, but for one thing. He was very jealous. Regardless of who I would talk to, even my cousins, he would make a scene. Then he took to drinking which he still does. He smokes so many cigarettes during the day that he keeps us up all night from coughing. I know it's from smoking for I had a doctor to examine him.

Year and half ago my father died and my mother didn't wish to be bothered with the store, turned it over to my husband to run and every time she takes a nickel out of the store he has fits. He claims the store is his. Now he doesn't give her a thing not even rent. Now doctor, my husband hasn't worked a lick any where in six or seven years except in papa's store. He didn't have anything when I married him. My father has always given me what I wanted even after I married. He even supported my husband, clothed him and my children and still he can't stand my mother. Can you tell me what kind of man is that? Now, if it wasn't for the children my mother would put him out of the house. I am all that my mother has living.

In front of people he talks that we don't give him time to go out anywhere. But the truth is he won't go when we tell him. He goes out two or three nights a week and I never ask him where he is going. I am not the nagging kind. All my friends think he's a perfect angel but if they knew him like I did they would soon change their mind. I did try hard to love him and for awhile when we first married I did, but he soon killed every smack of love I had for him.

Now let's go back to the other man. I love him so much that he is always on my mind. I can't sleep at night from worrying. His face is before me day and night, regardless how hard I try to put him out of my thoughts. Doctor, understand I don't believe in divorces where there are children. If I did I wouldn't be asking your advice. My husband doesn't know what's on my mind. I have kept it away from him on account of the children. Now I haven't done a thing that's dishonorable to him or anyone else. The only one that is suffering is me. Perhaps you think I am foolish. Maybe I am, but please advise me what to do and please do not publish this but answer by mail. Am enclosing stamped envelope. I know I have taken a lot of your time. Thanking you, I am,

Yours very truly,

Apr. 30, 1931

My dear Mrs.:

My position on such matters as you write about in your letter of April 11 addressed to me in care of the *Ladies' Home Journal* is simply this.

If a husband and wife are very unhappy, if the wife is quite convinced of her husband's uselessness or wickedness, I think the children are more harmed by their staying together than they would be by a divorce. I never advise any woman to get a divorce because if the situation is so bad that she can't stand it she will get one of her own accord and if, on the other hand, she wants to put up with it that is also her privilege. It seems to me that everyone ought to have a right to marry the person they love providing someone else is not injured thereby. I do not know enough about the details of your case to understand just why it is that you do not marry the man you love but if it is for the children's sake, it seems to me that the children would be very much better off in a home where the parents love one another than in a home where they hate one another.

Sincerely yours,

Lincoln, Nebr.
May 10, 1931

Dear Dr. Menninger:

I have read your articles and find them so helpful, I am going to ask you for help too.

I was married in 1925 to a man four years my junior. He was 25 at the time and I 29 years old.

He seemed to care for me the first three years and then we moved into an apartment. He began looking in the neighbor's windows and would get greatly excited at sight of a woman undressing or anything sexual between a man and a woman. I laughed at him and he began doing it when he thought I wasn't looking. During this year we knew few people as we had moved to a strange place. He was faithful to me that year I know. Finally this unrest got the better of him, he began drinking every day, ran around with an old sweetheart and a wild crowd. He asked me to leave him several times, saying marriage bored him, that he craved freedom and did not care for any one girl. This lasted 6 months. I left and was only gone four days when he appeared and said he had been out of his mind and made all sorts of promises of fidelity and begged me to take him back. I finally did but learned he had been meeting women afternoons all during our courtship and marriage. I was ill from worry and had a nervous breakdown and had to go away. I feel sure he was faithful while I was gone for he insisted on staying with mother and was so careful not to worry me. He quit his friends cold and went to work and has a good position.

I noticed several nights ago he was watching a 17-year-old girl across from us undress. He made an excuse to get up one night and I saw her undressing from my room. Next night, he did the same thing. I walked out to him and he had gotten up on a chair and was very excited. I am so worried about him anyway and I felt I just couldn't trust him any place. He got mother and she said he was only a normal man and I was making a mountain out of a mole hill. My sister said he was a weakling and never would be otherwise and that I will eventually have to leave him. I really feel this way at heart too. My husband said the other evening after I found him that he needed me terribly to help him, that if he had married any other girl he would never amount to anything but that I could do much to help him. He said the impulse to watch this girl was much stronger than his judgement and he felt sure it was a form of insanity.

His aunt eloped at 45 with a man 32, her inferior in every way. It ruined her life and her daughter killed herself over it. One uncle has been divorced twice and goes from one affair to another, putting forth no effort to get anyplace. His son (my husband's cousin) is a flighty foolish boy and has been confined to an asylum. Another uncle deserted his wife and six children. He has been in two asylums, is a religious fanatic and lives with various women. All of these people are university graduates, were unusually bright. Is it insanity? It just looks to me as if they are too selfish to put forth any effort.

My husband is a good husband in every other way. I live in dread and fear he may do these things again. But I am going to do all I can first and not give up until I know it is hopeless. I am keeping myself more attractive and sexual relations are very satisfactory. I am as attractive as the average girl and have no desire in the world to be unfaithful to my husband. I feel that if he is ever going to get control of himself, now is the time. He says he is trying to keep his mind from sexual things, that he has always been on the alert for a thrill and thought too much about it.

Can you tell me any books to read or give me any help at all? We could be so happy if he could learn to control himself. He loves me very very much, more now than ever before. He is so ashamed of the way he has treated me and wants so badly to be faithful I know. He has controlled himself for the past year and a half and he says he has never been so happy. But he seems to tell small lies so glibly even when it isn't necessary. He told me his stomach pained him when got up the other night.

I don't understand it all. Why should any man with a wife he loves be unfaithful. It seems to me he doesn't love her much but I am convinced my husband loves me. Is he insane too, can he be helped or am I wasting my time? He does not seem to be able to be strictly honest in many little ways and treats it as a joke. I am trying so desperately to give him some of my own strength but of course I can't do that. I find he often expresses himself in the very words I have used to him and know I can influence him some.

Could I be the wrong one? Should I look lightly on a few infidelities because he is so kind to me in other ways? I can't live with him under those circumstances, I would rather always live alone.

This letter is disjointed I know but I am so worried and have so many misgivings and doubts.

Thanking you for any help you can give me, I am

Very truly yours,

June 2, 1931

My dear Mrs.:

I have found your letter addressed to me in care of the *Ladies' Home Journal* interesting because I think it is so important for someone to give you the right advice just now when you are in such a quandary. Of course I cannot be certain about any case merely from one person's description of it but the facts you give of your husband's wanting to watch other women undress and so forth is of course a very well known phenomenon in psychiatry.

I would judge that your mother is absolutely wrong when she says that such a person is normal. Your sister is also wrong when she says that he is a weakling and will never be otherwise. I am inclined to think that your husband is absolutely correct when he says that it is a kind of craziness that he needs you terribly to help him. I think this is just so.

It is absolutely true as he himself puts it that his impulses overcome his intelligence and his judgment. Yes, to answer your question, I do think that you should look lightly on his infidelity and on this curious behavior of his so far as judging and censoring him is concerned but realize that he is having a struggle to try to conform to what he knows he should do and give him such help as you can in the way of friendliness, consideration, patience and love. No, I do not think you are the one in the wrong and I do think he loves you and needs you for a helpmate.

I must add in conclusion, however, that I think that such a case as you describe certainly ought to have the benefit of psychoanalytic treatment.

Psychoanalysis would help this man to discover the real origin of his curious impulses and if he knew the origin of them he would be in a position to control them, which he is not at present. Psychoanalysis is a serious business and should not be undertaken lightly but it is of incredible benefit to those who are capable of it. It is very important, however, to get into the hands of a man who is recognized as a competent psychoanalyst; unfortunately there are many who call themselves such who have not had the training and do not have their skill.

In regard to a book describing exhibitionism and also describing psychoanalysis, concerning which you ask, I might mention my own book, *The Human Mind,* where you will find these things discussed on pages 306–7.

Sincerely yours,

9.

Frigid Wives

Dayton, Ohio
Nov. 6, 1930

Dear Sir:

After reading your book and also your articles in the *Ladies' Home Journal* I am coming to you with my problem.

Sexual intercourse is not as it should be between my husband and I. Although I have been examined by three doctors and found to be perfectly normal sexually, also have read the books they advised and taken several kinds of medicine, I have never had the experience of an orgasm during intercourse. I have had this experience when sleeping, which wakes me up and continues after being awakened. My husband is of a passionate nature and requires intercourse often, nearly every night. I never refuse him this privilege although it means nothing to me. I'm sure our home would be much happier if I could be a normal person in that respect. I am thirty-one years old. I love my husband and I am sure he does me also. The doctors say I only lack the desire or libido. I feel as though if I had the desire the other would follow naturally. Doctors never seem to have faith in the medicine they give. I'm sure this must be a mental problem so I am asking you for any advice you will give me.

I have two children, my husband is a school teacher and I was also before we had the children. People say I am attractive and appear to be normal but this one difficulty makes me very sad and blue at times because I feel as though my husband is not enjoying married life as he would if I would be normal in that way.

Yours Sincerely,

Dec. 15, 1930

My dear Mrs.:

I have read with interest your letter addressed to me in care of the *Ladies' Home Journal.*

In most instances the inability of the woman to enjoy sexual intercourse is precisely what you have called it, namely, a psychological or mental difficulty. It is not so much a lack of libido as it is the proper expression of that libido. Everyone has libido, desire, but often it is inhibited. This inhibition or repression occurs in the unconscious part of the mind so that we not only do not know why we repress it, but many people do not even recognize that they do repress it.

A great many studies have been made about this matter in recent years. There are numerous books on the subject. Perhaps you have seen Dr. Katherine Davis' summary of the sexual life of twenty-three hundred women.[1] In it she tells that a large proportion of married women are never able to overcome this frigidity as it is called. On the other hand, many women do overcome it, some slowly and gradually, some suddenly. Some of them overcome it by a process of education. Towards this end numerous books have been written, particularly by a Dr. Robie whose books can be purchased at book stores; some of them, however, cannot as there was some squabble between the author and the post office as I understand it. They are very helpful, however, to some people. Your husband could probably get them for you and he ought to read them as well as you. Then there are numerous other books along the same lines, the titles of which do not come to me offhand. There is a pair of volumes on the technical aspects of the problem by Wilhelm Stekel called *Frigidity in Woman.*[2] I don't know whether it would help you to read them or not; I don't think it would do you any harm, however, but they may be a little too technical for you.

The other method of treatment is psychological treatment. Psychoanalysis is the particular method I had in mind. I wouldn't recommend it except as a last resort. What I mean is that I would try other methods first if I were you.

If they don't succeed, the thing to do would be to go to the best psychoanalyst you could discover and work the problem out with him because I am sure you are right in saying that your home would be much happier and so would you and so would your husband and so would your children.

---

1. Katherine Bement Davis, *Factors in the Sex Life of Twenty-Two Hundred Women* (New York: Harper and Row, 1929).

2. Wilhelm Stekel, *Frigidity in Woman in Relation to Her Love Life,* trans. James S. Van Teslaar, 2 vols. (New York: Liveright, 1926).

Naturally I can't expect to solve a problem as long standing and as deep lying as this but I can make a few suggestions that may help you. At least they will help you in taking the right attitude in your reading. Sometimes difficulties of the sort you describe are due to an inability to get away from the wrong idea about sex. Most of us were brought up to think that sex was disagreeable, was ugly, was more or less of a necessary evil. It is difficult for us to overcome that idea altho we know better now. We know that it is a beautiful thing and ought to be the height of love expression between husband and wife. In spite of this, however, our childhood conception sometimes prevails. In other instances, the inability to achieve an orgasm is due to a little too much haste on the part of the husband. I doubt if this is the case with you. It is probably chiefly a psychological problem as I have suggested and lies with you. It is not an index of abnormality or anything to be ashamed of. I think the very fact that you are sensible enough to write this letter so frankly is an exceedingly good omen. I believe you ought to get yourself out of it and where there is a will there is usually a way.

Sincerely yours,

San Bernadino, Calif.

Mar. 25, 1931

Dear Dr. Menninger,

I've enjoyed your splendid articles on mental health so much, and I am wondering if you could help me as you have so many others.

This may not seem important but it is to me, and whether it would come under the heading of "mental health," I don't know.

I am twenty-three years old, my husband the same age, and happily married. We have two boys, three years and one year old. My problem is one I guess of many married people—that of sex.

We mutually care a great deal for each other, but I am unhappy because I am so cold physically. The sex relation means nothing to me. I don't dread it because I've learned to accept it as a duty but I feel it isn't fair to my husband, and too, I don't like to be so unresponsive. It seems people who are passionate have more ardent natures, can love more deeply, etc. Not that I don't worship my husband, because I do, but I don't enjoy prolonged kisses, demonstrativeness, etc., and I want to intensely enjoy it, since he does so much and is happy with me.

What is wrong with me, Dr. Menninger? I seem alright physically. Had both my children with no trouble, and was in fine health while carrying them. They are fine healthy boys. Of course, ordinarily I'm inclined to be a little thin, and require a great deal of sleep. I just haven't an abundant store of vitality, but if I get enough rest, I'm alright (one doctor, when I was in

High School, said I had a lack of secretion of the adrenal glands, but that's all, except slightly anemic, but don't think I'm anemic anymore). I'm not conscious of any mental inhibitions in this matter, but wondered if earlier impressions might have something to do with my unresponsiveness. During adolescence and late 'teens I was unaware of any "sex awakening" or any inclination for the opposite sex. Parentally speaking, my mother was also very unresponsive, not even being very demonstrative with her children, but nervous and reserved always. I was raised by my mother, my father and mother having separated when we were small. However, my sister raised in another state by my father, of an ardent loving nature, has the same trouble in her married life.

What shall I do? I hate to think of going the rest of my life so cold. Why are some people so passionate and others [have] no feeling at all? I've tried hard but it hasn't been any use, can you help me? I want the fullest, richest married life that is possible, and it isn't normal when it's this way.

I will greatly appreciate any help or advice you may give me as I have implicit faith in your judgement.

Most sincerely,

May 2, 1931

My dear Mrs.:

I have read with interest your letter of March 25 addressed to me in care of the *Ladies' Home Journal.*

I get many letters such as yours and I am very much tempted to devote a whole page of my department to answering your questions some time. For the present I shall try to tell you personally a little about frigidity in women.

In the first place understand very definitely this; it is always psychological in origin and not physical. A great many women undergo all kinds of physical treatment in an effort to overcome it and sometimes they do suddenly overcome it because of some operation or some physical manipulation of the womb without realizing that what has happened is merely that because of suggestion or some other psychological effect of the treatment, they have recovered. I say recovered because I regard frigidity as a kind of disease. It is a very widespread disease, however, and affects a large proportion of American women. It is a great pity too because there is no doubt but that sexual intercourse and sexual contacts of other sorts ought to be just as pleasurable and just as enjoyable to the woman as to the man. Why are they not? Because deep in the subconscious part of the mind something rises up and forbids it. Something says you must not permit yourself to indulge in this. You must not enjoy this, you cannot enjoy this, it is bad, and so forth and so on. It is not necessarily true that you feel this way about it intellectually. Many women, like yourself, feel that sex is perfectly normal and proper and good and all right and yet unconsciously they feel it is bad or they feel that it is something they should not do and so forth and so on and therefore they cannot yield themselves to the pleasure of it.

Now the only way that you can get rid of this with any degree of certainty is by psychoanalysis. Psychoanalysis is a method of treatment in which the repressions which exist in the unconscious part of the mind are brought to light so that the patient is free from his own unconscious inhibitions. Psychoanalysis is a tedious, expensive, difficult treatment, however. It takes a long time and there are only a few men in the United States who are really first rate, competent psychoanalysts. One should not go to anyone except a competent, recognized psychoanalyst. This limits the possibilities of such treatment to a very, very small proportion of the number of women who need it. However, because I think it is worth all it costs and a great deal more, I strongly advise you to try to get it if you can.

If you can't, the next best thing is to have your husband talk with a psychiatrist in regard to his own technique of intercourse with you. A great many women do not get satisfaction in intercourse because their husbands are not very skillful at it. The technique of sexual intercourse is an art and while some women are satisfied with almost any sort of procedure on the part of the man, other women are satisfied only when the man uses a great deal of skill and art and science and everything else and frequently men simply don't know how to do this. Sometimes they know but they don't take the trouble. I know nothing about your husband's technique, of course, and usually in spite of the very best technique women who are really frigid cannot be aroused. It is worth trying, however, and I suggest that you let your husband read this letter and go to some doctor who will give him the very best possible advice. Some people have gotten very good suggestions by reading books by Dr. Robie who published several books before his death several years ago on the subject of happy sexual relations, with particular regard to the point I have been mentioning. You can probably get these books at any large bookstore and second hand bookstores often have them for sale also.

Because I am particularly interested in the problem you raise and in how much good can be done for people by suggestions by correspondence in such a matter, I should appreciate it very much if you would write me in a month or two and tell me what differences, if any, you have noticed in yourself and what you plan to do in regard to it.

Sincerely yours,

10.

Interfering In-Laws

Dear Dr. Menninger:

Just recently I have discovered your articles in the *Ladies' Home Journal*. They have interested me so much, and it seems so wonderful, the good that you must be doing in helping people with their home problems. I am tempted to bring you one more problem, since you are so kind as to invite one to do so.

I hardly know how long or how short to make my story, but I am tempted to tell you more, then you may be better able to judge the situation, and if some parts seem unimportant, perhaps you can skip them.

I was born a farmer girl, my mother being German, and my father of English and Dutch descent. You know the traits of Germans—how thrifty, home-loving, hard-working, religious, music-loving, etc., they are. My mother, and her seven sisters, and her one brother were all typical Germans in these respects. My father has always been very hard-working, fair-minded, and strong-willed. I hardly know what to tell you about the years of my childhood and girlhood. I am sure that our parents always did the best they knew for "us," for I have an unmarried sister, seven years my senior.

All through those years, there was such a "clinging together" in the relationship on my mother's side. There would be Sunday dinner after Sunday dinner, one aunt would invite them all, then the other aunt would invite all the rest, and so on. And I remember, after the "little girl" stage was over, what a bore they always seemed to me, because there was always the same thing over, the same people to meet, and so often.

The relatives on my father's side always seemed so much more interesting, and companionship with them was so much more bracing, because they spoke and acted more frankly, and didn't say and do the same things over and over, because they always had, or because someone expected them to speak or think or act in a certain way.

I will tell you a few more facts concerning others in my mother's family. When I was still quite small, and at an interval of a few years, two of mamma's sisters committed suicide. Ill health was given as the cause, but I have always believed it was because they were not happily mated.[1]

The first had married a second time—a man who was making efforts to gain possession of the property willed her by her first husband. The husband of the second had a very bad disposition, and I believe that that, together with her illness, caused her to do what she did.

The second left a daughter who married later. Her husband farmed her father's farm, and they all lived together until her husband committed suicide several years ago. They said he had started drinking, and had gotten into debt, and consequently violated law, that he would have been imprisoned if he hadn't taken this way out, but I believe the root of the whole trouble was that they all lived together, and couldn't agree, and one bad thing led to worse.

Another sister, after a number of years of very hard work on the farm—early to rise, and late to bed, etc.—was taken with slow paralysis, and was practically helpless for about eighteen years. The only daughter always remained at home, and did not marry until rather late, several years before her mother's death. Her husband would not have taken her away from her mother, even though she had wanted to, and even though relations between her father and himself were not of the pleasantest. Now they live in the same place, and the son-in-law farms the father-in-law's farm, and the two scarcely exchange a word. There is a terrible state of affairs in the home.

Perhaps I should be ashamed to tell you of these things, but I wanted to mention a few facts concerning the family first. Mamma's other sisters married more happily than the two mentioned, and I think the most conspicuous traits in their characters were always love and faithfulness to home ties, and they were strongly religious and conscientious.

Now I am approaching my own problem, although I have been long doing it. During my four years in college, and the college was only a few miles from my home, I remember that out of a sense of duty, because there was so much work at home on the farm, I spent most of my weekends there.

---

1. Menninger has written in the margin, "How could they be?"

During the last year in school, mamma developed the beginnings of the same ailment as her sister, a slow paralysis, and of course since that time she has gotten gradually worse until now she is confined entirely to her wheel-chair. I married four and a half years after graduating—having spent over three years of that intervening time at home—and my husband started in business in a town eighteen miles from home.

Then the problem began. My sister had taken up other work, and would have been very unhappy to have given it up to stay on the farm again— partly because she had found her new life so broadening, and partly, I know, because my father's stronger will, when she was under his roof, always made her feel as if she could not be free, and could not be herself as she can when she is at liberty to decide things for herself.

Different times my father had mentioned how he thought we girls ought to do all in our power to be of help to them, and that of course whatever there would be to give would be given to no one but us two.

Then from the time of my marriage I began to bite off more than I could chew. I can honestly say that whatever I did for them, I did, not for what I would get some day, but because of my mother's condition, and because I wanted to be of help to her. I began spending several days a week there, cleaning, cooking, canning, etc. I kept doing a little more and a little more. My husband never complained, but would drive the intervening distance, just as I would plan. Always, at house-cleaning time, I would stay several weeks at a time.

After four years of this, and mamma grew gradually weaker, we decided to give up our home, and live with them, my husband driving the eighteen miles morning and evening. To show you that this program was not all sacrifice on his part, he would hurry home, and either dig around in the garden, or else hurry to the river, for he loves to fish, and the river runs close by. I did not think it would be easy to do, but it seemed as if we had to do it.

I could never describe the feelings I had as we rode back of the moving-van that day. It was like going to my own funeral, for I loved our little home so much, and our dear little boy had been born there. And then when we reached mamma's, and she said, "Welcome home!" I could have screamed.

That following summer was a nightmare. Papa and mamma are both good and kind, and I hardly know what made it so hard to live with them. During the four summers, there was scarcely a cross word exchanged, except once when papa struck our boy—then I flew off at a great rate. Instead of cross words, I think I felt a constant resentment, as if they were asking something which I should not have been required to give.

The fact that I could not have for meals what I would like to have was a source of annoyment to me at first, but something to which I learned to adjust myself as time went on. Then being a home-body, I had never sought pleasure outside of my home, but found a great deal of pleasure in friends, and in offering hospitality to them in our home. But this pleasure was denied me almost entirely because company worried and tired mamma, especially if there were children. Soon I felt as if we could not accept others' invitations, because we could not return the courtesies offered us.

I could get little comfort from church, because we were able to attend so irregularly, and during that first summer, even if we did go, my eyes would nearly burst with tears that came from I didn't know where, and I wished I were anywhere else.

And so it seemed I could not be myself. When visitors came, it seemed as if I were a "nobody," and as if I didn't count. I hardly know how to describe it.

I wanted to do the best I could toward my father and mother, and most of all I wanted to be a loving and attractive wife to my husband, and a good mother to our boy. The work was so hard, and there was so much of it—and so many times I thought, if it were just the work alone, I could have stood that—or if it had just been the giving up of our home and all the hard things that went with the giving it up—I could have stood that alone, but both of them together seemed more than I could bear. I felt sure that if my husband had lost his care for me, I should lose my reason, or something even worse might happen, I felt, but he was always so dear and good that I could never doubt his love for me.

Even then, I don't know what might have happened if we had not broken away in the fall and taken furnished rooms in our own town for the winter. The first weeks after making the change were very bad weeks. I suppose a psycho-analyst could give reasons for the conflict going on in my mind, but I could not have told anyone the exact nature of it, or the cause of it. When we studied psychology, we learned that certain thoughts that are unpleasant to our conscious minds are often put away and become active in a subconscious way that may bring much harm, and this must have been a struggle between my desire to be happy in my own home, and my other desire to be of help to mamma by living in their home. And truly it was a struggle! I longed to be able to visit some psycho-analyst, or some kind of mind-doctor who might help me to see things right. But if I had asked my husband to take me to one, he would have made fun of the idea. I was even afraid that I might be acting strangely in his presence at times, without knowing it.

I remember the first Sunday we went back home after leaving there to take furnished rooms. A terrible feeling of revulsion came to me as we were nearing there—I felt as if I hated nothing in the world as I hated that home. Now wasn't my mind sick—and won't it be [a] wonderful day when there are a great many more people whose life work it is to try to heal people's minds, instead of just their bodies!

And so we spent four summers that way—meaning by summers all the time between Easter and the time when the snow flies and radiators freeze in the late fall—then taking furnished rooms or a small apartment for the winter in our own town. Each time those first weeks after leaving mamma would be bad weeks. Then after the adjustment was made, I would be so happy during the remainder of the winter, that it seemed too good to be true.

I have not told you that my father owns a good farm of 180 acres. A farm nowadays, especially with a poor renter on it—and there are very few good ones—is perhaps a liability instead of an asset. Then he has life-insurance to the amount of at least $12,000. I just mean to show you that he is financially able to get other help than mine in the house, if he would only see fit.

Through what I believe to be the kindness of God, and the sympathy and understanding of a few dear friends, I have gotten through those times without anything terrible happening, and now I have almost—not quite—reached the conclusion that as the wife of a man in business, and the mother of a little first-grader, I shall always insist upon remaining in my own home, and that I will help my parents in every way that I can without neglecting our own little household.

Does that conclusion seem reasonable to you, Dr. Menninger? It may or may not seem like an axiom to you, instead of something to be proven, or reasoned out.

Or does what I have told you suggest a person who is either too weak to do a small piece of the world's work, or one too anxious to have her own way to be willing to give up anything for another who is in trouble, and too selfish to do what is right. And the question of what is right, and what is not right, is so hard to decide sometimes, isn't it?

I want to thank you so much, for reading this long letter, and for giving your attention in such a kind way to help people.

I will be so glad for your reply, when you have time to send one.

Very sincerely,

Feb. 20, 1931

My dear Mrs.:

I have read with interest your letter of January 26 addressed to me in care of the *Ladies' Home Journal.*

I think your conclusion is exactly right. I think it is not only a source of great unhappiness but a great deal of mental unhealthiness for so many members of a family to live together. You say on the first page of your letter that the root of the whole trouble in your mother's family was the fact that they all lived together. Not only did they do so, but apparently you are carrying on the same tradition.

I think you are entirely justified in getting away from your father's home and staying away. I think if you don't do so you are likely to bring a great deal more trouble on yourself and your family than you have already had.

There comes a time in every young person's life when their emotional development should be such that they can leave the home and build a new family unit of their own. If for some reason or other there are hindrances in the development of this plan there are sure to be conscious and unconscious hostilities arise somewhere which bring about unhappiness.

In the May number of the *Ladies' Home Journal* there is going to be a long article on the subject. I shall not use your letter but you will discover that there are several others there very much like yours. You are somewhat imprisoned by your own family. Part of that however is due to your own attachment. An attachment that you have been a little reluctant to break. Consequently, I think your resolution to go away and stay away is an excellent one and I hope you carry it out.

Sincerely yours,

Vancouver, B.C.
Feb. 2, 1930

Dear Dr. Menninger,

Could you tell me how to overcome my antipathy to my husband's family? I am very happily married and have two fine boys, aged five and three and a half, yet the prospect of contact with my husband's family seems always hanging over me like a dark cloud. Last spring while preparing for a visit from my mother-in-law I had a nervous breakdown accompanied by a severe attack of sciatica which lasted for two months and a half. When she visited us before—when my younger boy was three months old—I had an outbreak of frightful boils which did not clear up till she had left. And after that when anyone of the family came to stay with us I promptly had a boil. That seems to be over now. You must not think that they visit so very often for they don't. In seven years (I have been counting up) we have had some of the family staying here for thirteen months. Eighteen members have visited us, usually one at a time, occasionally two or three together. We have visited at the family home three times for three weeks each time. It is the prospect of another such "holiday" that occasions this letter. I feel I cannot face it, yet it is a perfectly natural thing that my husband should visit his home and he is unwilling to go without me. His people are quite as good as mine and have hosts of friends who admire them yet my one desire is to keep away. I have always tried to conceal my feelings and think I have been successful as they all treat me in a very friendly manner. I can look ahead and see that we will be thrown together for the whole of our lives so the only thing for me to do is to overcome my shrinking. Have you any advice for me?

Sincerely,

Feb. 20, 1930

Dear Madam:

I have read your letter of February 2nd addressed to me in care of the *Ladies' Home Journal.*

My advice to you would be to stay away from your husband's family as much as possible. You recognize this antipathy, you recognize that it arises from illogical causes which are deep in your personality and the only answer is that you must either go thru a process of ridding yourself of these deep lying causes or else you must stay away from the people who cause you such acute distress.

To remove the real causes of your antipathy might be a very prolonged, expensive process. I think it is much easier simply to stay away. If your husband is intelligent, I am sure he will understand and help you to arrange matters so as not to hurt your mother-in-law's feelings.

I shall not publish your letter but I shall take the liberty of quoting one or two paragraphs about the way in which these boils appear as a result of your unexpressed hate. I think that is very interesting and a phenomenon the significance of which is usually clear. I'm sure you will not object to this.

Sincerely yours,

Illinois
Feb. 20, 1931

Dear Doctor Menninger:

Am I in the wrong and if so, what is your advice?

I am a young house-wife and mother of two children; one six years and a baby of eight months. I am twenty-seven years old and been married seven years to a man one year my senior. He is a graduate of Harvard, finishing in three and one-half years with honors, which proves he has a good mind I think. He has been in the teaching profession but did not enjoy the work so resigned last year at end of first quarter. He intended to devote his time to writing a novel the idea for which had been growing for some time. Little has been done on the book and all his time he devotes to his hobby which is the radio. He takes no interest even in his appearance.

This fall he did not try for a job and our income is very small from a little farm his father left him. I have to use strict economy and I do all my own sewing and make everything but shoes and stockings for the children. Also in my spare time I sew for other people the money from which goes for the comforts of the family.

Our house is quite small with just two tiny bedrooms one of which we give up to my husband's mother and the other belongs to the children. We use the daybed in the living room.

My mother-in-law has a fine big house of her own but is always unhappy and grieving over the loss of her husband five years ago, "can't even have her son," and her poor health. Two different doctors failed to find anything wrong with her except a need of glasses which she thinks would not help her any. She is a bit more cheerful when she is with us, but my husband and I dare not talk alone in another room or spend a quiet evening reading or she will sit and hold her head and appear to feel badly. Her son then leaves the house and I must entertain her till she gets tired and goes to bed.

Now this is a little of the picture of my home life. The following is my reaction to it.

I love good times, beautiful and happy surroundings, but I feel I am doing more than my share in supplying all the scenery and action in the home and there are no good times. I like to work for things but I want cooperation. I have to create all the cheerfulness and happiness for the mother-in-law, and in [the] meantime, I am discouraged about our future. I want to be with other young people and laugh and sing and be attractive like I did when I was in school.

If I mention to my husband that I feel this way he says I am selfish and I cause him to worry.

What shall I do, play the game even tho it is disgusting to me or take the children and leave the mother and her son alone together for awhile. I think I could earn enough by sewing to supply our necessities.

Thanking you for your time.

Yours sincerely,

Mar. 20, 1931

My dear Mrs.:

I have read with much interest your letter of February 20 addressed to me in care of the *Ladies' Home Journal.*

If your account of things is correct I should say that you are exactly right in everything except your proposed solution. I think you must see first of all that your primary object must be the maintenance of a home, and a happy home. Now the presence of your mother-in-law there certainly detracts from the happiness of the home and I think on the whole it detracts from the integrity of the home. In other words, I believe that mother-in-laws in the home are very dangerous persons even when they are possessed of the most agreeable personalities. They have a very bad effect on each member of the family, including the children. Therefore, I think in her own interests and in the interests of her own house, a wife should object very seriously to having her husband's mother stay with them.

In the second place, I think you should recognize that your husband's behavior is strongly suggestive of being that of a seriously neurotic man. Quitting a job because he doesn't like it when he has nothing better in view, setting out to write a novel and then neglecting it, devoting himself to a hobby when he has no income and reproaching you for your very justifiable desire to keep the home together, all indicates that he is not acting in an entirely healthy-minded fashion. He probably does not quite know why he does these things but believes that he is acting quite rationally and sensibly. Perhaps, on the other hand, he knows that he isn't. Please do not understand me to say that your husband is crazy. On the contrary, he is probably very sane, and not nearly so disturbed about his unprofitable investment of time as he should be. But this is not something to scold him about. It is something to help him with if possible. I am going entirely on what you have told me in your letter, of course, and it is possible that you may have unintentionally misrepresented something. But if it is as you say, I think your husband most certainly should consult a psychoanalyst. Whatever you do, I don't think you ought to leave him as you suggest. I think you ought to insist that his mother leave if it is at all possible. I don't think you have been entirely wise in your own reactions. You say if you mention your dissatisfaction to your husband, he says you are selfish and cause him to worry and evidently you think this is reason enough for stopping. I think you ought to cause your husband a little worry. I think you have indulged him too much. You have been too willing to be made a martyr of. You have been too willing to do a lot of work and sewing to support the family which he should be doing. This permits him, unintentionally and probably quite unconsciously, to depend more and more upon you just as he evidently depended more and more upon his mother. Therefore, you have helped him along in the wrong direction. You must help him to realize the responsibility that rests upon him and help him to have the courage to face it and shoulder it and go on like a man instead of playing about with the radio like a child. As I have already indicated, I doubt if you will be able to do this unassisted and I think the best means would be to take advantage of any inclination he may show to want some help by having him consult a good psychiatrist or psychoanalyst. I don't know just where [your town] is but I presume it is somewhere near Chicago and there are several good men in Chicago to whom I should be glad to refer you if you decide to do this.

Sincerely yours,

Montana
Apr. 11, 1931

My dear Dr. Menninger:

My plea seems to be the usual one, after ten years my marriage is about to go on the rocks and frankly I do not want it to. When we were married we were madly in love with each other. My husband is an architect and very hard-working and conscientious. He is well liked by his business associates. He is very set in his ways, things are either right or they are wrong, there is no halfway measures.

After we were married three years a baby girl was born and died, three years later a son was born. At that time both the child and I were about to pass on but we didn't. While we were in the hospital my husband seemed to be the usual proud daddy but as soon as we returned home things were different. Of a necessity the home revolved around the child. I had always been an excellent housekeeper and cook but I found it impossible to do things as I formerly had.

Up to the time of the birth of the child my husband and I had never had the slightest trouble, not even the tiny bickerings that creep into every home. Now things were changed, when K. would come home at night he would be irritable, if the child cried or interrupted him when he was telling me something he would shut up like a clam and refuse to speak the rest of the evening. This made things very unpleasant for me and as I too was tired I didn't have the patience with him that I formerly had and I would occasionally snap at him.

My husband has developed into a stubborn, fault-finding person. Nothing the child or I does is quite right, while he doesn't always say anything we have no difficulty in knowing that he is displeased. The child is an adorable four year old, sweet-tempered, well-mannered and minds me beautifully. He loves his daddy, but it does seem that the two of them are constantly arguing. Sometimes it is laughable and then again I get disgusted because his father doesn't spank him and make him mind. I don't believe in interfering when he starts the correction. I tell him to spank the youngster and have it over with but he refuses.

Like most marital difficulties the mother-in-law enters into the picture. My mother is a widow and in all frankness I must say that she is not the most comfortable person to have around the house. My husband has taken a violent dislike to her. I never paid a great deal of attention to it, just tried to have her here while he was at the office or out of town. I never realized to what an extent this dislike had gone and when he explained I willingly agreed that she should not come here anymore. After this talk I thot we were on a road to a better understanding and then my mother had to step into the picture again and raise a big fuss. I tried to be as diplomatic with her as possible and explain the situation, but she threatened death and destruction to the entire family and it was necessary to call in the police. Three years ago mother was injured in an automobile accident and I don't believe she has been right since that time and seems to be getting steadily worse. At this time my husband was out of town. Our town is small and we are very well known but I know that no one but the parties concerned knows about this as the police commissioner had my mother taken out of town by my brother. Of course I felt that I had to explain circumstances to my husband as he might find out in some manner and it would be worse than ever. Since that time he has been absolutely impossible to get along with, he is forever giving dirty digs about "cheap people" etc. That hurts. I can't help what my mother does.

I have always been popular with the opposite sex and my husband has never seemed to be the slightest bit jealous, in fact he rather got a kick out of it. I do all the specification writing at the office, working perhaps a week or ten days out of every month, the rest of the time we take care of the correspondence at home. I take an active part in civic affairs, entertain and am considered capable so my husband has no cause to feel ashamed of me in that respect.

I truly don't know what the trouble is between us, all I know is that he treats me like dirt beneath his feet, sarcastic and yet polite. I have tried every means I know to restore peace and happiness in our family but as I don't know what the source of the trouble is and he won't tell, what am I to do? I still care for my husband, but I don't see how we can go on this way even for the sake of the child. I am young, I want happiness too. If I thot there was a chance of conditions bettering themselves I would willingly stay.

If you can get any sense out of this letter and have any suggestions to offer I would be more than grateful and can assure you that I will give your methods a sincere trial and be willing to let you know the results.

Sincerely yours,

May 13, 1931

My dear Mrs.:

I have read with interest your letter addressed to me in care of the *Ladies' Home Journal.*

It is quite obvious that your husband is jealous of the child. This is a very common form of infantile reaction on the part of husbands and I don't know what you can do about it, except to appeal to his intelligence. Intelligence unfortunately is not very powerful in controlling human behavior but perhaps if you make it very clear to him he will see it.

I must go on and say that I think your own reactions are far from being very hygienic. I think your husband is absolutely right in not wanting to spank the baby and I think it is a curious little quirk in you that makes you feel like doing so and think that it ought to be done. For you to say that you get disgusted because his father does not spank him seems to me to indicate a certain spark of cruelty in you which I don't think you should tolerate in yourself, not because it in itself is so bad but because it is so likely to stimulate in your child hostilities and reactions which are going to be increasingly difficult to manage as he gets older.

Furthermore, I think you are not at all justified in permitting your mother to live with you. I think it is a very grave mistake from the standpoint of marital happiness in practically all cases. All husbands take dislikes to their mother-in-laws, or at least most of us do, altho they do not always express it so frankly. It is not clear from your letter whether she lives with you or not but if she is a direct irritant for your husband as you say she is, I would certainly see that they are together as little as possible.

Now I come to the sentence in which you indicate that you think your mother's mind has been afflicted and that you have treated it as if you thought it was some kind of a disgrace and concealed it from people. I think in this you play into your husband's hands. I don't think you should have permitted yourself to regard it as something disgraceful. I think you ought to face it very frankly as one of the disasters which overtakes people sometimes and which ought to be dealt with in a sensible, frank, open way. It is not a disgrace, it is not cheap, it is not bad, it is not shameful. You ought not to treat it so.

I don't think your family situation is in a bad way at all. I think you are having some of the maladjustments which are very common in your particular period of married life. It is quite obvious that you ought to have more children and I think you will find that matters will adjust themselves.

Sincerely yours,

Iowa
June 18, 1931

Dear Dr. Menninger:

It has taken me a great deal of time and effort to come to the writing point. I have now made my mind up that your decision is to be my deciding factor. The question facing me is: Shall I leave this home and my husband and start life again for myself, or shall I remain? The facts bearing on this case are these:

My education and training:

I have had stenographic training and several years experience in the Government.

I play the piano, guitar and mandolin.

I draw, paint, sing, dance and write.

I speak three languages besides English.

These things my mother and father had me learn. My father wanted me to be a lawyer. My mother wanted me to marry nobility. Father died before I finished school. Mother married within a few months of his death. She is dark, beautiful, charming and speaks seldom and slowly. Neither she nor my father has ever caressed me to my knowledge. He was sixty when I was born. She was nineteen. He was extremely wealthy. I always had too much money, too many clothes and too many ideas.

My ambitions and hopes:

I planned, of course, to marry well.

Travel is my main objective in life.

I don't care for fame, but I do care for comfort.

I'd like a little happiness and quiet before I die.

Here is the condition I am now in:

I married a boy thirteen months older than myself because he loved me and I loved him.

He brought me here to live with his parents; his mother is fifty, his father is sixty. He is the only child and was born after ten years of married life.

He is totally dependent for decisions and initiative upon his mother.

She has trained him to be so. She has told me that if he leaves, she dies. He has told me that he will never leave mother because she needs him and he worships her.

The place:

This place is a run-down farm on deep Iowa gumbo roads.

It is sixteen miles from a small town of six thousand population.

In the spring, winter and fall there is no way out of here excepting on foot.

The house is seventy five years old and is alive with rats, mice, and a great many varieties of spiders, all of whom feast upon me as I sleep, with the result that my face and hands are swollen a good bit of the time. My mother-in-law says there is nothing to be done about it. The mice eat my papers, my plants and my clothes. There is no plumbing. There is always a pot to carry for my husband who has been trained to use it rather than exert himself to venture out doors.

All water must be carried from a well which is an eighth of a mile from the house.

The entire place is a mixture of cow manure, horse manure, chicken manure and hog manure, and is odorous of these during the entire summer and spring and fall weather, especially after rains. Mother-in-law doesn't believe in house cleaning. Her cooking is not clean. We don't fight, because I always give in, rather than.

Entertainment possible:

I can have my choice of these two alternatives: we have four neighbors. . . . they can come here or I can take the lantern and wade the snow or rain or whatever, to call on them. The sole topic of conversation is Tommy's last turn of colic, or the price of eggs. They read nothing. They rock and stare at the stove. They can't play cards. They have no instruments. I cannot seem to arouse a great deal of enthusiasm over the quantity of eggs gathered during the day. This is not a bit of an exaggeration, Dr. Menninger. It's as true as life. It is life.

The family:

Mother-in-law. She is kind-hearted and strives to do the best she can. She really does. She is, first, the ugliest woman on earth to look upon. Second, she is the most curious. Third, she is the most talkative. Fourth, she is the most maudlin. She has spoiled her son so thoroughly that no woman on earth will ever please him, or can. She undresses him when he is tired and puts on his night things. She brings him drinks, cigarettes, matches, stories, food; whatever he calls for, rather than have him stir himself and get it for himself. She loves to do this.

She must have your attention all day long. If you don't give it, she stands over you and repeats your name until you do. If I try to read, she will come over and say, "Whatcha readin'?" I always respond. "Oh," she will say, "Well, that reminds me of a story I onct read in the Popular Monthly." And she will tell a long and rambling tale. It doesn't matter if I want to read. She wants to talk. If I play on any of my instruments, she still wants to talk. I always stop and listen, not because I want to or even because I feel I should, but because I know that if I don't she will insist until I do.

She will let me have no privacy or solitude. I can't have a word with my husband because she follows him about like a spaniel.

She has even informed me that she wished he had been her husband instead of mine. She has him answering to "Pretty boy" and "Precious pet." I am "Pretty girl." Understand, my mother paid me no personal attention in all my life. Then this. . . . muck. I have been called down stairs in a hurry only to have her ecstatically point out of the window at her son carrying a pail of water, gurgling, "Aint he cute!" She is son-obsessed. Sonny is mother-obsessed. He has taken out a goodish bit of life insurance since we were married. At her insistence. It is all in her name. I didn't even know he was getting it until I carried the policies in with the mail. Not that it matters. Nothing, does, I suppose.

She works like a Trojan slave. The Augean stables would be just a tidbit for her. She cuts down trees and makes them into kindling. She picks up the hog cobs all day long for fuel. She carries all the water. She does two-thirds of the men's work in the barnyard. I have never in all my life seen such a Herculean woman. I can't begin to tell you half the labor she consummates. She swears like a muleteer and uses the language of a street urchin.

Father-in-law: He is fat, lazy, dirty, chews tobacco, is always grouchy, in excellent health, brow-beats his wife continually, has a fight every single morning to start off the day, abuses his son daily and his stock frequently, swears, loafs, talks his head [sic] kicks me out as regularly as the moon changes. He calls me "son of a bitch" and threatens to knock me down every time I happen to differ with him. So much for that. He has "kicked" my husband and I out five times so far. And my husband cringes and begs back into good grace.

My husband: He is lovable, very babyish and soft, sentimental, six feet two and weighs two hundred pounds. He loves his mother passionately and he loves me greatly. I know this. He has absolutely no backbone. He has told me that he has always depended on his mother and now he always will. I am his second wife. His first wife divorced him after living here three months. Her grounds were that his mother threw her out. The first wife was a community favorite. Raised here. Can you imagine the welcome I received when I arrived?

The future: This is a 160 acre farm. It is mortgaged for twenty-five thousand dollars. The taxes are almost five hundred dollars a year (with interest). The interest on the twenty-five thousand is over a thousand dollars a year. There is, besides that, two notes due at the defunct bank. Do you see that no matter how hard the whole lot of us worked, the mortgage could never be paid off, because it now takes all that is made to keep the taxes and interest up? Do you see that at any time the place may be lost completely? Can you see my husband is spending the years that he should be using in building up a business which would support us the balance of our lives in running this decrepit farm, which may be lost at any time? There is absolutely nothing to look forward to for me. If his father dies, it will mean even less liberty for W. and I, and more work. If his mother dies, it will simply mean that I step into her worn shoes and perform the labor of ten men. And this work will warp and eventually kill me. There is never money. There is never even good food. The diet of salt pork and potatoes has made me hopelessly anemic. I lost twenty pounds the first month I spent here. The furnishings are hideous and poor. I had a good home.

I think I could stand it somehow if I weren't watched and commanded by my vigilant mother-in-law. If I go up stairs for a moment alone, she calls me down by complaining, "Mother is lonesome." And that's another thing. She never calls herself I. It is always "Mother." Furthermore, both my in-laws have told me they will on no account have children here. So that is that.

Because of the splendid example set by dear old Mother, I work in the field with the men. It is simply expected of me. I husk corn. I shock oats. I seed oats and clover and alfalfa, I help cock it [sic] and put it in the barn. I ring hogs. I herd cows along the roads in spring and fall because we have no pasture.

I am soul sick and tired even to the hairs on my scalp of the dirt, the constant watching and compelled attention, the constant questioning and talk, the continual fighting and swearing, the abuse of the English language, such as, "I are got," "I ain't," "Them there roads," "These kind," and the silly, silly baby talk his mother uses on W.

There is no hope that I will ever have a home of my own with him. Shall I stick it out with determination and an out-thrust chin? Or do you think it would be better for me to resume my stenographic work in some city? I know I can do this. I was an excellent stenographer. You have to be fairly good to pass the Civil Service, you know. My family lived in every portion of this country, so, understand, it isn't just restlessness that is irking me. My mother-in-law has me to the point that tears stand helplessly in my eyes sometimes more than once a day. Simply from frustration, you see.

I really am sorry to have to bother you. I have always solved my own problems up until now. And now I am afraid to trust my own judgment. Please do answer me. And if I am to blame, don't spare me in any way.

Sincerely,

July 24, 1931

My dear Mrs.:

I have read with a great deal of interest your letter addressed to me in care of the *Ladies' Home Journal*.

If I knew as definitely what I wanted out of life as it seems you do—comfort, a little of happiness . . . and quiet, and found that circumstances over which I had some control had thrown me into an environment where these things were quite impossible, I would most certainly put to work the talents and experience that you seem to have and thus secure for myself both peace and comfort.

Reared, as apparently you were, in an atmosphere of comparative luxury it is difficult to understand what has made it possible for you to endure such living conditions as long as you have but whatever it may have been will probably prove a stumbling block when the time for a break comes.

Whether or not your love for your husband is a greater one than his for you is a question but in any event the situation sifts itself down to whether or not your love for or need of your husband is greater than your need for peace and comfort and whatever may be your conception of happiness.

I think if I were you that I would go back to work. Distance will surely lend enchantment either to your present situation or to the new one into which your work may take you.

Above all I would certainly consider myself very fortunate to have come through what has undoubtedly been a trying experience with poise and self-confidence. I would look upon it all as having been very much worth whatever it has cost you because love and marriage are worth any cost even if they turn out badly.

Sincerely yours,

Louisville, Ky.
June 20, 1931

My dear Dr. Menninger:

I have read with a great deal of interest your writings in the *Ladies' Home Journal.* I have a brother that I am very much concerned about and am wondering if you could help him. He is a drinking man and has been drinking for a number of years. He does not stay intoxicated all of the time, but about every two weeks or three is the longest period that he ever goes without getting on a spree which generally lasts several days.

When we talk to him about getting help to overcome this terrible habit he always says that he does not need help, that he can quit any time, but I know that he cannot because I know that he wants to and he promises that he will quit but is not able to resist the temptation.

He is the kind of a person that should not touch any kind of a stimulant, he is highly nervous and excitable and was that way from a child. His work is very strenuous being connected with a brokerage house. He is considered very keen and of having a brilliant mind and a quick thinker.

He has a charming personality. He has a lovely family, two boys 11 and 13 years of age and a daughter 16, they are all very fond of him. He owns a lovely home and would be the perfect husband and father if it were not for this one thing. He does, however, have one thing which seems to irritate him and which causes him to say awful things when he is drinking and that is his mother-in-law, who has to live with him. His wife is the only child and her mother is dependent on them for a living and when my brother is drinking he talks to her perfectly awful and says disgraceful things which makes it hard for the rest of the family. It is true that this mother-in-law is very irritating and disagreeable and does not like my brother any more than he does her and when she is around there seems to be an undercurrent all the time, but thank goodness she has gone away for the summer and we are in hopes things are going to be better.

No doubt, you will think this a very silly letter, but I would so love to find a way to help this adorable brother because if he keeps on it is going to kill him and I am afraid will affect his business career. He is 37 years of age—just in the prime of his life.

If you can suggest any way for us to appeal to him or if you could touch him in any way we would be so grateful. I am enclosing an addressed envelope and would appreciate a direct answer. Would prefer not to have this letter appear in the *Journal*.

Yours sincerely,

July 27, 1931

My dear Miss:

I have read your letter addressed to me in care of the *Ladies' Home Journal* with sympathy.

I get a great many letters from people in regard to friends of theirs whose excessive drinking they recognize to be a form of mental ill health. They are quite right in so regarding it. But what they must recognize is that the excessive use of alcohol is not exactly a disease, but only the manifestation of the disease. Fever is not a disease but it shows there is a disease process in the body and the craving for alcohol indicates the presence of a disorder within the personality, a psychological conflict of some sort which the individual feels incapable of solving. Consequently he takes refuge in a form of escape. Now it is very characteristic that these individuals are exceedingly amiable, likable, capable people and often give very little evidence outside of their alcoholism of the need or intensity of the conflicting emotions within them which make them so susceptible to the boon of alcoholic intoxication.

In your particular case I think one of the irritants which obviously adds to the difficulties is well known. I think it is a very expensive way to take care of a mother-in-law. Your sister-in-law should make almost any sacrifice rather than keep her mother in the home under these conditions. It is always bad business and in this case it seems to be particularly bad business.

But I also want to warn you that this is not all there is to it. If it wasn't the mother-in-law, I suspect it would be something else. Mothers-in-law don't drive sons-in-law to drink. There is always the fault within the personality of the drinker which makes him incapable of handling external difficulties in a satisfactory way.

I have been at some pains to make it clear to you that the person who uses alcohol as a sort of psychological necessity does so because something is wrong within him, because I think the only hope of curing these individuals is by a psychotherapeutic process which gets at the root of the difficulty. This is no easy matter even in the best of hands. It will probably take a year's time and will probably necessitate your brother going to some other city to live during the time he takes his treatments. He probably won't want to do it. Both he and his wife will probably feel that they can't afford it. All sorts of objections will arise in his mind and perhaps in yours too.

Nevertheless, my own belief is that excessive alcoholism such as you describe is an exceedingly serious problem which can only be treated successfully by making a great effort and an intelligent effort. The method of treatment I have in mind is psychoanalysis. Not everyone has the intelligence to profit by this method of treatment but for those who do it has more to offer than anything else I know. I certainly think that it does little or no good to merely lock such individuals up in an asylum or a so-called Keeley cure.[1]

Sincerely yours,

1. In 1880, a Doctor Leslie Keeley announced that he had discovered a remedy for alcoholism, the secret compound "Bichloride" or "Double Chloride of Gold." Alcohol, he argued, poisoned the nerve cells, which became addicted to it. The addiction could be broken by this compound; although Bichloride was available by mail, a surer cure was offered at "Keeley Institutes." The original was in Dwight, Illinois, and by the turn of the century, every state in America had at least one, as Keeley's cure gained widespread fame. After Keeley's death in 1900, the popularity of the "Keeley cure" diminished.

11.

Problem Parents

Florida
Nov. 2, 1930

Dear Dr. Menninger:

May I appeal to you for help in a mental adjustment. The trouble lies in my all too quick temper. As a child of 2 or 3, I first showed it violently—being the youngest of 7 and the only girl, I was alternately spoiled and bullied. But as I grew older I learned to control it. My parents both died when I was 7 and I was sternly disciplined thereafter.

I had thot my temper conquered until increasing deafness brought with it increasing irritability. Now that I am almost totally deaf I am less irritable, depending on a phone and some lip-reading. Also, I am for the first time in my life deeply content and utterly happy in the possession of a small son. My first and only. But as he grows older I find my violent temper returning when weary with a hard day's work and care of him. My husband is much away from home and we can't afford any one to relieve me of the care of the boy, now 2 years.

I try so hard to be calm and quiet with him but any child, no matter how dear or how good, can be exhausting to an older person, and I am 37.

I have studied and worked with children all my life and do enjoy the days with my own so—if it were not for these flare-up tempers.

I try to avoid conflicts. I rest in the afternoon for a bit. We are outdoors a great deal. We eat plainly and intelligently. My husband and son both have very quiet nerves and are slow to wrath. Please tell me what I can do to control it? I would appreciate any help.

I enclose a self-addressed envelope.

Yours truly,

Nov. 26, 1930

My dear Mrs.:

Your recent letter addressed to me in care of the *Ladies' Home Journal* interested me very much.

To some extent, no doubt, your irritability is an expression of the resentment which you once felt toward the person who disciplined you after the death of your parents, towards a new object. When we become tired our unconscious buried motives have a chance to get out and if you have long buried these feelings you can keep them down pretty well until you get tired or overburdened and distressed and then these resentments take on any convenient goat. You probably make your husband the goat sometimes or the child the goat but the real goat is whoever it was who punished you when you were seven. You feel so strongly against these people that you didn't even tell me who they were in your letter.

I don't know anything that you can do about it beyond recognizing this fact and trying to get sufficient rest because I doubt if it is severe enough or serious enough to necessitate a thorough psychological housecleaning. I think on the whole you are probably very healthy-minded. You are taking this matter of your deafness very bravely and sensibly I think. I marveled at that when I read your letter. I don't think irritability is such a serious symptom, don't be too severe with yourself about it. Remember that there is nothing in the world that your husband and the child too for that matter will crave so much in a woman as a cheerful, smiling face and sweetness. They would much rather see that than anything else. To lose your hearing afflicted you but it does not deprive them; but if you lose your smiling you will deprive them of one of the greatest things in their life. Remember that and do the best you can.

Sincerely yours,

P.S. Some people you know take out their "mad" feelings by beating rugs or beating a golf ball or mowing the lawn. If you feel it coming on, perhaps you could resort to something of this sort. For your child's sake and your husband's I would try to hide it some way or other; for your own, I think I would take it out on some inanimate object.

Missouri
Nov. 20, 1930

Dear Dr.,

As you suggested in the *Ladies' Home Journal* that you help make mental adjustments for people, I want to tell you our troubles. My husband is such a trial to us and it is affecting the oldest daughter and very likely the other three children. And sometimes I wonder if I am right myself and how one knows and how one can prove who is and who isn't.

I shall try to start at the beginning. As far as I know there is no mental trouble in my family, tho that does sound conceited. I am afraid I grew up in too ideal a home and my trouble now is so new I do not know how to manage it.

My husband's father was a drunkard, tho he reformed about middle age and died before our marriage. By the way we have been married seventeen years and he is 44, I am 43. His mother was one of those decided nervous wrecks who still lives here in our town. She has always caused more or less trouble in our home, trying to make him feel if anything went wrong it was *my* fault. I do not like to quarrel so just leave her alone and seldom see her—so she is seldom mentioned.

My husband's boyhood was not happy—I do not know whether it was the father's or mother's fault, but they did not get along well and I remember him saying once that when in adolescence his father once whipped him until he lay there seemingly lifeless. He gets from his home environment the idea that he is never wrong. When things are not right it is someone else's fault. He has the feeling of revenge very strongly developed. Only the last seven years has our life been so unhappy, when he lost his job and we now have a dairy farm. To illustrate his revenge if we get a milk order from someone he is prejudiced against, he refuses to sell to them. That does not hurt them but it hurts our children—the wrong principle you know. And I do not always have time to cover it up from them.

When we married it was a true love affair, altho he is naturally cruel and selfish, it did not show much and being the other extreme I admired his sternness. I knew his mother was against me but thot that would right itself and had no other warning of what I was getting into. We should not have had children. My husband has a flat back head so maybe he can't help it because he isn't good to them. One more thing: all his five sisters and brother have had serious nervous trouble by or before the age of forty except the oldest, who has a very bad disposition. This is all to make you understand the husband, who once tried to kill himself and since I have often thot would try to kill me. You know how feelings pass from one to another and when he was angry at me about something I have often felt he was just aching to let himself go, so he could get his hands on me. He keeps a gun in the milkhouse but I never pretend to care and always try to seem indifferent tho I fear he can read my feelings. Thru it all I love him for sometimes he is wonderful to me and I always try to forget unpleasant things and feel maybe I imagine worse than it is. Also he loves me, as far as I know he is true to me.

But—it is not myself nor him that matters, it is the children. They are the coming generation, we may die any time. I sometimes think all the trouble is because he is jealous of the children yet I crave his companionship and he knows it, so I have turned to them for the devotion I do not get from him. Anyway they are my job and I want to give them the advantage of everything I know and can do for them. I was a music teacher and try to give them all the music I can.

We have four children—14, 12, 9, and 7. Two are more aggressive like their father. The middle two are more quiet like me. Their father seems to have to always have to spite or blame someone for things. For a year or so it was P. Jr. It keeps all of them on a constant strain for they are more or less sensitive and rather affectionate to each other. None of them ever seem to blame their father tho for his harshness except E. who openly talked to me this last year about him. I try to excuse him and tell her he loves her and that it is because he is tired and worried. And finally I told her I was afraid he grew up that way and could not help it. She has seen a little of the meanness of her grandmother when the children visit there.

One day when he had been unusually cross (and that generally happens when they are not much wrong but when his nerves are raw) she talked to me about him, "Mother I wish he was like other girls' fathers. Why can't we live like other people do? And he is so mean to little D. And I just help M. and D. to go hide if you are at the milkhouse when he comes in. Mother we children are not going to grow up right. It is robbing me of my confidence and it will the others too." O, I had feared that very thing. Yet every day I hope tomorrow will be better and try my best to make it so. Our daughter has always been so active and fearless. Last spring she refused to obey something he told her. She told him he was a bully to the children and he was mean to me. He struck her to the floor. Since then she is easier to manage but it took her spirit. She has lost her confidence with her schoolmates and does not mix much. If she goes to a party, she is just a wall-flower. Usually she stays at home and whenever she does go, says she did not have a good time. I feel so sorry for her, but I don't know what to do. I have thot of divorce but I could not support the children. Now the effect that affair had on the father. He is better to me but worse to her. He wants her to do all the housework before she goes to school, wash dishes, make three beds and sweep. Then she has to walk 1½ miles. I don't let her do it, then when he notices she doesn't he gets cross with her and makes her do whatever he says. I work in the milkhouse after breakfast of mornings. It is wrong for me to help her deceive him but it isn't right for her to have to do all that and I have time when they are gone. Now last night I found her teaching one of the others to deceive me. Ingratitude—yet she had not thot of that. But she is taking on the manner of her father when she does not feel well. She often tells me she isn't happy, that she hates all men.

Her father uses lots of cigars and medicine and eats lots of candy (does not drink). But he does not like for the children to make candy (I seldom buy it). Last week he came in and our daughter was making candy. He had been specially short-tempered for several days at her because she had taken part in some school exercise which had greatly restored her happiness and self-confidence. The school work had. She is a rather talented girl in dramatics and music and is a pretty child too. I had been doing some of her work so she could practice at school and he had found it out, cause of his anger. When he found her making that candy he told her if she made that candy he would bring the black-snake whip up and use it on her. I immediately sent her down to the cellar to get something, like I always do—try to turn things off. I told him if he started such a thing I would call the sheriff. A look came into his eyes I never saw before. He went out on the porch then called me to come. I went to the door and said very quietly, "I won't do it." Our daughter had heard and she came and was sobbing brokenly saying, "Mother I won't let him hurt you." He seemed to be satisfied then after he had hurt her like that and went on. He has been better since but I can't run the risk of that happening again. Surely I have told you enough for you to get the situation. After that incident she went to her room crying as if she could never stop and she seldom cries. She said, "Mother if he ever hurts you I'll kill him."

Since then she has often been almost impudent to me, she seems to blame me because I don't do something about it but what can I do? I can't change him. Should I divorce him? We all love him but her. I fear I could not support them. My father might take us, he is alone, but is a school teacher and a good one but is 70 and may not get a school another year.

Our daughter's only joy outside her home is the movies. Should I let her attend often? Of evenings when the father is at town our homelife is quite happy believe it or not. We are literary and musical and get on fine.

Yours truly,

Dec. 19, 1930

My dear Mrs.:

I think your letter of November 20 addressed to me in care of the *Ladies' Home Journal* is one of the most terrible letters I have ever read. I do not mean that the letter is terrible but the things you describe in your letter. Such cruelty on the part of a father toward his daughter, such selfishness, such rage, all indicate to me a very serious disease of the personality.

I certainly think that you ought to protect your children. I don't think you ought to protect them by deception. I don't think deception is ever a good policy. I think what your daughter says about growing up wrong and learning to hate all men is exactly right.

If she likes to go to the movies and take part in school plays and so forth, it would seem to me very wise to permit her to do so. In fact I would encourage her to do so. If what you say is true, however, I imagine that her life is almost ruined now and I think it is highly important that you try to save the mental health of the younger children.

I never advise any woman to get a divorce. That is a matter for you to decide, with the aid of your lawyer. All I can tell you is that it sounds to me very unhealthy mentally for you to put up with such abuse and very bad for the children's mental health to permit them to be subjected to it.

Sincerely yours,

Danbury, Conn.
Dec. 14, 1930

Dear Doctor Menninger,

I will try to state my problem as simply and shortly as possible, but to me it is complicated and long, for it goes back so many years.

It's about my mother. (I hope you won't publish this for she might recognize herself tho' I doubt it, and that would be terrible.)

Mother is very gay, charming and attractive. She was always so marvelous to me that tho' she demanded me at times when I longed to be with young friends I gave it to her willingly. She always bragged to people what pals we were and how much we meant to each other. However, when she was crossed she had what I used to term spells and would scold and talk on and on terrible until I'd give in and cry and beg forgiveness. Another item—she always complained of not feeling real well, a pain here was surely cancer etc. She has had a great deal of illness, operations etc., and my father always made a great fuss over her at the least little thing. Also she really is very nervous and excitable.

Well, The Man came along and I married him and moved away. Mother came to visit and all was not well. Nothing serious, but a tension was there. The next visit she stayed three months. We are only a normal, average young couple trying to get a home started and a bit ahead. That visit ended in a terrible "rumpus." When I visit at home everything is lovely. Well, she came this year with dad and they stayed two months. There is a baby now. Work was hard for me cooking and cleaning for so many, expenses were heavy. Mother would work herself sick making clothes for me, anything to make me lovely, but not with the house work. Said she wasn't able. We didn't dare disagree with her about anything or she'd make a terrible fuss. She criticized everything my husband did, the way we raised our child. If we mentioned finances in front of her she begrudged what we spent for their food. All my friends were criticized, if we went anyplace we did "nothing but gad," if we stayed home we weren't performing our social obligations. If my husband bought even a pair of sox for himself "he got what he wanted for himself but didn't want me to have anything," etc. ad infinitum. We were so selfish etc., until I thought I couldn't stand another day. My husband only stood it because of me. Then she said we didn't want them for Christmas and went into a tantrum that lasted three days. And for the first time in my life I told her the truth. She threatened suicide and ended by having a "stroke" tho' I honestly didn't think she was sick at all.

Since she left she has written me letters that have kept me upset all the time. Such as "not to send her Xmas presents as she wouldn't open them, it would hurt her too much from a daughter who didn't want her for Xmas." And "Xmas had always meant so much to her but would ever after be a sad memory." These letters have upset me so that I have actually been physically ill. I've tried to reason it out and get over it, but I can't seem to. For I love her, I've written how sorry I am and won't she forgive me and the answer was "I hope some day you feel you have done right but why didn't you do this, that and the other thing."

So, Doctor Menninger, can you help me out. I don't doubt that we didn't do everything just right, but we tried and it didn't do any good. What is the matter with my mother, or do you think it is I? I'm sorry I said anything in answer to her accusations for the only result was that she feels she failed in her raising of me. I used to be sweet and lovely but I've changed so since marriage, she says.

My husband and I live in peace and harmony and adore each other. We hadn't asked them for Xmas because we had no idea they would stay so long and we just could not afford it. What shall I do? I can't bear to have her go on thinking such terrible things about us. Am I the problem or is she or are we both?

Thank you so very much.

Sincerely,

Jan. 12, 1931

My dear Mrs.:

I have just read with amazement your letter of December 14 addressed to me in care of the *Ladies' Home Journal*. I say amazement because you describe so vividly a situation which I think should be dealt with very positively and very immediately if a serious disaster is to be prevented.

I am quite certain that your mother will do everything possible to ruin your happiness and your home. She does not realize that she is doing it nor why. Nor on the other hand would she care. Your mother is quite obviously one of those women whose charm and attractiveness has led to them being hopelessly spoiled, who has, in short, never outgrown her infancy. Having temper tantrums and writing such ridiculous, childish letters to you in an effort to make you feel bad for having done what you most certainly should have done are quite typical. I think it is highly important that you protect the happy home that you and your husband have started by keeping your mother out of it. The fact that you have a remarkable husband and the fact that you yourself are tolerant and patient is no reason why you should be foolish or blind to the fact that your mother is so selfish that she will ruin it if you let her continue. Don't be angry with her, don't be combative, don't be unkind. Just say this is my home and things are thus and so and I must do thus, and so forth and don't be swayed by her infantalisms, tantrums, and so forth.

You will find this phenomenon discussed at length in my book, *The Human Mind*, pages 307 and 312.

Sincerely yours,

New York, N.Y.
Jan. 29, 1931

Dear Dr. Menninger:

Some time ago I noticed your article in the magazine and was truly interested in it because I realized that soon I was going to have a vitally serious problem to discuss with you—serious to my family.

To begin with, I shall tell you my age, although this story does not concern myself—merely to show you the attitude and point of view is from a youngster and not an older person. I am twenty years old and have graduated high school four years ago—and worked ever since.

There are three other girls in the family—22 years being the oldest, me next, then S., 18, and E. 15. B., the baby, is nine.

Here's the story. For the past six years Mother has acquired a mania for playing cards—poker. In that time she's lost more money than Dad could make—and has lost something far more dear than all the money in the world—the respect of her children for her. She is out every weekday playing, gets home at 6:30 just in time to grab on an old house apron to pretend she wasn't out when Dad gets in. She heats up the food she's prepared in the morning, or starts making some make-shift supper for us. Two girls are working and the others stay home. On Saturdays she goes out at one P.M. and doesn't come home all day, sometimes not til 3 or 4 A.M. Sunday morning.

It has happened more than once that Dad gave her a large sum of money—perhaps for the rent—or some large item—and she's squandered it away. In the mornings, she cries for money, stating that she can't run a house without a cent but Dad doesn't want to give her good, hard-earned money when he knows what will be done with it. We used to give her our money on pay day, but soon lost the habit as we got disgusted when we saw what she did with it.

Her "friends" are cheap and common. They would cut each other's throats for their dimes and quarters—calling each other foul names.

Here is the worst part of it. She got accustomed to borrowing to pay back her debts—borrowing from one to pay back another—sometimes I don't think she ever pays them back. She's asked one of my admirers for fifty dollars when he proposed to me thinking, I suppose, that if I accepted she wouldn't have to pay him back. I never knew this until three months after I refused him. His sister called up to ask for the money, and inadvertently blurted out the fact to me. I arranged to meet her that week and paid back half the money. I never heard from her or him again so I don't know if mother paid him back the rest.

Then I was engaged to another very nice chap, but later broke off because I realized he was too old for me (32). I have every reason to believe she's borrowed money from him due to a telephone call I intercepted from him to my mother last week. Since it has been eight months since we parted there was no reason for his call unless it was to ask for his money back since he knew I would not consider him. Then—and this is the final blow—I was sick for a short time. My employer called up to find out how I was, and spoke to my mother. She came into my room, and gushed all over saying how lovely he was. I should have suspected something but didn't until he told me she had asked him for a loan of $50 that evening and said she didn't want us to know about it. He told me anyway, to sort of apologize for not being in a position to do so (I thanked God for that!). She denied asking him in a hesitant manner. I know she's lying. How am I supposed to know I am not entertaining some of my intimate friends to whom she owes money?

There are fierce arguments in the house very frequently. We seldom eat supper together because a peaceful meal is an unknown quantity to us. There is hell to pay almost four times every week. We've threatened to leave her many times because she's always said she'd never leave the house for fear she'd be divorced for desertion. Dad has pleaded with her over and over again, granting her anything if she will stop. She agrees in the evening and in the afternoon of the next day she is out again. Dad has offered to pay back all her debts—no questions asked—if she stops. But she denies owing money—yet every month or so, Dad gets a call from one of *his* friends requesting the money she's borrowed from them. She's cost us countless hundreds of dollars—and countless sleepless nights.

Isn't it outrageous that children should have no respect—only pity for their mother? She neglects the home and the children—one of whom is so anemic and frequently must stay home from school. Dad's teeth bother him and he requests her to make him certain foods—but she makes what is easiest to make in the morning so it can be heated in the evening.

She's the first to "throw the stone" at others, but oh! let someone say something about her and she's wild. We've tried everything we know. Dad would give her money, at her request that if she had money in the house she wouldn't have to go out and gamble for it. But he pays all the bills except the ice-bill. Even the laundryman calls at night to be paid.

He's left the house vowing never to come back—but always does. He started separation proceedings but at her earnest cries, he stopped. He's tried not giving her a cent, but she borrows it. We've even thought of having those games raided.

There have been more times than one that I've gone to my girl friend's home to sleep because I got disgusted with the eternal squabble. We all make wonderful salaries, but never have a cent because there are always bills that must be paid twice because of her selfishness. Dad has even tried taking her to those games twice a week in the evenings if she wouldn't go in the daytime—but it always winds up the same way.

Tell me, are we wrong perhaps? Is there something we should do, or should have done that we don't know about? Is there a remedy for it. Please help us—and we will be your eternal debtors.

Sincerely,

Feb. 24, 1931

My dear Miss:

I have read with interest your letter of January 29th addressed to me in care of the *Ladies' Home Journal*.

Your problem is rather an unusual one but there is no doubt at all in my mind what you ought to do. First of all you ought to straighten out your own attitude. Your letter is so sensible and your general sense of things is so commendable that you must get a few other things straight before you know just how you are to handle this matter.

Aggravating and exasperating as it is, you must understand that your mother's behavior is just as much a disease as if she had cancer or delirium tremens. In fact she can't help doing what she is doing as much as you can help it. She is like a person who is addicted to morphine or alcohol. Sometimes we get very angry at them and think they ought to be able to stop but they can't. They will go to any length to keep it up. I wonder if you have never read a story by Charles Dickens called *The Old Curiosity Shop* in which the daughter discovers her own grandfather to be an inveterate gambler. If you haven't read it you certainly should.

To get back to the point however, until you recognize that your mother is sick and needs that kind of understanding instead of scoldings and blame and hostility and loss of respect and all the other things which you describe you are not going to know what to do. But if you realize that she is sick then you will treat her like any other sick person, you will try to get her treated for that sickness and that will require a great deal more skill than you folks in the home are likely to be able to manage. You see you have all played into her hands. You have given her money, you have permitted her time after time to repeat the same performance, you have scolded her and abused her which relieves your mind and hers too for a while but didn't prevent her from going into the same thing again.

It is very probable that you will have to put your mother in a private sanitarium or in a State Hospital for a period of six months or longer. This may not be necessary but I think it probably will. If she wanted to get well very badly you might be able to get her treated outside of an institution but I think she will just sneak off from the treatment and go back to her gambling. She will find it irresistible. So I think you had better make arrangements to put her in a sanitarium somewhere. I am not sure it would not be a good thing to get her a long ways off from New York where there would be no chance of her getting in touch with her old cronies. This is the first step in breaking this habit. The second step is for the doctors in the institution to try to help her understand the nature of her own affliction and the reason for it. If they are not successful in accomplishing this she will go back to it when she gets home.

So there are two things to be done. Now you know how to attack your problem. Just how you will manage to do it will depend upon many circumstances. The first thing for you to do is to see the necessity of doing something of this sort.

Sincerely yours,

San Francisco, Calif.
Feb. 5, 1931

Mr. dear Dr. Menninger,

I need your aid so badly. If I can conquer these mental abnormalities that a terrible childhood environment planted, I believe I shall lead a particularly useful life—for I'll strive in every way to bring about correct childhood influences for others. If I don't get help—

Mother wasn't a mother to any of us. We all suffered, each in different ways. My eldest sister—she, Mother called her "Comforter"—and leaned on her like a ton of bricks—was so used to toil and brain-killing fatigue that she married a man who used her as a farm animal.

My brother is just a tramp, and a slave to drink.

My next sister is all right in mental outlook, but she has Mother's nagging, argumentative, forever aggressive, outlook.

I reasoned these things out at an early age, and swore I'd escape. Because I was the youngest—and an illicit child as well—I somehow had an arrogance.

But I was touched, too, by the same curse of a mother who should have stayed single and led a strongly individualistic career.

Because mother had sinned, and had me, the child of a physician once well-known in Texas—her sin preyed upon her. She got mixed up with the fanatical Free-Methodists—and, when I was 3, told "Dad" W., her husband. That was the last straw, he left home.

Then I became "Ishmael" and I remember being told, at about 4 years, by Mother that she wished to die, and she'd pray I'd die, too, and wouldn't I want to die with her? She did not want to leave me behind in the cruel world.

Religion took stronger and stronger hold, but it didn't remedy her "health," her nagging, her moroseness. Life was just meant to get ready for Heaven and to avoid Hell.

During High School, I did my homework evenings to quarreling between mother and sister H. If I asked for a little quiet—both jumped on me. And I loved school. I wanted to be Something. I always believed I could write and be—well, famous. I still do.

I built a world of dreams for the Future to counteract the terrible present. I planned—since I'm being patient now, I'll get my happiness later. I'll be really and truly *loved,* and I'll be famous—because I deserve it, by what I'm putting up with now. So, sometimes, I was gloriously happy—with my feet enmeshed with family friction, I didn't even feel. That's how I thought I'd escape.

I graduated at 16. From then until I was 19, Mother was insane at times. Doctor Menninger, I've seen her quarrel at one of us all evening til we lost patience and made a good reply—then clutch her heart, perform a brilliant—but broken by a chair, or a hand on the wall—fall to the floor—and there she'd lie—calling on God in a voice terrible to hear—all because I said, perhaps, "Oh *Hell!*" after hours of provocation.

Her spells of gloom would last for weeks. We'd work to support her—and have that waiting for us at night. Yet—with her graying hair, her white, wrinkled skin—she looks the *real mother.*

I wasn't allowed shows, operas, or musicals. I longed for them—I wanted culture. Wanted to rise above my family group. First I wanted to attain the prestige my real father's children enjoyed. As adolescence passed, I set up higher standards still—and I've kept them.

My one pleasure she allowed was car-rides with the boys who had autos. Whatever course of queer logic was that, Doctor? No dances—no shows—but *car-rides* on moonlight nights—to secluded spots! Often such excursions would cap a day when I was nearly frantic with the depths of tragedy to which she insisted we were all plunged. I would do almost anything to escape. Almost—but not quite. I was still determined to be worthy of the real love that would come.

I worked 3 years to go to college and was no nearer than before. Off and on during the time I lived away from home, and in those periods expanded in will-power and my own personality.

At 20 I ran away. Merely across town to the University Campus, where I took a room in the girl's dorm. I'd gotten 1 year of school but I worked 8 hours a day while doing it, and when I studied on Sunday, mother fasted on Monday. (Afterward, I found out she ate a heavy breakfast before beginning her heart-rending fast!) All was for sympathy.

The 3 years on the Campus were wonderful. I was awarded a scholarship of $100.00 for promise, grades, and because I was the only entirely self-supporting girl. During that horrible first year before I ran away, while I was working 42 hours a week, carrying a 2/3 full study schedule, and bucking a "backslidden, nervously broke down" parent, I had placed, in grades, 5th highest of the Fresh Class of 2,000.

The Dean of Women knew my troubles. She had advised me to run away long before I did.

Then I made my blunder. Instead of plunging right on I fell in love. A boy I'd already gone with intermittently, since I was 15. The blunder came one Xmas. I had no home to spend Xmas in. The Dorm was deserted. Only one or 2 girls out of that jolly sixty remained. I tasted wine, that Xmas eve night, for the first time. And then—I didn't want to go straight home to that lonely, empty Hall, and my queer little basement room. I wanted to drive around a little.

We were gloriously in love and gloriously reckless and I regret none of it.

But V. had enough sense to want to wait until we had something to marry. And he had a jealous, ill, demanding society-type mother. He had Family, and Money—all begging him not to marry me.

After three years I began to doubt. I shouldn't of. I knew my V. But I did. And when a friend threw a nice, ordinary, young man across my path, who fell in love and rushed me—I allowed myself to be corralled into marriage with him.

Now—we pay the piper.

In my regret and unhappiness all the submerged childhood limitations are coming up.

Melancholy. Fear. Oh—the fear of death, rides me continually. Not fear, exactly—but *hatred* of it.

That is my problem. Unquestionably, my husband and I must part. I needn't ask much advice on that. We don't quarrel but we don't hitch. V. understood—H. merely sympathizes. V. and I wanted fame. H. wants a good job.

V., of course, is lost—but I love him, and I can't be wife to another. And I've got to write. I'll go crazy if I don't. And married to H.—I don't.

But this fear of death, surely, you can help me with.

It came this way. I was taught, "The world will end before you die," and I grew up thinking I'd never die. Science in college was too much for the notion to last, and with a shock I realized there was no God, no eternity, no immortality—nothing but oblivion.

And I want to *live*. To make up for those horrible 20 years in happiness, *now* and *forever*. I don't want to die. I want to be young and vibrant and hopeful and to love the man I love forever. That's the logical thing.

Mother wanted me to attend funerals when I was adolescent. That horror lingers. And the memory of a dying chum mother insisted I see—oh! All around me she brought the fact of death. Now, at night, all such fears come and laugh at me—laugh at the determination for success and true love that carried me thru adolescence, and still carries me on.

And how, doctor, to forget this horrible past? How to wipe out the blunder of marrying the wrong man? My husband agrees now it was all wrong, and he'll cooperate. But what folks will say! And what of my little baby boy—and anyway, a divorce won't bring back the man I should have married.

I'm so afraid you'll say, "You can be happy in this marriage," but that is not it. There's an unfastidious mess about not loving your own husband.

So it's the hatred of death, I want help on. And how to be brave and have courage to make the decisions mother wouldn't ever let me make. How to straighten out the life my mother tried to tangle hopelessly.

The dean of the college of Journalism at Washington says I have very great chances for success as a writer. And that is my burning desire above all else, since I've lost V. Because the Dean does feel I can be successful, I thought perhaps you'd think me worth helping.

Gratefully,

P.S. I'm quite willing to answer all questions—or to be a case-study for a psychiatrist's note-book. Anything to help myself—or others. I took much sociology in college, and my professors were charmed with my papers on "Influence of parental friction on the adolescent child"—so I'm prepared to cooperate with you or any other who might be interested.

Anything for a little relief, for the chance of living a normal life at last.

Feb. 20, 1931

Dear Mrs.:

I have read carefully your letter of the 5th addressed to me in care of the *Ladies' Home Journal.*

Your letter is very interesting because your life has been very interesting. Tragic as it has been it interests you a great deal too. I wonder if you realize that. I wonder if you realize that you are imitating your mother in one respect. I refer to the matter of dramatizing your life and the things about you. Your mother's dramatization was somewhat more crude than yours but the style of your letter, the melodramatic appeal of your questions and your descriptions all indicate that whether you realize it or not, you are thinking of yourself as the heroine of the tragedy. There is no harm in doing that if it does not let the emotions which the play stimulates carry one beyond the facts of reality. I think this is what you are doing. I think you are an emotional girl, whose early life was certainly very much shocked by very terrible experiences, who cut off her own nose to spite her face and who is now making a very dramatic thing of it. You certainly made a great mistake in deserting the man you loved to marry a man that you thought was more available.

Having done so, however, should afford you some material for studying yourself. Why did you do it? What are your seriously dangerous propensities? I do not think that the fear of death is a very serious one. I think that is a childish fear which is likely to pass off very soon and is of no great consequence anyway. I think it is much more important to see why it is that you cut off your nose to spite your face, that you do foolish things which cause you so much trouble. If you could discover this, if you could get a little better balanced, if you could see yourself in a little perspective and not so dramatized I think it would help you.

If I did not think you had the intelligence to apply this information I would not give it to you. I am very much impressed by the good grades that you made at the university and by the ambition that you had to get an education and get ahead. I think it is very desirable that you do some writing. Whether or not you leave your husband is something I can scarcely advise you about. If you are very unhappy and don't want to live together I should think it would be simpler to separate than to try to go on doing something which distresses both of you. But whether you live with him or don't live with him, the important thing is that you express yourself in writing. Someone said it was a good thing for a person who wants to write short stories to write two or three hundred and throw them away and after that they will be all right. That is merely a way of saying that the first stories you write will not be so good as they should be but if you keep on trying and trying and write a great many you will find it a great help for the emotional pressure which you feel and it may be a source of income and a source of achievement and fame such as you so much desire. I might point out in closing, however, that happiness does not necessarily go hand in hand with fame. It might be a great deal better to do a little writing that gave you pleasure than to do a great deal in an effort to achieve fame.

Sincerely yours,

Orange City, Iowa
Feb. 9, 1931

My Dear Dr. Menninger:

After reading your page on Mental Hygiene in the Home, I decided to write you in the hope that you can help me with my problem of unhappiness.

I am a girl twenty-four years old. Since my mother's death four years ago, I have been responsible here at home. Our family consists of my father, a brother just of age, a sister in High School, and an old, but very active and helpful grandmother.

In these years, my father has lost his grip on life. He is subject to moods of melancholy and discouragement, and magnifies little trifles into calamities. Because of this he had to give up a good position and take one as an inferior clerk. This was a tremendous blow to his pride and made his condition worse.

After graduating from High School, I worked for two years and had just started my college course when I was called home. I have never given up the idea of continuing, and have tried to get a few hours of credit at various times. At present my activities are three-fold: housekeeping, eight hours of study at the Junior College here, and music. (I am giving a dozen lessons in piano every week and am church organist on Sundays, in order to be independent of my father as far as my personal expenses are concerned.) I will admit that this is a very full schedule. My friends continually warn me, for a similar period of activity two years ago caused an overactive thyroid condition which put me in bed for two months. I could do all this, though, if matters would always run smoothly. But they don't. Last year my sister gave me much uneasiness. Before I awoke to my responsibility, she had gone through three adolescent years practically undisciplined, and had developed an ungovernable temper and a sharp tongue. This often made her very unhappy in her school associations. This condition has improved somewhat this year, but her independent spirit is still often hard to cope with.

But now I've had to add arbitration to my list of duties. My brother is young, fun-loving, careless, and thoughtless, and there is a wide breach in sympathy between him and father. Now when he is gone often and late and spends money recklessly, father magnifies these matters and sees sure destruction of character and the like, and lies awake at nights, brooding over the matter. But, instead of speaking to the boy, father pours it all out on me and I have to smooth things out. I can sympathize with the attitudes of both, but a scene with either taxes me to the limit. And how I hate these strained silences!

And I hate to think of what it is doing to me. Dr. Menninger, I never have "dates." Oh, I'm not socially ostracized. There are frequent feminine bridge parties and a very occasional party of unmarried people of both sexes. But I think I may admit that they do not satisfy me any more than they would satisfy any girl. And, really, how ironical. I am learning all the ins and outs of housekeeping when I'll likely never have a home of my own in which to use this knowledge.

And how I envy other girls' gaiety. How I wish I could be gay, frivolous, carefree, and without a single worry except what color my new party frock should be.

Dr. Menninger, I never could *talk* to any one this way. But writing to some one I don't know has not seemed hard. Please criticize and advise me frankly, even if it may hurt my feelings. I'm tired of commendation.

Thanking you for your time, I am
Sincerely yours,

Feb. 24, 1931

My dear Miss:

I have read with an unusual degree of interest your letter of February 9th addressed to me in care of the *Ladies' Home Journal.*

As I read your letter I wonder if you haven't undertaken some responsibility which you have carried about as far as you can logically be expected to carry it. After all you are not the mother of your brother and sister and you are not the wife of the man for whom you keep house. Don't you think you might be doing them all a kindness if you would cast an increasing amount of responsibility upon them and devote an increasing amount of energy to the satisfaction of your own life?

It seems to me that it would be mentally healthy for all of you if you would do this. For a certain length of time after your mother's death I am sure you did the only thing that could be done. The beauty and unselfishness and discretion of your life shows very clearly in your intelligent and coherent letter. I get the impression that you are still laboring under certain notions of duty and responsibility which I am not so certain exist. You have a certain responsibility to yourself for the development of your social and educational and business and artistic life which are really much more important than your responsibility to a family all grown and perfectly able to take care of itself such as you describe.

Sometimes we labor under very mistaken notions of duty and responsibility, and do others as well as ourselves a certain amount of harm. I think you are quite justified in envying and desiring the gaiety which other girls have and I think you ought to give yourself a little more opportunity for achievement. I think you ought to begin to live your life for its own sake rather than in the sense of a housekeeper and mother, as you have been doing.

In the May number of the *Ladies' Home Journal* I am going to cite a case of this general sort which may interest you but before then I hope that you will have begun to make some withdrawals from the present situation and be enabled to do more what you want to do. It does not need to be done immediately or suddenly but you should progressively work in that direction, and remember that sometimes the kindest thing you can do in regard to those who depend on you so much is to decline to continue to act as their mother when you are in reality their sister.

Sincerely yours,

Montana
Feb. 28, 1931

Dear Dr. Menninger:

There are two mental-hygiene problems in my family, which are a source of worry to the rest of us. In the *Ladies' Home Journal* I note your page, and hope you can help us.

The first is my youngest brother. I shall begin at the beginning. He was the youngest, and was, as long as he was at home, completely dominated by our mother. Our father was gentle, understanding, lovable and impractical. Mother dominated him too. She always settled family questions, made all the decisions. When my brother graduated from high school, he was sent to my mother's brother, a very wealthy man. He (my brother) had always made money, had "jobs" even as a little fellow, and my uncle promised to groom him for an executive position in one of his numerous enterprises.

My brother, let us call him J., was put to work in a factory, he was to learn the business from the ground up.

None of us know exactly what happened, but in the course of four or five years his letters became so incoherent that the family became alarmed. Mother went east and brot him home with her, somehow mentally affected, queer.

He had not been at all mechanically inclined, and, so my uncle said, did not do well in the factory. Instead of putting him at some clerical work he was kept for years in the shops, where he was utterly out of place. Another thing, which happened just before he graduated from high school, was the war. Mother talked him out of going. His pals went, and he didn't. He felt it very keenly.

Well, after he came home, he worked outdoors for a while, seemed to be better. Then someone suggested that he go to the University and get his degree, as the rest of us had done. He partly worked his way thru, made excellent grades, majored in *psychology*, was principally interested in *abnormal* psychology.

He has taught since graduation, for six years, I believe. *And only twice has he held his position thruout the complete term.* Usually he writes at Thanksgiving. "They have it in for me, are trying to oust me." Sometimes "they" refers to the superintendent, once it was the Masonic Lodge, again the Catholics! And he resigns at Xmas, by request. Frequently he falls in love with one of the teachers, writes long letters about marrying her, when he has perhaps taken her to church a couple of times and that's all.

The pitiful part is that he *tries* so hard to make good. At first I would write him out of the fullness of my own teaching experience, that making friends was as important as teaching, and from his letters I know he tried to socialize himself. But then I found out that mother and all the rest were writing him reams of advice, and he was conscientiously obeying it all to the letter, ludicrously (when it happened to be a love affair), disastrously, as far as his teaching was concerned. So I stopped.

It seems that he just can't co-operate with fellow teachers. And he's always falling in love. Now that's dementia praecox, isn't it? One doctor said, "He'll outgrow it," but he's past 30 years old and not a great deal better. I have studiously refrained from giving him any advice or suggestions. But I wish I had some intelligent and expert information concerning such cases. Would he do better at some clerical work? What can the family do to *help* him find himself? Or should we leave him alone?

And the second case is my mother.

I have already described her to a certain extent. Now there's this additional information, she was very ill last summer and as a result her vision is terribly distorted and she is unable to see well enough to do anything, but wipe dishes. She has always been *very* active and you can imagine what this means to her.

At present she is spending the winter with my sister in the South. But she is homesick for the ranch and has written that she wants to come back this summer, and end her days with me and my family.

Now, please don't misunderstand me for an instant. I love my mother, I think the world and all of her. She has lived with us since my father's passing, until I took her east last fall, where she could have more and constant expert medical attention than it was possible to have here, we are 125 miles from the nearest doctor.

But life *is* a problem when she is here. She bosses me, she always has. I know it, and accept the fact. It pleases her and doesn't hurt me, and I love her and won't hurt her. *But*, I have a husband who *won't* be bossed, by *anyone*! And three children for whom her bossing is *not* the thing.

They are far from perfect. They are well, industrious, imaginative and noisy. But oh dear me, noise and dirt and imperfect table manners and grandmother just don't agree.

Husband is out of the house almost all day, so he gets along with grandmother fairly well. She *knows* he *isn't* the kind that can be "bossed." But what about the children, and principally, what about grandmother?

I can rely upon the children to do their best. They, too, love her. But in spite of that, I'm afraid she will criticize and correct everything they do. I'm afraid, at her age, it's too late to change. But there's this about it, I don't believe she *realizes* the *effect* on the *children*. How can I, without wounding her grievously, let her know that *I* am the one to correct the children? And if so, how can I do it, so it will achieve permanent results?

There you are. And if you can help me see any way out, over, or around, you may save *my* reason. I haven't slept decently for weeks.

Very truly yours,

Mar. 31, 1931

My dear Mrs.:

I have read very carefully your letter of March 5 [*sic*] addressed to me in care of the *Ladies' Home Journal*.

I think the diagnosis you have made of your brother's case is probably correct. At any rate the symptoms are very characteristic. You probably felt confirmed in this opinion after you read the April number of the *Ladies' Home Journal* in which I described a somewhat similar case. I think your family is to be congratulated that the boy has made as good an adjustment as he has, or perhaps I should say that he has been able to avoid a complete collapse and retreat from reality. The main thing in these cases is to encourage as much self-expression as possible. No one knows exactly how to treat them, or at least we know very few general principles about their treatment. If they become severe, so as to become completely maladjusted, they are better off in an institution. If they can possibly be kept outside in any useful capacity whatsoever, they are much better off.

In regard to your mother, I think it is exceedingly unfortunate from the standpoint of your family's happiness and your children that she is coming to stay with you. I think the grandmother problem is always a troublesome one. Your mother writes you that she is coming to end her days with you, thereby gains your big-hearted sympathy and compassion. So far as I can understand, however, there is no reason to believe that her days are likely to come to an end in the near future and she may live twenty years. I think you are quite right that the effect of grandmothers upon children is apt to be a bad one, whether they are bossy like yours is or whether they bestow too much affection as others do, or whether they interfere with the mother's relationship with the children, or whether they antagonize the son-in-law or whatever they do. They generally do do something. If you can possibly stall this off I believe I would. If you can't and she is going to come, I would certainly take steps to make my own position in the family definite. I do not think you should permit her to boss you, no matter how much she wants to or how willing you are or how little it disturbs you. I do not think your children should be given to understand that she is managing you. You should be their mother and the manager of the home. Just how to manage this is going to require a great deal of skill and something of a change of attitude on your part because it is quite apparent from your letter that you are a little inclined to knuckle under to your mother's opinion and wishes and your mother is probably the kind of woman who will get her way if she can possibly manage it, by direct means or indirect. You can do this I believe and I have less fears in your case than in some, however, because your letter shows so much evidence of intelligent understanding of psychological principles.

Sincerely yours,

Illinois
Mar. 19, 1931

Dear Dr. Menninger:

For years I have longed for someone to whom I could reveal my family history and background so that I might be helped to see myself in the proper relationship to that background as neither too high nor too low, too good nor too bad. I cannot meet people well because I feel inferior, not mentally, because I believe I am at least average, but socially.

My husband is the only one to whom I have confided the facts about my family. I could not have married him without doing so for fear of eventually wrecking our happiness.

Here are the facts:

My earliest memory of my father before he left my mother with four children to support when I was five years old was that of a drunkard, brutal and uneducated. Our life was a hand-to-mouth affair from then on. My recollection is that my brothers were in and out of reform school for petty thievery and pranks while I was in and out of orphans' homes.

The task of rearing us was obviously too much for my mother. She struggled for a time to support us honestly and finally sank as low women may sink and accepted money in return. The police matron finally took my youngest brother into custody and placed him in a private home in a distant city. I have not seen him since.

My oldest brother could not endure the home atmosphere and ran away. We had only a letter every year or so. He was interested in music and in some miraculous manner found means of supporting himself and studying wind instruments at the same time, until today he is regarded as one of the best musicians in the country and plays in the leading bands. He has married a lovely girl.

I admire him immensely and yearn to keep in touch with him. But the trouble seems to be that he has not confided in his wife as I have in my husband, and fears that should we associate together she might learn facts concerning which he is so sensitive [of] and lose confidence in him.

My third brother seems never to have had the desire to rise above his environment. In all of my mother's wrong-doing he was her confidante. Today, he follows in my father's steps. He would spend every cent I advanced him for drink.

My mother died when I was sixteen. My grandmother took me in. By this time I had finished the eighth grade of school and had been working at various jobs for two years. Then I became restless and took a business course which helped me to a better position. At eighteen a Y.W.C.A. secretary induced me to use my small savings toward a high school education at a nearby self-help college. In five years I have finished high school and two years of college through the aid of several scholarships and summer earnings. Then by borrowing money to continue my school work, I received my B.A. degree three years later at the University of Illinois.

I married a most lovable and understanding husband the following fall, though I continued to work for a while to repay my college debt.

Today we have a precious boy almost two years old. My husband also has a university degree and was born for success.

I hope I have not been too lengthy. My trouble is this: I cannot move easily among the people whom I most admire and respect because I feel I have no right to be among them. If they were to learn of my background I feel I should die of shame. While others converse easily of their mothers, fathers, sisters, and brothers I sit in embarrassed silence because I have nothing that I can proudly tell. Imagine associating for years with people to whom you *cannot* mention your family. What must they think of me? But what can I do? My story might bring sympathy one moment and furnish exciting bridge table conversation the next.

This problem tortures me at times. My hope is that there is some way that I can attain mental peace. That is why I appeal to you, Dr. Menninger. If anyone can help me, you can, I am sure. I shall be very eager to hear from you.

Trusting that I have given salient enough facts for a reply, I am

Very sincerely yours,

Apr. 10, 1931

My dear Mrs.:

I have read with a great deal of interest your letter of March 19. In fact I think it is one of the most remarkable letters out of the many hundreds that I have received recently in my capacity as counselor to the readers of the *Ladies' Home Journal.*

First let us give credit where credit is due. I think you deserve a great deal of credit for having told your husband the facts about the case. I think that was exactly the right thing to do. Furthermore, I think you are a most fortunate woman in having so intelligent, so understanding, and so sensible a husband. I am sure he will make a success of whatever he does.

Then I think both you and your brothers, particularly the musician, deserve a great deal of credit for taking advantage of the opportunities that presented themselves and working your way up. In fact I think I must point out to you that your mother and father cannot possibly have been so bad as they seem to you if they could have brought forth such children. You may give them very little credit for what you are but you must not forget that after all you are the child of your parents and while environment is responsible for most of what you have done, your heredity is probably not so bad as you think it is. Alcohol addiction and prostitution should be, I think, regarded as the unfortunate and deplorable reactions of certain types of individuals to unbearable circumstances. Anyone might become a drunkard or a prostitute if the pressure of circumstances about them was sufficiently great. I think if possible you should remove from your own mind the stigma of disgrace and dishonor which the ignorant public erroneously associate with these two afflictions. They really are afflictions and not sins. If you could see it that way, I think your first difficulty in social adjustment will be removed.

I think someone needs to point out to you that it is not necessary to drag one's parents into discussions even if one is not ashamed of them. I do not think you should be ashamed of your parents but on the other hand, I think you should not have the feeling when other people talk about their parents that you should bring up yours. That is simply a kind of bragging which we must permit some people to do, often knowing full well that they are lying or covering up things. You have the advantage of an enormously greater understanding of life and it ought to be a comfort to you to have no feeling of necessity that you must discuss your past history and your family history with strangers. It is certainly none of their business. What they think of it has nothing to do with the problem. It is a question of what you think of it. If you think of it in the right way, you will not feel inferior about it. On the other hand, you will feel rather superior. You will realize that very few people with your start could have achieved the healthy-mindedness that you seem to have in most respects. Very few of them could have won the love of as fine a husband as you seem to have. Feel proud and confidant of yourself and feel sympathetic and tender, not bitter and ashamed of your parents. With this attitude toward things I think everything will look different. It is surely a very much healthier-minded way to do.

I should appreciate it very much if you would think this over a little bit and then write me how well you have been able to apply these suggestions.

Sincerely yours,

Albany, N.Y.
Aug. 20, 1931

My dear Dr. Menninger

I am in great perplexity and am sure you can help me if you will be so good. I will try to be concise.

My parents have never been truly congenial, and after the three children grew up and left home, cohabitation became a great burden to them both. They did not separate, but my mother found a home and work in which she was happy, and my father, a naval officer, went to sea for several years. I am the eldest child and only daughter, and my father is deeply devoted to me. I admire him very much and we are very companionable, but I have, strangely, never had a strong affection for him. Of course I have always done my best to conceal this, and have tried to be a satisfactory daughter. At the age of nineteen I became a nurse, and want to continue in the work, which I enjoy tremendously.

After my father's return from sea there seemed nothing for me to do but to give up my work and live with him. This I have done for six years. At first I was very unhappy and rebelled against the inactive and monotonous life of housekeeper and companion of an elderly man. I have not so far wished to marry, and as I am now thirty-three I do not find close friends among married women with children, nor among unmarried ones who are usually so much younger than myself. However, during the last year I have become more contented. We have a nice home and garden and I have found more to interest and occupy me here than for some time. I had about decided to give up hope of ever getting back to work, and was trying to become perfectly contented.

A few weeks ago my father asked permission to tell me something which he feared would upset me. He seemed much agitated and not like himself at all. I listened with as much equanimity as possible, though I confess I was dismayed. He said that all his life he had had what he considered unnatural, effeminate likes and dislikes, particularly the love of attractive feminine clothing. Some years ago he bought some women's silk underwear just to look at and feel. After a while he began to wear it, and his love for it increased until he began to buy dresses, shoes, hose, jewelry and even corsets (which he doesn't need being thin) and to wear them in the privacy of his room and around the house at times when I was out or away. Several times he has gone out at night. He bought and wore a wig and shaved off his mustache. He told me that his passion for this masquerade had become so great that he could no longer conceal it, but wanted my consent to wearing it around the house. I was terribly distressed and frightened, but tried to be broad-minded enough to regard it as a mere eccentricity, of which we all have plenty. When he came home at noon I was prepared for the worst, but when he appeared before me in the wig and cosmetics and complete outfit my nerve deserted me and I screamed and ran from the house. For several hours I tried to make a decision, and at last felt sure I would have to go away from home and insist on my mother returning to take my place. But when I came back he was so contrite, promising never to do it again that I gave up my plan and tried to forget the episode. For several days I brooded over it, and could see that he did so too. Then I went away for a week hoping we might both recover. Last night when I returned he told me at once that he had used the things during my absence and wanted to keep on with it. I consented and promised to be more sensible. Today he has done it, and though I have been quite calm I feel as if my life had toppled in ruins. It seems horrible, unspeakable and monstrous. I can't bear to be near him or even go into his room where I know the things are hidden. My own clothes seem almost loathsome to me. My home and all the little duties connected with it seem strange and repugnant and I cannot see how it can go on this way.

Now what I want is your advice as to the seriousness of my father's trouble. He is 60 years old, has a splendid mind, masculine interests and tastes, and is physically very well. He is rather asocial and has not many friends here, his work is not demanding at present, but he has a keen delight in making furniture and spends most of his time in his workshop. He is ambitious to become an expert and perhaps practice after his retirement. But with all his virtues I can see that this strange passion will eventually overcome him. He has been in the garden in the daytime, which shows that he is becoming indifferent to public opinion. Please tell me Doctor, what is the cause of it and what will the outcome be? Should I try not to mind and let him indulge it as much as he wishes? Am I justified in being repelled by it? Indeed he seems no longer my father but a mental patient whom I am obliged to care for. Will I become used to it and not mind, or will I feel worse as time goes on? If I ask him not to do it in my presence he won't, but he will be miserable and repressed, and of course at his age it cannot be overcome, unless the cause is removed. He says he has been denied a satisfactory married life, and has never had extra-marital relationships except of the most harmless kind. My mother is a fine and charming woman and not averse to living with her husband, but he seems to dread having her here even for a visit. Do you think I should put my foot down and go back to work, thereby forcing him to take back his wife? I think he would prefer to live alone. In that case he would be lonely and bitter and resentful because the one person he really cares for had left him. Do you think there is any chance that he and my mother would be able to live in peace and contentment for the short time left to them? She professes to love him, and would really do so I think if he could lose his antagonism to her. In any case I would like to be free myself, to live as I please, for I don't feel the least bit free or natural living with a man who wants to be a woman. He is a fine looking man and dresses well. Why can't he be satisfied with that?

Please, I beg of you, not to publish any part of my letter in the *Ladies' Home Journal*, for he might see it and would surely recognize it. He does not consider himself unbalanced and would be deeply hurt if he knew I did so.

I will be so very grateful if you can help me.

Very truly yours,

Nov. 19, 1931

My dear Miss:

I am very sorry to have delayed so long in answering your letter in view of the fact that at the time you wrote me you felt the matter was something of an emergency. I have been so crowded that I have only just gotten to your letter. I found it interesting and I think I can make some valuable suggestions to you.

In the first place it seems to me you are faced with three problems: the problem of your father, the problem of your own life and the problem of your mother. Let us take yours first. I think you must have noticed when you wrote your letter that when you came to explain how it was that you gave up the work you loved so much and went to live with your father you were somewhat at a loss to make it appear logical or to give any good reasons for it. You protest that at first you were very unhappy about it but came to enjoy it. I think a little introspection will show you that this act which you apparently regarded as being dictated by a sense of duty was really done out of certain personal motives. You had a career which you gave up; your father was perfectly capable of living alone and even if he wasn't he had a wife who was well and able to take care of him. If you are at all familiar with psychological literature in general or with the Electra complex in particular I think that you will be able to recognize the formula. You take your mother's place and live with your father.

In doing this you undoubtedly felt that you were doing your father a favor; but I think in reality it was not such a kindness either to him or to yourself. You had a career started which you interrupted. To continue as his housekeeper can mean for you only a few more years of mixed happiness and sorrow which you get out of this situation and then you will be out of a job as well as out of a career.

In the second place do you not think your mother and father should decide their own housekeeping problems? As you say, your mother is willing to come back and take her place with your father. If he is not willing to have her that is his business and not yours to decide.

And finally there is the matter of your father's peculiarity. As you will notice I have put it last in the letter; this is because I think it is the least important. It is as you say a psychological abnormality but one which is quite common and one which is rarely serious except insofar as it invites public ridicule.

You are quite justified in abhorring it because society does abhor perversions of instinct but you should abhor it just as a surgeon abhors a cancer. It is a disease and you are quite right in taking the attitude that he is to be treated as a patient.

I do not like to give advice beyond indicating some of the factors not always seen by my correspondents but I could go so far as to advise you to ask yourself why you don't develop your own life and let your father and mother develop theirs and if you conclude that this is the best thing to do why not put the matter up to them frankly, announce your own plans and help them if you like to form theirs but withdraw yourself from implication in them.

It is very rarely that I invite additional correspondence from the many people who write me in care of the *Ladies' Home Journal*, but I should like very much indeed to know what the outcome of your case is. Won't you write telling me what developments have occurred in your father since you wrote before and how you feel about the suggestions I have made in this letter?

Sincerely yours,

New York, N.Y.
Aug. 21, 1931

Dear Dr. Menninger:

Please advise me as to how I may overcome a growing antagonism toward my parents, particularly my father. This feeling distresses me as I realize all that my parents have done for me and how much I owe them for the advantages and care they have given me. I feel doubly obligated because they adopted me when I was a few months old and have brought me up as their own. They have no other children. I know nothing about my real parents but believe they are dead.

Most of my life, except for two years spent in residence at college and the past three years that I have been supporting myself, I spent at home with my parents. There have been periods of visiting, of course, when they would be away from me for some time and I would also visit friends so we are used to being separated. However they have always been a bit upset because I do not seem to get homesick. The years I commuted to college I lived at home, not from choice but because I had no way of supporting myself and father said mother needed me to help with the housework. As father was pastor of a suburban church there was always a lot of entertaining to be done and also church work. I did not enjoy the church work particularly but did it to please my parents who said I was a hindrance to their work if I did not show interest and take part in it.

Three years ago my father retired and moved to a small town in New England. He has found work to keep him busy and he and mother have a fine circle of friends and plenty of social life. However they are disappointed because I will not give up my position and come home to live with them. There is no work in the town for me and I would simply have to stay home and do housework and be dependent on my parents for everything. The thought of that is unbearable to me as I have a good position in New York and love my work. It gives me a real chance to use initiative and make decisions and it has been difficult at times; the kind of difficulty that one enjoys because it gives one a chance to use his brain to find a way out.

The thing which makes living at home very difficult for me is the constant supervision of my affairs. Mother tells me what clothes to wear and father directs my activities. If I say "I'm going for a walk in the woods this afternoon," my father will say "No. We have other plans. I want you to call on Mrs. S." Or Mother will ask "Would you like to do so-and-so" and before I can answer my father will say "Of course she does," and it is settled just like that. If I object there is a scene and they say I am being contrary and opposing their plans. Father will not allow me to do anything for myself and he objects to my swimming or walking in the woods "because you might get hurt." I sometimes feel I would respect him more if he weren't such an old woman. He has never been athletic himself and I am naturally athletic, though not masculine in my dress or apt to take foolish chances.

My parents want to direct my thoughts as well as my actions. They are fairly broad in their religious beliefs but are a bit rigid in their observance of Sunday. They act hurt if I confess to differing with them on points of conduct such as women smoking, petting, etc. It is like being dead to live at home because I feel I have no chance to develop my own powers or to be myself at all. I am expected to be an echo of their opinions and standards. I try to explain all this to them and they get angry or hurt and say I am losing my morals. They say I can do as I choose but I have found that if my choices do not coincide with theirs they make it very uncomfortable for me and see evil where there is none. I have always wanted to have a "sound mind in a sound body" but at home there is no chance of having either. They are nervous and irritable and I soon get the same way and I wish I were so far away I could not see them at all.

No doubt I am irritating to my parents. There are always two sides to every story.

The most irritating thing for me is the way my father constantly kisses and fusses over me. He tries to hold me on his lap as if I were a child and he never comes near me without kissing me. I did not mind it so much when I was a child but now it irritates me. I am naturally affectionate and respond to a lover's affection but I cannot be so affectionate with my father. It seems silly. Probably when my parents are dead I will miss this affection but I don't like it now.

Mother is not at all demonstrative. I used to wish she were more so when I was a child. She is more understanding about my desire for independence but she feels I am selfish. She feels that as she and father gave up things for me when I was small, I should give up my plans now that they are getting old. I know how it looks to them and to the neighbors and perhaps I am selfish. Mother is always worrying about what people will say or think and is disturbed because I don't care particularly what is said as long as I feel that what I do is harmless.

I used to spend my vacation traveling, on the sea if possible, and I usually go alone as it seems like more of an adventure and I love to meet new people. My parents do not approve of this and think I should spend my vacation at home. Lately I have divided my vacation and spent part time traveling and part at home, but I have found that at home I spend most of the time housecleaning and washing and doing odd jobs mother has saved up for me. I resent it and feel it is unfair and have offered to pay someone to come in and do that sort of work but my parents won't allow it.

All this makes me unwilling to marry. Mother urges me to marry and settle down so that when she dies I can make a home for my father. I have had several love affairs but cannot bring myself to marry. I feel that I do not want to be tied down by another family. Have had too much family already. Hate the idea of being dominated by another man as my father has ruled me and yet I would not want a man who was a door-mat. Sometimes I feel that if I could find a man who would be a real companion marriage might not be so awful. However the family do not approve of the men I pick out. The ones they like are too effeminate.

Did not intend to write such a long letter but there is nobody in whom I can confide. My father tells my affairs to anyone who will listen and then wonders why I do not confide in him.

How can I overcome my fear of marriage and this dislike of my parents? I do not miss them at all and really don't enjoy being home at all.

Sincerely yours,

Aug. 19, 1931

My dear Miss C.:

I have read carefully your letter addressed to me in care of the *Ladies' Home Journal*.

What I kept wondering as I read your letter was why does this girl keep arguing with herself about such an obvious matter. She lists all sorts of arguments to justify her in doing what I should consider the most natural thing in the world to do, namely, to develop her own life, her own standards, and her own family.

I think it must be because you feel a little guilty about your relationship with your parents and it is not quite clear to me why you should feel guilty, except that they try to make you feel so. I should say that that was a case of undue sacrifice. Your parents deserve a certain amount of affection, attention, thoughtfulness, remembrance on your part but they don't have any right to your life, as you very well know. I think you do them an injustice on account of your sense of guilt by giving them yourself with bitterness. What you don't want to give them, don't give them; giving it to them with a grudge is like giving a dog a piece of meat with a thorn in it.

I suspect also that one reason that you are so rebellious is that you are more attached to your parents than you realize and what you are fighting is partly your own desire to be dependent, rather than your own desire to be independent. If you are really independent you can afford to be gracious and if you are really independent you will have no fears of being tyrannized over by a husband in a home of your own.

Sincerely yours,

12.

Problem Children

Grand Valley, Colo.
Sept. 18, 1930

Dear Sir:

Your article interests me greatly. Here—it seems to me—is a chance to obtain workable advice in dealing with my children.

M. is seven years old. Everything she does is well done and with enthusiasm at first. The difficulty is to keep her at it and up to the mark. For instance she is taking music lessons and does so well. Her teacher hates to have her give up. But we are inclined to drop it because of the fuss and tantrums over practicing. Seems it's one fuss after another when we want her to do anything regular like practicing her music and little duties about the house. She doesn't balk at school though and makes very good marks in everything except handwriting.

She will pester people out of all patience, actually seems to like annoying at times. One bad habit is asking questions whose answers she very well knows and butting in when people are talking.

Her grandmother is always contrasting her with her sister who is two years younger.

Sister will take all sorts of kidding and laugh over it. M. will sulk or cry.

Sister will try to please. M. will try to annoy.

Sister is not resentful when punished. M. will sulk or go into tantrums.

M. used to get terrible hysterics when she was two to four years old merely over not being allowed to have something not possible to give her, like crying for the moon, but now just borders on them occasionally.

We have trouble getting her to tell truthful accounts of things. But I think she is greatly improved on that point. But she got such a name no one will believe her anymore. Once she told the school a bull had attacked her sister and badly hurt her and caused a lot of inquiries to come in over the phone.

As a matter of fact the bull had only looked at them through the fence.

She don't seem to care a damn what people think of her as appeals to her "pride" have no effect. How can one build up a sense of pride and morals that will keep her straight in later years? She won't have many friends if she does not stop being so annoying. Like in her play—she will try to force everybody to do what she wants and often makes her sister miserable that way.

Perhaps there are too many bosses up where we live. Grandparents, mother, uncle and aunt. And they often tease her to distraction. As I said the baby laughs but M. cries or gets tantrums.

Very truly yours,

P.S. We are a Christian family. Grace before all meals. Family worship every morning. Church and Sabbath school every Saturday (grandparents are Seventh Day Adventists). Children are very well behaved on such occasions.

The old-fashioned religion of reward for good—sure punishment for bad—is preached day in and day out by grandmother. My teaching is confined to bedtime stories with a moral. She adores stories and gets the point unasked or questioned by me. Personally I think she is doing pretty well but when they keep telling how *"terrible"* she is I get worried and fearful. *They* are the grandmother and uncle.

We are a family with a long history of respectable people.

Oct. 6, 1930

Dear Mrs.:

I enjoyed reading your letter of September 18 which you addressed to me in care of the *Ladies' Home Journal,* chiefly because you first stated your problem and then analyzed it quite well. You say there are too many bosses which is quite evident. Then you go on to say that the bosses tease the child to distraction. This is almost enough. But just a little above that you say that she has a sister two years younger who is held up to her as an ideal and compared with her and who has winning ways and whom everyone likes and this child is urged to be like her sister. And finally what you say about the fact that you think yourself that the child is doing pretty well but the rest of the relatives think she is doing pretty badly and alarm you about her, these things are quite enough to cause the conditions described.

I think your letter is almost a practical one showing the ways in which the child tries in vain to express its great dissatisfaction and unhappiness in the situation for which it is not responsible. When you think of the limited powers which are available to a child and think how this particular child is hedged in by a superior altho younger sister (I say superior meaning superior in disposition and perhaps in talent, at any rate in the impression it makes on older children) and an uncle and an aunt and a grandmother and a father and a mother, all of them big and powerful and strong and who exert various kinds of influences upon her and who have various kinds of expectations of her, I say that it is no wonder that a child, particularly one who has gotten started off on a bad reaction, continues to make herself as disagreeable as possible as the only means to her available of expressing herself and obtaining any sort of satisfaction or power in the world. You may be pretty certain that all the child's reactions are directly attributable to the ways in which people about her are treating her or have treated her. I shouldn't want to criticize your religious customs but I gather from your letter that there is a great deal of talk about the right thing to do and the moral thing to do; I would suggest that you strive for a goal of happiness for the child. How can this child secure happiness and comfort? Certainly not by being pestered and scolded and annoyed. That sort of treatment only induces her to pester and tease back; because she hasn't some of the restraints that you have, you will probably win in the long run.

If you can't get rid of some of the grandparents and uncles and aunts, I think it might be a good plan to get rid of the child. I mean, I think it might be a good thing for the child to put her in another home for a while or in a private school. She certainly ought to be separated from this sister of whom she is so jealous and with whom she is so unfavorably compared. If she must stay where she is, the comparisons ought to stop.

All of this will require a lot of maneuvering and a lot of work on your part and you may need some help.

Sincerely yours,

Bristol, Conn.
Oct. 31, 1930

Dear Sir:

I am interested in mental hygiene, particularly in regard to its effect upon child behavior. I have three boys whose ages are ten, nine, and seven years. They are very active boys and according to their I.Q.s are considered very bright, but their behavior is not all that is to be desired.

My husband is away much of the time and this leaves the discipline of the children to me. I am not a born disciplinarian and do not seem to acquire the knack of it readily. While I love my boys dearly, I do not care for boys as a sex and therefore do not understand their ways. I have learned much since associating with them but feel that I have much more to learn.

The nine-year-old boy, the middle one, causes me the most trouble, and I think that if he were different, not only he but all of us would be happier.

According to a physical examination, his health is good but he is considered a very nervous child, although at times it seems as though something besides nerves must account for some of his actions.

At home he frets and finds fault and opposes most everything I want him to do from the time he awakes in the morning until he is asleep at night. He takes delight in annoying his younger brother in all ways possible and even threatens to kill him. I presume jealousy is the cause of this and have tried to create a "big brother" feeling in him toward his younger brother but to no avail.

He does not like to read but is interested in anything mechanical. He also likes to paint and color and seems to appreciate beauty in colors and scenery. He is seldom quiet for any length of time and seems happiest when he is causing others to be unhappy.

When he is the only child at home, he is very sweet and likable, but just as soon as the other children appear, the trouble begins. Apparently he can behave when he has to, for his school mark in conduct is Excellent. There is also a noticeable improvement in his behavior when his father is at home.

I am wondering if I unintentionally cause my child to behave as he does. Any suggestions you can make will be greatly appreciated.

Sincerely,

Nov. 20, 1930

My dear Mrs.:

I have read with interest your letter of October 31 addressed to me in care of the *Ladies' Home Journal*.

I think the key to your letter is contained in the last paragraph in which you say, "I am wondering if I unintentionally cause my child to behave as he does." Frankly, I should think from what you say in the rest of your letter that you undoubtedly do. Just how I cannot be sure. I am struck, however, by the very remarkable sentence in your letter, "I do not care for boys as a sex." What on earth do you mean by that, Mrs. W.? In what way do you care for boys? And do you think of them just as a "sex"? I think this indicates a very remarkable and peculiar psychology on your own part which you most certainly should get straightened out before it does incalculable harm to your children.

You see, a mother who has three little boys and who then says she does not care for boys, almost writes the story with those words. And when she refers to them as a "sex," she still further indicates to me that there is something radically wrong in her. I am sure that your sons unconsciously recognize and react to this attitude on your part. It may be that because of your dislike for them, your unconscious hostility toward them, that you have over-compensated and treat one, or perhaps all of them, with a tenderness and kindness and indulgence which is really dictated by your feelings of guilt.

Now all of these things could be straightened out I am sure if he could go to someone who makes a specialty of problem children. There are many excellent opportunities for things of this sort right in New York City and you live so close to there that I very much hope you will go and see someone about it. There are so many good people that I hesitate to make any suggestions but in hopes of encouraging you to carry out this suggestion if possible, I am going to mention a few of the more outstanding ones. Dr. David Levy at the Institute for Child Guidance and Dr. Marion Kenworthy are among the best but they are probably too busy to see you. Dr. John Levy is a very good man, Dr. Edith Spaulding is an excellent woman psychiatrist.

In addition I would strongly recommend to your attention a few books dealing with the subject. For example, I would read *The Nervous Child* by [Hector] Cameron as soon as possible;[1] then I would read *The Modern Parent* by Garry Myers; next I would read a collection of essays which Mr. [Nelson Antrim] Crawford and I have recently edited under the name of *The Healthy-Minded Child*, published by Coward-McCann and Co. I think these will help you a great deal and I am sure they will open a new view of the thing to you because I can see from your letter that you are intelligent and thoughtful and anxious to do your very best and almost entirely unaware of the unconscious way in which you are standing in your own light. It is because I am so very anxious that you change things that I have written you so long a letter.

Sincerely yours,

Illinois
Oct. 31, 1930

Dear Sir:

Your articles in the October and November *Ladies' Home Journal* were of interest to me, and I am very happy that we are invited to ask you questions relating to our own family problems.

1. A little daughter about 11½ years of age has for over a year now had recurring spells of fear of death. For instance, last night after being in bed an hour she asked me to come to her, and when I went to her bedside she said she seemed to be "worrying" again, her heart was beating hard she said, and she was shaking visibly as if she had ague. I have never seen this shaking before. She always calls it "worrying." Usually I must explain all over again what death is but last night after asking if she had done

1. London: Oxford University Press, 1919.

something she shouldn't and receiving a negative reply I was able to quiet her by a "pretend" shopping expedition and finally she dropped off to sleep. But usually as I said we must go into the subject very thoroughly. We have tried to maintain a Christian home for our three children, still trying to keep up family prayers once a day and "grace" before each meal—everything very brief, and I have tried to omit Heaven and Hell, and death, because I do not know much about them. At the very beginning of the trouble our physician examined her and found nothing wrong and no physical signs of adolescence. I think there are still none. She is well but a little small for her age. In school she is in the 6th grade and ranks high in her class. Is there any way in which I can discover the cause for these sudden fear spells? I've not been able to decide anything. She is naturally sensitive to beauty, to music, and I've tried to help her from introspection. She is busy most of the time, and happy.

2. The other problem relates to our oldest boy of 17. Just to what extent does a boy of that age owe his parents obedience? He has always been fairly obedient if handled tactfully. But he has within the last three months taken the stand that he has a right to spend part of his self-earned pocket money on the "luxury" of smokes. Tobacco has been tabu in our family all these years, and we have begged him to postpone his smoking until he has his growth. He is convinced by his own observation(!) that it is harmless. What can we parents do about it? Legally, I understand we have a right to all his earnings—only $11.00 the past month—and we are in financial need of all the assistance he can give. But we do not feel we can force him. He is already through one semester of college work and would easily pass for 19 or 20, and most of his associates are that age.

If you can suggest solutions to these problems or refer me to books where I can find help I shall be grateful. Allowing him to "get by" with smoking, will, I fear, complicate problems with a younger brother 15½ when he takes a notion to be independent.

Thanking you
Yours Truly,

Nov. 28, 1930

My dear Mrs.:

Your letter of October 31 addressed to me in care of the *Ladies' Home Journal* interests me very much.

First let me consider the problem of the daughter, 11½ years old, who wakes up with these spells of fear of death. Your daughter is undoubtedly suffering from what we call anxiety attacks. These indicate a considerable disturbance in the depth of her mind, in what you probably call her sub-conscious mind. It indicates something radically wrong in your treatment of the child. It is probably something of which you have not the remotest idea. You very much need help in the matter and I strongly advise you to take the child to a psychiatrist. I gather from your letter that you suspect the child of sexual behavior about which I gather that you have had some discussion with her. I do not know in what spirit you discussed the matter and I cannot tell whether or not that is responsible for these panics but I am sure there is a great deal more to it than merely the discussion of death. In fact I am quite certain that it is not death that your daughter fears at all but something which is identified with death in her mind.

Now the other problem is one about which I can give you more specific advice. You ask me to what extent a boy of 17 owes his parents obedience. I should say that he owes his parents obedience to just that extent to which he has been convinced of their wisdom. Other than that I do not believe that a child owes his parents anything. Perhaps I should say he owes them only respect and courtesy, and he only owes them that if they have given him in his turn respect and courtesy. Many of us parents do not treat our children with courtesy.

I share your feelings about a young lad starting to smoke but I don't see what you can possibly do about it. I think for you to interfere with him, take his money away from him, would be a far more serious sin, if I may use that word, than his smoking is. Let him smoke if he insists, tell him that you do not approve of it and tell him why and there you had better stop. Neither you nor I know exactly what the bad effects of smoking are. We had better not pretend that we know what they are. All we can say is that we wish they wouldn't do it because some people think it does have bad effects and that it might have a bad effect upon him. If he feels that it is the best thing to do, however, in the light of this wisdom, let him do it and don't take a grouchy or injured or grief-stricken attitude about it.

I think you could get a great deal of help on this matter, particularly in regard to the attitude which you take toward your children, by reading some of the recent books on child culture. I will tell you some of the best ones. One is a book by Garry Myers, called *The Modern Parent*. I think very highly of it and I would advise you to read it first. Next I would suggest you read a book called *The Healthy-Minded Child* which Mr. Crawford and I edited but which really consists of a number of essays by different authors and is published by Coward-McCann & Co. at $1.75. Then another book which I recommend is a book by [William E.] Blatz and [Helen] Bott, *The Management of Young Children*,[1] and read each month the magazines known as *Child Study* and *Parents*. Of the two I think the former is the better but both are very good.

1. New York: Morrow, 1929.

I think there is some work being done in the high school in your city by a psychiatrist or by a psychiatric social worker. I cannot tell you just how it is but I am sure the principal of the high school would know. I think you might ask to discuss the problem with her. I shall be interested to know what you think.

Sincerely yours,

Illinois
Jan. 14, 1931

Dear Dr. Menninger:

Please do not think me ungrateful for not sooner acknowledging your kind letter. Your invitation to write again surprised me and I've been re-reading your letter and searching memory and mind for what might be wrong in my treatment of my daughter H. Also I've been watching and questioning her, trying not to suggest some wrong ideas as I did it.

I got into touch with the social worker at the High School as you suggested, and she has spent several hours with H. on two occasions. She considers her a happy, normal child but did not care to do any analyzing. The psychiatrist who comes here once a month, comes for consultation with High School and Junior College students only, so it would have to be a very unusual privilege for H. to see him. As she has been considerably better lately I thought I would try now to see what I can do myself to help her.

No, I did not mean to imply that she was indulging in sexual habits. I do not think so.

The books you recommended to me—I am trying to get hold of through the libraries here. When your letter came I had from a Chicago library Dr. Sadler's *The Mind at Mischief*,[1] and in the time at my disposal I covered a good share of the book, especially all the portions on fear, and also his chapter on complex hunting. The book served to refresh my memory on much I learned from Dr. Josephine Jackson some fourteen years ago when I spent three weeks studying with her. I have tried to put into practice what I learned of her, but seemingly have failed.

---

1. William Samuel Sadler, *The Mind at Mischief: Tricks and Deceptions of the Subconscious Mind and How to Cope with Them* (New York: Funk and Wagnalls, 1930). Sadler, a surgeon at the University of Chicago Medical School, asserts that self-help books are plentiful for "fear, worry and the common phases of the functional nervous disorders" and that there is abundant literature about psychoses. "It is my intention, in this work," he writes, "to discuss abnormal psychology of the more benign sorts, 'the tricks of the mind' " (vii).

From the time H. was two, for nearly six years we lived in the Orient—India. Sometimes she had a white playmate of her own age. For several months on two occasions she had none and often no suitable Indian playmate. Not a few days she and I were alone in one bungalow (excepting servants) and one or two ladies in another bungalow some blocks away, the sole white persons in a city of 35,000 Indians. So there has been unusual opportunity for her to be warped by any mistakes in training. She seemed always to be rather a happy child, too sensitive and not too robust.

When she was about three years old an Indian boy brought to her an experience which she seemed to forget completely as soon as she told me, but which haunted me a long time. As my work was with men and boys I scarcely let her out of my sight after that (figuratively). I tried to guard her unobtrusively, but perhaps I didn't.

Twice I have questioned her about the start of this fear of hers some 18 months ago. She says it started after she attended a Chautauqua (in a park in another city) and they had music which she "didn't like too well" (a xylophone probably) and she thought she was going to be sick as she felt nauseated for some unknown reason and she wondered how she was going to get home to me. I recall what she apparently doesn't, that a few weeks before this two young girls were on their way to this same park, and a man in a car stopped them enroute and said he was going there and would take them. And he didn't. One girl was assaulted. The whole story came out in the local paper which said the girl might die. At that time I had business duties which took me away from home several hours each day so H. was left with neighbors a lot. I told her never under any circumstances to accept a ride from a strange man, and also said she could not go to the parks that summer unless accompanied by an adult. The previous summer she had gone with chums to the playground there. I have no doubt this incident was discussed before her. When she wanted to get home to me from the Chautauqua later on she probably felt that if it wasn't safe to go there alone, it wasn't any safer to leave it alone. I do not know whether this sort of thing and what she may have overheard about it might start these anxiety attacks.

The thing that broke the vicious fear circle in H.'s mind some two weeks ago was a re-examination by our physician because she complained daily of pain in various parts of her body. He told her then that she had such a fine heart it would be hard for her to die. That seemed to be a new idea to her. She did have some temperature that afternoon. The cause of the pains has not been found yet.

I do not know whether you would be interested in some of the things she has said about death, but will mention a few of the recent ones. She said that sometimes when she was going to a neighbor's or to school, something told her she might not live to get back home. I told her rather jokingly it was just her brain teasing her, and that brought the tears to her eyes. She asked one night if death was like falling asleep when you couldn't do what you wanted. I said I didn't think so, but if it was she wouldn't care. She told me emphatically she would care, it would be awful not to be able ever to do what she wanted to. Another night—"Mamma it seems as though the only way to stop worrying about dying is to die," and that time she said she didn't think she could stand it to stop worrying all at once (implying the reaction of joy would be too great?). She started a habit of breathing heavily in the middle of whatever she was doing. I asked her once as she sat reading "Kitty and Her First One Hundred Years" why she did it, and she looked up and said "I seem to be worrying." Some days later under different circumstances I asked her again and she said "I do it to be sure I'm there." There has been a decided break in this breathing habit since our visit to the Doctor, it is not done so often nor for so long a period, but she does it a good deal in her sleep—without crying out or dreaming so far as she can recall.

Most of the worrying comes on in the evening—a week ago she looked up at me as I was tucking in her bedclothes with a sort of strained look in her face and said, "Do you think I'll live until morning?" I told her I certainly thought she would and reminded her of what the doctor had said. Then I told her of all the different things I was planning to do the next day and she soon fell asleep. I realize this is not getting at the root of the trouble but I feel she needs her sleep, and she often wakes up full of "pep" after a bad half hour at night. Just now there seems some unusual fatigue—it is harder to get her out of bed though she is bright enough afterwards.

Now I would like to ask whether I dare try to hunt for this fear complex. If I could get it up to consciousness it seems to me it could not be more difficult to deal with than some of the questions she asks about death, when I must be careful not to start some other complex! I have been hoping that soon there would be a break as there was in the beginning when the matter seemed to be forgotten for a long time. The only other alternative I can see is to plan a program which gives her no time to think such things, but that means driving, which I feel she can not stand just now, because of unusual fatigability.

I think I did not say before that when this "worrying" began she also started writing "poetry." She would rush into the house for paper and pencil and write as fast as she could. At the beginning of 1930 she received 6 months' subscription to *Junior Home Magazine* for some verses she sent in. We had that magazine a good share of her six years in India and she likes it. Our physician at that time wanted me to discourage her poetic efforts as he had a number of university students, budding authors, who were problem patients, but I didn't see it his way. Though I have remembered his warning and tried not to drive her to it, and not to praise her unduly. I feel apologetic over the length of this letter, but scarcely see what to omit if I hope for suggestions from you.[2]

Yours Sincerely,

Ogden, Utah
Nov. 1, 1930

Dear Doctor:

I am a journal reader and have just finished reading your article on mental hygiene in the October issue. I think this department or series of articles is highly beneficial to say the least. I have a problem which I should like to submit to you.

My only child, a son age 5 years, has a peculiarity in his disposition which I find it almost impossible to cope with. For example I might ask him to do some simple thing such as wash his hands and he refuses instantly and I cannot persuade him to do it and it usually ends in me losing my temper and probably slapping his face (which I am extremely ashamed of). This happens more times when there is someone present than otherwise but it seems to be a sort of deep obstinacy and it sometimes occurs as often as three or four times a week tho that is beyond the average. The extremely harsh physical punishment is the only thing that seems to bring him around.

I hope I have made the case clear enough so that you can tell me how to intelligently handle it.

Nov. 26, 1930

My dear Mrs.:

I am glad indeed that you wrote me as you did on November 1 in care of the *Ladies' Home Journal.* I think I can tell you exactly what the trouble is.

I think you are forgetting that your child, like yourself, has an ego. He too wants to be somebody. He wants to show you that he is somebody. Consequently, particularly when there is someone to witness it, he stands on his own feet regardless of the fact that it is costing him pain.

You see there are many times when it is much better to yield to the child than to force him to do something. You may be entirely correct in that the particular things should be done, but you are quite incorrect in attempting to force him to do it. In doing so you may accomplish your end because

---

2. If Menninger replied to this letter, his answer has not been preserved.

you are stronger than he, but he resents it and he will hate you for it as long as he lives. His hate will be deeply buried, it may be unconscious. He may never show it toward you but he will show it toward someone. Don't give him the opportunity to develop that attitude toward you.

Instead I should try to show the child why I wanted that particular thing done. If you can convince him of it without browbeating him or without slapping his face or without being overbearing, he will be glad to do it. If you can't convince him of the why of the thing, if you do not succeed in showing him why it should be done and it is not a thing which will actually harm him or someone else, you had better let him persist in his unwise way until he has learned the lesson from someone else than you, by the bad results of his mistakes.

You see this is an entirely different attitude toward the child than you apparently have. You use the expression "this is the only thing that seems to bring him around." I am not at all sure that it is at all a good thing to want to bring a child around. You had better let the child bring himself around than to try to bring him around. Your own wish for power is so strong, you see, that you take it out on the child and you have created in him an equally stubborn desire for power and he battles with you. Sooner or later he will be stronger than you are and so you had better look out. The way to look out is not to enter into any such contests as this.

I am quite sure that you would derive a great deal of benefit from reading some of the recent things on child culture. I can strongly recommend a book by Garry Myers, called *The Modern Parent* and another book almost as good by Blatz and Bott called *The Management of Young Children.* You may also be interested in a book that Mr. Crawford and I edited and in part wrote, called *The Healthy-Minded Child,* published by Coward-McCann & Co., New York City.

Sincerely yours,

P.S. Also let me recommend to you the magazine called *Child Study* published by the Child Study Association of America and the magazine called *Parents.* Of the two the former is the better but both of them are good.

New York
Nov. 4, 1930

My dear Dr. Menninger,

In order to give you a clear insight into this case I shall begin by telling you the history of my oldest son from infancy. At eleven months of age my mother-in-law had charge of him while I had pneumonia and he was with her and her nine sons and daughters until I was able to take him again eight months after. During that time they all talked, walked, and sang to him and taught him all kinds of tricks until he was apparently a very clever child, though I am sure you agree it was the worst possible thing they could do for his nerves. They never attempted to train him, though he was quite used to using a chamber before he left me, but just changed him so often that they called him "Old Faithful." As he grew up we could all see that he was a nervous child but hardly connected his bed-wetting with that till it was almost past remedying. However, he has been wetting his bed at intervals of at least twice a week, ever since. We put him to bed, being sure he has been to the bathroom, and at bedtime, that is, when we retire, we always took him up and saw that he again emptied his bladder. About two o'clock, or whenever I had to get up to the other children, I would go to him and attend to him and even then he would sometimes be wet in the morning. For one year he went without wetting his bed. This was about two years ago and I believed that he had finally attained the age at which the Doctor said he would cease as lots of children do. However, without warning of any kind, that is, sickness or shock, he started wetting again, and has been at it ever since. He is now twelve years old, will be thirteen in February. He is a most affectionate child, returning two or three times a morning to kiss me good-bye, is lovely when alone with me, but a vixen when fighting with his brothers, of whom there are two. He will not go to the movies, for which I am very thankful, and when he has been taken has been so upset that he had to leave when it was half over. He is very brilliant in school, having first standing and an average of 97% all through last term in eleven subjects. He has no difficulty whatever with his lessons, seemingly assimilating them, rather than studying them. He never seems to have to study a thing at all, merely reading it suffices. He is strong, plays football and likes it immensely though I am so timid about his doing so. He has learned to swim this summer and does not seem to be afraid of the water at all, though I am extremely timid of it. He hates to stay alone in the house or come in the house when no one is here; won't go to the barber's by himself, requiring one of his brothers or myself to go with him.

I am very nervous myself ever since I had that terrible attack of pneumonia and had shock after shock while I was recuperating (seeing my nephew nearly run over, having the man upstairs commit suicide and my nurse and housekeeper leaving me to attend to him with the ambulance clanging outside the door, etc. etc.). Then I have had four children since, all splendidly strong and healthy children, thank God, but that in itself is enough to wrack anyone's nerves. I was a musical prodigy at fifteen, an elocutionist and then an expert stenographer, writing all the specifications for the Bankers' Trust Building, J. P. Morgan's Building at Wall and Nassau, etc. etc. To come down to the humdrum job of minding five children and an eight-room house with no appreciation after the approbation I received in my other capacities is not stimulation enough for a person of my temperament. Can my outlook on life have had anything to do with my son's present nervousness and resultant disability? He does not seem a bit sorry when he is chided for his slackness or carelessness or whatever you may call it but still is very sensitive, I know. I think he just tries to brazen it out and pretend he doesn't care. Last night he went up to take his bath at quarter to seven as he had a big game of football on today, and wanted to rest up. I know he attended to himself before he went to his room, at ten o'clock I heard him get up again before he turned out his light to go to sleep. At twelve-thirty Daddy went in to see if the boys were alright and my son was wet. Daddy changed him, putting clean sheets on his bed as we have always done, never have I permitted him to lie in the wet clothes as I understand many people do, and this morning, he was soaked again. Isn't that trying? It means so much extra washing. This morning I made him take his things downstairs himself and put them in to soak. Then after breakfast he had to wash them out, rinse and blue them, and I hung them out for him. I did this a number of times this summer thinking thereby he would be more careful; but it didn't work any better.

One Doctor raised the foot of the bed, saying the sensitiveness of the organ might account for his trouble. A second gave him medicine. One of my maids told me that in the home from which she came they made all the bed wetters take an icy cold shower at night and sleep in the Infirmary until cured which was usually a very short time. This I did and it was after that that my son stopped wetting for the year period. We, of course, thought we had solved our difficulty, but it didn't work the next time we tried the same recipe, nor did any of the other advice do any good after the third or fourth night.

If I am out in the afternoon when he returns from school, he will go all over town; to my Mother's, Sister's, or stores, till he finds me. This happens so seldom that we all laugh about his following me up.

I have been dieting for nerves and high blood pressure, which normally is 185 although I am only 41 years old, the Doctor maintaining that that must be my normal pressure or my legs and hands would swell and I would be otherwise uncomfortable. He says there must be something else wrong with me and my body has finally accommodated itself to 185 degrees to balance the defect. Can this be right? I am feeling better now than I have been in two years. Had a breakdown last August, 1929, and went away for a month with only the baby and maid as my blood pressure was up to 225 and the Doctor said I would have to stay in bed for three months. However he consented to the change of scene and I have been greatly improved after the rest began to work. I admit I am enough to make anyone nervous as I take my job so seriously and mind the children so conscientiously, never going away and leaving them at all. I'll admit I should, but I'm worrying so about them when I'm away that it doesn't do me much good.

Can you psychoanalyze his case? Did I say he was domineering and very bossy with the younger children? He has to help a bit around to the extent of drying dishes about one time a day, empty the garbage can the same number of times and about once a week sweep the front porch, but grumbles all the time because he thinks he has a little more to do than the other younger children. He reads every minute he has from play and makes a splendid impression on all the relatives and friends with whom he stays at vacation time. They are always willing and seemingly anxious to have him despite the inconvenience he sometimes causes, though here's something strange and very annoying to me, he seldom if ever wets his bed when away for a week but comes back here and starts all over again.

Please let me hear from you. Most sincerely,

Nov. 26, 1930

My dear Mrs.:

I have been extremely interested in reading your letter of November 4 addressed to me in care of the *Ladies' Home Journal.*

The whole problem of bed wetting is one which we can scarcely cover in the contents of a letter. I would like to direct your attention to a discussion of it in such books as Hector Cameron's *The Nervous Child,* and Douglas A. Thom's *Everyday Problems of the Everyday Child.*[1] Look for it under the heading of Enuresis, which is the medical term for bed wetting. If you are not extremely familiar with these two books, I would advise you to read not only those two articles but the entire book. You might also read Mr. Crawford's and my book called *The Healthy-Minded Child.* . . . I am asking you to read these partly to get suggestions as to how to handle bed wetting but more particularly to show you how to understand this problem in your son.

As I read your letter I am impressed by the fact that you yourself are a very tense, energetic, over-conscientious person with a great deal of ambition and drive and what is called personality. Bed wetting, talking in very general terms, is very frequently an expression of a refusal on the part of a child to grow up or at least a refusal to give up some of the things associated with childhood. Now the thing which your child most probably is reluctant to give up is his dependence upon you and his monopoly of a certain interest from you. Wetting the bed is the act of urinating in the

1. New York: Appleton, 1927.

unconscious and has what we call an infantile sexual significance; I cannot very well explain in a few words what I mean by this except to say that it is a thing which the child unconsciously enjoys. Consciously your boy does not enjoy wetting the bed but unconsciously he does, and he doesn't want to give it up. I do not think you make it easier for him to give it up by some of the things you do. I do not advocate punishment but on the other hand I do not see why you would permit your husband to get up and go and change the boy's wet bed for him at night. Why make it any more comfortable; I would rather make it less comfortable. I think if I were you I would totally ignore it. Let the boy himself handle the sheets and the nuisance of it. Let it be his problem and not yours. Don't inquire about it, don't look after it, just forget it. Then it ceases to be a weapon, a claim on your attention, and an unmitigated nuisance to him himself and he will give it up I am sure.

Sincerely yours,

Erie, Pa.
Dec. 17, 1930

Dear Doctor Menninger:

In February's issue will you please help a lot of us mothers out? We would like to know what you think of spanking as a means of discipline when reasoning and coaxing fails. We tried the other methods without results, we now spank and get results. According to some child psychologists we are wrong but others say we are right.

I will tell you how we spank and will welcome any criticism or suggestions. I have only a few rules but I insist that they be obeyed. These rules are against lying, stealing, talking back and getting in late. They do not break the first two rules but they did talk back sometimes and come in late. They do not break these rules since I started spanking. My four children are 13, 15, 16, 17 years of age. The older two are very troublesome at times. The 17 year old is a girl, 16 a boy, 15 a girl, and the 13 one a boy. When I think they deserve spanking, I take them to a separate room and explain their offense. I then make them undress from the hips to the knees, lay facedown on the bed and I use the strap on the bare buttocks. They are allowed to cry as much as they desire but are not allowed to struggle. If they struggled, they know they would get double. The strapping makes the buttocks hurt and sting but does not injure them any.

A half hour after the spanking I always go in and make up with the spanked one. They are always willing. I do not harp on the things they have been punished for. I figure they have received their punishment and that the penalty has been sufficient. The spankings are never mentioned outside the house. I know that other mothers have found it necessary to follow my methods. I will be anxiously awaiting your opinion on spanking.

I was greatly surprised to read in the January issue that letter from a mother who never had given her 14-year-old son any sex information. Even if he is 14 his mother or father should furnish the information he needs. The information he may have received from other boys is probably half wrong. She should at least warn him against practicing masturbation. Mothers do not seem to realize that to most boys there is a fatal fascination to commit this wrong. My husband says that he doubts very much if there ever was a boy who did not commit masturbation once in a while. Of course, they seldom do it after their parents explain to them why it is wrong. The boys usually start doing this because older boys teach them to do it.

I always explained things to my children. When they were small I always bathed the boys with the girls. Thus, in their early life, they knew that boys' and girls' bodies were different. They thought nothing of it. When they asked about babies, I explained it to them. When the boys needed information about masturbation etc. I explained it to them. I adopted the same methods with the girls.

Because of bathroom doors sometimes refusing to unlock, we do not have a key for our bathroom door. No one but my husband or I goes in when the door is shut. I still go in and help them bathe. They have perfect confidence in me and always ask me about things which they do not understand. There is one question I would like to ask you. My two boys are not circumcised. Should they be and if so why? If it is necessary, I would like it to be done when they are young instead of waiting. Hoping you can answer my questions.

Your friend,

Jan. 9, 1931

My dear Mrs.:

I am very glad indeed to have your letter of December 17 asking me what I think of spanking as a form of discipline.

Frankly I think it is a very bad method of accomplishing results. I don't deny that it sometimes appears to help a child break a bad habit but I think it is very likely to damage the child psychologically in a way which is much more serious.

I think the method you describe as using yourself is a very bad one. You say that you spank the child in a certain way and then a half hour later you go in and make up with him. This business of hurting a child and then being nice to it creates a very bad psychological [undecipherable] in later life. If I were you I would discontinue it. I would not hurt my children at all. If they did not deserve a certain thing, I would deprive them of it but I would not be an aggressor against my child if I were you.

You will find a considerable discussion of the psychology of this in a book which Mr. Crawford and I edited called *The Healthy-Minded Child.* You will find that we investigated how a great many parents treated their children's bad habits. You will also find that many parents are very cruel to their children and these cruelties have sometimes appeared to have a good effect immediately but a very bad effect later.

Let me commend you on your very healthy-minded attitude in the matter of the sex education of your children. I agree with you precisely. You will also find this matter discussed in the book to which I refer.

Do not get the idea that I think you have harmed your children. You asked me, however, what I think of spanking and I have told you. I think that all psychiatrists and psychologists agree now that spanking is bad, not because it hurts the child but because it represents to the child an attack on the part of its parents. He is apt to resent it and take revenge without being conscious of these emotions. I do think you will injure your children if you continue it.

Sincerely yours,

Lexington, Ky.
Feb. 2, 1931

Dear Dr. Menninger:

I am hoping you can help me decide how I can help my little boy, D., to overcome one of his various faults which has worried us often. D. will be six years old next August. He is evidently a bright child, as his kindergarten teacher insisted he was so superior to the others in the kindergarten that he must enter the first grade this term. This was done, and D. seems to be getting along well so far—altho, as the second term began only a week ago it is rather early to judge this. However he enjoys school, and comes home less irritable and tired than when he was in kindergarten. The kindergarten teacher, who is a woman of some twenty years experience, could not seem to praise D. too highly. She called him a "delight and a joy"— "wonderfully responsive"—"so interested in everything" so "unusually well-informed"—and many other pleasant things for a mother to hear. While I realize D. is, perhaps, what she says along these lines, I cannot agree with her further remarks that he is "such a good sport"—"cooperates so well"—and "has perfect mental health." D. seems to me to be exactly the opposite of these last remarks. With such a striking contrast between the attitude at school and at home it seems evident something is wrong. Either I am a failure as a guide to him, and bring out his worst side, or he is spoiled and shows his bad traits at home—the better ones coming out where he is better managed. This I can't decide for myself.

I realize that I am far from an ideal mother. I was an English teacher before my marriage—a dreamer, fond of music and of writing verses. I was untrained in housework—my parents having been very comfortably off—my father is a college dean. I married a good and lovable man but one who does not earn much money. We have struggled with mountains of debt ever since our marriage. [My husband] had to borrow a large sum to take his M.S. degree and get into the sort of work he wanted. Then we had another child—a premature baby who struggled with one illness after another and finally died at two years old with a streptococcic infection—a year ago. Last year D. developed a bad case of eczema—he had been perfectly well, before this. After having various doctors, a skin specialist, and a course of ultra-violet for him, a bright physician removed his bad tonsils and adenoids and the eczema disappeared—only traces having recurred for the past six months. I have learned to keep house, to wash, iron, cook and sew fairly well, altho' I do not care for this type of work. I like neatness and find pleasure in keeping the house clean, but dislike the lack of mental stimulation when I am shut up by four walls. However—we get along fairly well under my ministrations, and are practically out of debt at last. I am very impatient by nature and find it difficult to be patient with D. but I do try, constantly, as I feel my duty toward him strongly. I try to make him as happy as possible too. I read to him a good deal. I try to endure his constant messes about the house without protest, and I try hard to make him follow all the rules of hygiene carefully so that he may not be ill again. He seems quite well, now, and is 1 lb. overweight according to the school nurse, at present. My husband is patient usually with D. as he has an amiable disposition.

Why is it that D. is such a cry-baby at home? When I refuse him something he bursts into tears or into a passion of rage—kicking and stamping. He does not always act this way—often he gets along smoothly for quite a while—I usually suspect fatigue and try to make him rest when he has such an outburst. Is there another cause for this? He is also a very poor sport with his playmates. If they don't do what he wishes he cries or says he won't play. I have tried to explain to him that they won't like him—that he must be a good sport—etc., etc., but he still behaves in this manner. He has a very strong will and wants everything his own way. I have tried hard to discipline him—I use a switch on him as a last resort. Often I just make him go to his room and stay. But I often feel worn out—life is one battle after another! He doesn't want to wash his hands—to drink his orange juice—to go to bed—etc., etc. Yet when I don't urge him, he will eat an orange with relish, fall asleep from weariness if not put to bed when I think he should go—and complain of dirt on his hands or face. My method has been not to give up but to "die fighting." I have tried to make D. feel that he *must* do the right things at the right time—but it is such a wearisome battle to enforce my wishes. I don't wish to paint too black a picture but I do think he is getting too old to continue being such a baby and so stubborn so much of the time.

I "raised him on books"—sent for all the pamphlets possible on child care and training and tried hard to make him a happy, well-disciplined child. I believe strongly in discipline as I was a spoiled child myself and had to learn to make myself do the right things after I was grown—a very hard job and one I never want D. to have to suffer thru. He is very like me and I sometimes fear I am too severe with him because I dread he will develop the faults I had such trouble to overcome after I married. On the other hand—am I strict enough? On the face of it you would say a child who cries and fusses so much must be spoiled. Or is it just a wrong viewpoint on my part?

D. has a very vivid imagination also. He tells tremendous stories about everything—sometimes this seems worse than at other times. I treated this lightly—tried to explain the difference between fact and fancy—to play "true and false" games with him. But he can't even tell me a straight story about what he got for lunch at school—which is a very irritating problem.

I would greatly appreciate any advice you can give me in handling

1. D.'s cry-baby and poor-sport tendencies—at least at home.

Am I too severe or too lenient in your opinion—if you can judge from what I have told you.

2. D.'s too vivid imagination.

How can I confine this within the bounds of reason so I can at least get a straight answer about common details of his day at school or of his play when he is outdoors.

Very sincerely yours,

Feb. 24, 1931

My dear Mrs.:

I have read with interest your letter of recent date addressed to me in care of the *Ladies' Home Journal*.

I shall do my best to answer the questions you raise. I must call your attention to the fact that you, yourself have noticed that the boy gets along very well in school but not very well at home. The obvious conclusion is that something is wrong at home. That is a rather disagreeable conclusion and you would rather like to squirm out of it but I think we must look at the facts as they are. I think you are quite right in your assumption that there is something wrong with you. Let us see what it could be.

As I read your letter over again carefully I notice that you are very fond of the words "must" and "ought." At the same time you say that you were a spoiled child and were not treated with any such severity as you are treating your boy. You say you wonder if you are not too severe with him. Elsewhere you say your theory is to die fighting. My frank opinion is that there is entirely too much fighting in your attitude towards the boy. It sounds as if you were at war with him and that you wanted to gain a victory of some kind.

Of course, you could win a kind of a victory but evidently the child can win a kind of a victory too, and he is doing so. I think you ought to make a very radical revision in your own point of view. My impression is that being a spoiled child yourself you don't want anyone else to be. You don't want anyone else to have the same indulgences that you had. Not because of the consequences as you tell yourself but because of a certain amount of jealousy. If you can see this attitude of hostility that you have toward your son it will help you a great deal in dealing with it.

You say you have read a lot of books on the subject. You do not say what books you have read. Let me suggest that you read a book called *The Modern Parent* by Garry Myers. Professor Myers brings out very clearly how parents mistreat their children without intending to. . . .

Just why he cries and why he is what you call a poor sport, etc., I cannot tell but if I were you I would not put too much emphasis on it. I think those things will straighten out as he gets older providing your attitude straightens out. And as for his vivid imagination, I should thank God for it if I were you. If you could possibly do so, get away from the notion that the world is a place of "must" and "ought." The "musts" and "oughts" in the world are not things which someone says but they are physical and social and chemical laws which the child will learn if you will let him alone but if you try to force certain notions of what you think he must and ought do down his throat you are going to have a rebellion on your hands and evidently you are already having it.

Frequently, in such cases the best possible way to treat the child is for the mother to take some psychological treatment herself. This may surprise and shock you a little bit but you would be surprised to know how many mothers I see who are really being treated because of some behavior disorder on the part of the child. If you have never thought of this before I know it will give you food for thought. I hope it will not make you too critical of yourself or have too much of a sense of guilt. I am sure you have been doing the best you could but I am trying to show you how you can do better. Please take it in that spirit.

Sincerely yours,

Stillwater, Okla.
Mar. 23, 1931

Dear Doctor:

Can mental hygiene help me? My problem may seem trivial but it is very real to me.

I am twenty-eight years old and married to a wonderful husband. People are always telling me how lucky I was to get him. We are the parents of two daughters, only one living.

Our little daughter is a sweet lovable child and I adore her but how I long for a son! Every time I hear of the birth of a son to one of my friends I am seized with an indescribable jealousy. I realize of course that this is very wrong.

I have experienced much pain and suffering during my life, mostly during the periodic process. I get little sympathy and help from physicians. They seem to take such suffering for granted. This is my real reason for fearing to bring daughters into the world. The prevalence of periodic suffering is alarming. I know very few women who escape.

I do not believe in rearing any child alone. I hope for a brother for my child. Dear Doctor isn't there some way that my dream may be made to come true?

Very truly yours

Apr. 14, 1931

My dear Mrs.:

I have read with interest your letter of March 23 addressed to me in care of the *Ladies' Home Journal.*

I think your own personal experience makes you exaggerate the suffering that women experience from menstruation. As a matter of fact, the vast majority of women don't suffer any pain at all at menstruation. I think part of your trouble may be of psychological origin. I don't mean by this that you imagine it but I do mean that you expect to suffer and were taught as a child that it was a sick time, as it is sometimes erroneously called, and so forth. Therefore, this makes you unduly sensitive.

It would be my advice that you have several more children. I think four is the ideal number, two boys and two girls. I am speaking now of what is most normal and most advantageous for the child. If you had four children, the chances certainly are that one of them would be a boy and three of them might be. If you have girls, however, I think you ought to be thankful. Personally I prefer girls.

Sincerely yours,

McPherson, Kans.
Mar. 30, 1931

Dear Dr. Menninger,

After reading your article "Self-Adoration" in my copy of the April *Ladies' Home Journal* I am moved to write you. There are problems of my children that need to be explained and smoothed out but I am sure it would be of no use unless we got at the root of the matter, myself.

I am (I don't like to put it that boldly) one of those self-adorers. And *I don't want to be*. What can be done about it? I am twenty-eight years old, reasonably healthy both physically and mentally, averagely intelligent and the mother of three children. From what I have been able to figure out about my father and his mother, I dare say I have an inherited tendency in that direction augmented by the loss of my mother at the age of five and a life of extreme poverty with my harsh and inconsistent father and a typical fairy-tale stepmother. (I do not excuse myself, mearly [*sic*] help to explain.) I have always been avid for beautiful things, I am afraid, not only to see and hear but to possess, and have never had any.

The one extreme physical passion of my life through which I could have diverted the greater part of my capacity for loving to another unfortunately ended with premature importunating. I have never yet decided whether virtue or egotism prompted my refusal.

I married to have children. And having had them there are times when I actually don't want them!

For I do indeed treat them with a mixture of harshness and inconsistency, sentimentalism and indulgence. I work with all my might to be the right kind of mother but always what you help me to interpret as my love comes between me and them.

For instance: all my babies are strictest kind of schedule babies breast fed at proper intervals with correct additions of the proper foods at each age. But when my first baby, an extremely precautious [*sic*] little girl, would refuse the food offered her, over and over again I felt affronted. When after nursing two minutes (and before God I wanted to nurse her) she would scream and refuse to nurse farther, I would become so exasperated I wanted to hurt her (only after dr. after dr. had assured me there was nothing wrong with either her or the milk).

So it has been for six and ½ years with all three children. I want to love them and of course I do in that extremely possessive manner. I want to be intelligent, fair, kind oh all those things that a mother ought to be. They are beautiful children and I dare say as good as average and above average in intelligence (their teachers bear me out in this) but I know they could be much finer with proper love and control. I don't say understanding for I do understand them rather well but can't control my own impulse enough to act with judgment. Is there anything at all that I can do? I don't say help me to happiness for I am sure I can get such happiness as I need out of helping them be happy.

You have doubtless wondered where their father fits in this picture. As a matter of fact, he doesn't fit. He asked me at least once a day for five months to marry him. (I worked with him.) I told him of my former love and assured him I believed it would be my last. He wanted me anyway and I wanted what any healthy clean blooded man could give me—babies. The triple tragedy occurred when it turned out that he didn't want babies at all, any time, and physically I seemed unable to keep from having them! He has one love—money—and as his earning capacity isn't great we keep him from obtaining it. I know it's a mess but I believe it can be made not more than averagely bad, if I can only come out of myself.

I do all my work, washing, ironing, sewing, gardening, the whole lot, have positively no recreation except reading. He spends all his evenings at the shop by choice for he did that before marriage, even had to go a while each evening before he could keep a date. Can you help me to help myself?

Sincerely,

P.S. Of course you could discuss to some length whether it were a greater sin to give one's self unmarried to a man one loved or to give one's self in marriage to a man one didn't but that wouldn't solve the question in hand. Obviously the course with the greatest self-control involved would be to do neither. But when one isn't especially gifted with self-control the latter course would at least be the more expedient.

May 2, 1931

My dear Mrs.:

I think your letter addressed to me in care of the *Ladies' Home Journal* is one of the most interesting I have read in several weeks. Whether you know it or not, you show an unusual degree of intelligence. It takes such intelligence to write the postscript you wrote in regard as to whether it is a great sin, as you call it, to do one thing or another and add that obviously the greatest self-control would be to do neither.

Now I think you must use this intelligence of yours in the problem before you. If you can use your intelligence a little more and your emotions a little less in these problems you will suffer less and you will do better.

The very fact that you recognize as clearly as you do the tendencies toward hostility toward your children is in itself something of a preventive. I doubt if you are likely to be very harsh with your children for the very reason that you do recognize it. Of course you are going to be harsh sometimes but the mothers that I am afraid of are those who deny that they are ever harsh and go on being as cruel as the devil all the time. With you it is quite different. Your children will be likely to forgive your harshness because you yourself are so genuinely anxious to avoid it. . . .

Finally I must add that I am not convinced that you are doing either yourself or your husband or your children justice by working so hard. Perhaps it is necessary, I do not know. But I suspect that to a slight extent you may be working hard in an effort to punish yourself for some of the indulgences and selfishnesses and other reasons for a sense of guilt which you speak of earlier in your letter. Of course if you enjoy the work you are doing then there is no reason why you shouldn't do it but I do not think it is right to your children to over-tire yourself with such activities so that you are psychologically [in]capable of maintaining the even poise and interest in what your children are doing and thinking and talking.

Sincerely yours,

Orlando, Fla.
Apr. 1, 1931

My dear Dr. Menninger:

I am a woman of 35, with two children—boys aged 3½, and 19 months. They are unusually healthy, I believe, as the older of the two never had a sick day, not even a cold, until he was almost three. The youngest has never been really sick but one time, and recovered quickly then. They are outdoors most of the times, and sleep well. The older one averages 15 hours of sleep, and is not easily awakened. He has one bad habit, only, thumb-sucking—which has never been constant, but is very persistent. If he is crossed in any way, or is very hungry, he puts his thumb into his mouth. However, he is getting much better about it. He occasionally wets his bed or his clothes. Otherwise, I believe he is normal. I am sure he is average, or above, in intelligence. The younger one has better habits, and weighs more for his age, but does not sleep quite so soundly—averages about 14 hours.

But the thing I am writing you about is this. There is a neurasthenic tendency in my family. I, myself, suffered a complete nervous breakdown before my marriage, which kept me confined in sanitarium or with a nurse for two years. Doctors told me that my children would not be affected by my illness, as I was completely cured, and normal at the time of my marriage. My trouble was diagnosed as melancholia, probably brought about by albumin in the urine, as a result of influenza.

But my father's parents both suffered from diseases which brought about disorganization of the nerves at the end. My father died from a kind of creeping paralysis, during which he lost control of his speech and of his limbs, but never of his sanity. Could read up til the last two weeks of his life. He has two brothers who are suffering from the same trouble. My own brother (one of three) died after an operation which was performed in an attempt to cure him of epileptic attacks which he had had for about 10 years occurring only once or twice a year. One of my other brothers has had two breakdowns similar to mine, but is well now. The other brother and two sisters suffered from no nervous disorder. My mother is 75—has lost none of her faculties, and is rarely sick—seems much less nervous and childish than most people I have observed of that age.

Pardon this lengthy recital. But I wanted you to know my children's background. There is no distinct nervous tendency in either branch of my husband's family, so far as I know. He is not at all nervous himself.

Would it be possible for you to give me an idea of whether my children will be subject to nervous disorders from such an inheritance, coming through one line only? If so, what additional measures can I take to guard them, besides protecting their physical health?

Sincerely yours,

P.S. I think that the nervous tendency in my father's family extended back through several generations.

Apr. 30, 1931

My dear Mrs.:

I have read with interest your letter of April 1 addressed to me in care of the *Ladies' Home Journal.*

I think you very clearly recognize yourself that your boy's thumb sucking is a defiance gesture. The best way to treat defiance gestures of any kind is to ignore them. I think from what you say that his bed wetting is the same sort of thing. If I were you I would ignore both of them. The more you make of it, the worse they will be. I do not mean that you cannot destroy the habits by making sufficient fuss about them, but I think the damage you do to the personality in this destruction is even worse than the thumb sucking. It will go away in all probability if you just have patience and tolerance.

I think the probability of your children inheriting any serious nervous disturbance is very little if any greater than that of any other children. I think the chief thing for you to do is to keep them in as mentally healthy an environment as possible. I think nervous trouble is usually acquired rather than transmitted by heredity. There is a book on this subject which I think you might enjoy reading, namely, *The Inheritance of Mental Diseases* by Abraham Myerson.[1] But I can save you the trouble of reading it if you will just believe me when I tell you that the main thing for you to do is to raise your boys as well as you can, by studying child-guidance literature as much as you can, and forget all about this inheritance business. You can't change that now anyway, and as I have already said, I don't think you have anything to worry about on that score. . . .

Sincerely yours,

Seattle, Wash.
June 28, 1931

Dr. Menninger—Dear Sir:

Please advise: My 9 yr. old (just turned 9) granddaughter tells *lies*. We love her dearly. Her mother, my daughter, is the soul of honor—lovely in character—cultured—excelled all other students in school—fine musician—likewise my other child is absolutely honest and a brilliant student—beautiful.

My other granddaughter also is *truthful* and *leads* her classes—is 7—has had two promotions in this year of school.

The 9 year old is *average*—slightly above at least not below, very *sensitive*, learns music well. *Minds always* and at *once*. A great help about the home, and of social companions. But she is *untruthful* and is often gossiping against her playmates *to other* children and to her mother.

For example: She will go out and eat *cake*. Her mother will say "Who ate the cake, did you C.?" She will blandly say "no" and when pinned down will cry and declare V. did it.

Her mother is very kind and never punishes her, just talks kindly. She *lies* continually.

She did not like to take her medicine, "Did you take your medicine, C.?" "Yes, I took it," but she *did not*.

Her mother is so worried for fear she will grow up dishonest. In every other way she is good. She is dependable in all other ways—attractive—very trustworthy with baby.

Her father is a minister's son. His sisters used to deceive their father—used to go to dances on the sly—or pretend illness, so as not to go to church. Her father is honest so far as I know—devoted to his family, industrious, a good mixer.

It is not fear of punishment surely. She attends Sunday school. Loves to read the stories of good little girls.

Please advise and *thanks*.

1. Baltimore: Williams and Wilkins, 1925.

July 21, 1931

My dear Mrs.:

I have read with a great deal of interest your letter addressed to me in care of the *Ladies' Home Journal*.

In the first place, from your description I would say that your granddaughter is a very lovely little girl. However I think you may be placing too much responsibility upon her shoulders—you say she is "a great help about the home, dependable, very trustworthy with baby." This may have the effect of making her over-conscientious in her anxiety to live up to adult standards.

Sometimes children tell fanciful stories with no intent to deceive. However in the case of your granddaughter I believe you are furnishing her with a quite powerful incentive for lying. She is trying to hold the approval of the elders in the family, which she feels she can do only by conforming to their exalted standards and demands. When she falls short of what she feels is expected of her, as any little girl is likely to do, she cannot bear to confess her shortcomings and thereby lose your love and confidence. Added to this is the fact that she has a younger sister who has had several promotions in one year in school and who is always truthful (i.e., has no temptation to tell lies) and that she, therefore, has a very strong rival for your good opinion which she values so highly. You say she does not fear punishment because her mother never punishes, but as you can see, to a sensitive and affectionate child your disappointment is a most serious punishment. I would suggest that you lessen the tension she feels by paying little attention to her lying and at the same time make more allowance for her childhood and inexperience in living.

Sincerely yours,

13.

Nonmarital Relationships

Aberdeen, Md.
Oct. 21, 1930

Dear Sir:

I have been reading your article "Mental Hygiene in the Home" and am writing you at once as to my own case. I do hope there is something you can do to help me.

I am a woman 35 years of age. About two years ago I suffered sort of a breakdown and was away from the office (I am a stenographer) for about 6 weeks. In August 1929 I took a ride one Saturday afternoon out through the country with a young man. We became friends thereafter. Last fall he told me about having a case for years with a young lady who had practically given him up. He had offered her an engagement ring and she passed him up. He heard nothing from her for several months. We kept going together at different intervals and this past spring or early summer she decided to write to him, and I now have reasons to believe they are sweethearts again. I hardly think they are engaged as yet. This young man has called 3 or 4 times since hearing from this young lady. I must confess this has been at my suggestion. Perhaps I should be more independent, and have vowed I would be, but inasmuch as I feel sometimes a hungering to talk with someone, I have asked him to my home, and knowing him so well, I felt like I must talk with him. I have not been engaged to him or been asked to marry him, but there was encouragement on both his side and mine.

Now I feel a wreck over the matter, and days and days it seems that the sun does not shine right, so to speak. I have lost interest in everything, and my only wish many times is to die. Buckets of tears have poured forth, and I feel that this is the worst thing I have ever had to happen in my life. This sounds doleful, but in view of the piece "A Daughter" in the article mentioned above, I felt that my case was somewhat similar, and that

235

perhaps you could do something to set me straight. You see this is a matter I can't discuss with everyone. It is something that I can't make amends for, and that is what so often grieves me—there isn't anything I can do about it. And to make things worse this young man works practically outside of my private office. I feel like the girl in the article, that I must be inferior or something, and everything in a social way hasn't much attraction for me. I go out, but am very unhappy, even though I do try and fool the public. I have been painting Christmas cards and also take china painting lessons on Saturday afternoons.

I feel I must not give up my office work. I am just a girl in moderate circumstances, my father is dead. I do not live with my mother, although she is living. I see her often though.

One reason, I think, why I feel so badly over this matter is because of the fact that just when I was down and out someone came into my life to make me happy, and now they have gone.

I have been advised to go away, but I feel that what is the use when I'll have to come back to the same scene again.

I think, too, that had I had the proper reserve nerve force I should probably been able to have stood up against odds.

What should I do? Should I ignore this young man entirely? I have tried this, but I believe I feel worse by it, yet, should he take a turn to marry, I should have to, so I feel at sea what to do.

I'll ask you to please keep this matter entirely confidential, and might say that only two or three of my friends really know about how I feel on this matter. The two friends with whom I live know about it, and know how distressed I am.

Thanking you very much for a reply, for which I enclose a stamp.

Yours very truly,

Nov. 4, 1930

My dear Miss:

I am very glad you wrote me and told me so much about yourself and about your problem. Writing it down this way and looking at it objectively ought to have helped you quite a little. It did, didn't it?

Didn't you see when you had finished writing this that a part of your depression and anxiety is dependent upon the uncertainty of things. You are still rather hoping that he loves you enough to marry you. You are afraid that the other girl may beat you out. You have been so much afraid that you have perhaps lost some of your pulling power, if I may use that expression, because of your anxiety and feeling of inferiority.

Now as I see it, there are several things that you could do. You could remember about the fox and grapes for one thing. There are lots of young men in the world and while they don't come along quite as fast as street cars, you are probably just as likely to meet another man as you were to meet this one. In fact I wouldn't give up the ship yet. I think if I were you I would try to make myself as attractive as possible and get this fellow if I really wanted him. You can be pretty certain that if you aren't able to get him, by being at your best, your prettiest, your sweetest, that you wouldn't be happy with him if you did get him. If the uncertainty is what is troubling you, why don't you bring it to a head. Why don't you frankly ask him if he is going to marry the other girl? You might even ask him in a caustic way if he intends to marry you. This would relieve your uncertainty and anxiety about it if you can't stand the suspense.

Back of this love affair, however, I think there is something else. One paragraph of your letter says that just when you were down and out someone came into your life that made you happy. You didn't tell me anything about the down and outness. If the only thing this young man has done for you is to make you feel that your life is worthwhile, I think the basis of your love affair is not a good one. Love does do that but it is only a flattering of the ego. Love must be a great deal more than that if the ultimate results of love are going to be permanent and satisfactory.

I hope some of these suggestions will change the color of things for you and I shall be interested in knowing the outcome of this matter.

Sincerely yours,

San Bernardino, Calif.
Nov. 3, 1930

Dear Doctor Menninger,

Oh, please listen and see if you can straighten this matter out for me. I've worked it over and over in my own mind, but I can't quite figure why it had to happen like this. I read your article in the November *Ladies' Home Journal.* I guess I'm like the girl you talked about. I don't understand the relations of women and men in the world.

I have a darling brother who is two and a half years younger than I am. (I'm twenty-four this Nov.) He has never been real strong; consequently, our whole family have always waited on him hand and foot. He is spoiled but I love him just the same. We have always been the best of pals. For years we had the same room with twin beds. I was taught that my body and his were different because he was a boy and I was a girl; that there was nothing to hide; and that I wore clothes because everybody else did and I would look queer, besides being cold sometimes, without any.

I am one of those very practical kind of people, always matter-of-fact, not a bit clever. You know, almost dumb when it comes to kidding and joking. I believe what people tell me when they are serious and sometimes when they are not serious. I have always taken a great deal of responsibility. My mother had to help my father in his business and I was responsible for meals and my brother.

I never have [had] a great many friends, but those I do have are very good friends. I think everything of my mother and father. My mother is like my brother, very clever and jolly—well liked by everyone. Dad is quiet in a crowd but at home he's heaps of fun. My family likes me but they think I'm awfully dumb about lots of things and I am.

In high school and college I was very busy. I worked my way through school. Much too busy to be bothered much about boys. Anyway my brother grew much taller than I. He is really clever and reads a great deal. Most people think he is the older. He always took me every place and I was very proud of him. The few boys I ever did go anywhere with couldn't hold a candle to my brother so I didn't think much of boys in general.

Last year I was ready to teach school and I got a position here in San Bernardino which is fifty-four miles from my home. I didn't know a person in the town. I had never been away from home for any length of time. I got a place to room and board. I didn't like it but my mother did. My work was in a Mexican school and at first I could not understand a word my third-graders said to me even though it was supposed to be English. I didn't have enough money to go home every weekend nor could my folks come over all the time. The teachers weren't particularly friendly and of course I was afraid of everything and everybody. Then along came F. He was the physical education teacher at school. He came over one night to show me about baseball. He is over six feet. A tall, blond, lovable sort of person. We liked each other from the very first. He was not only sympathetic but actually helpful. Of course I had never been waited upon or fussed over in the least. F. did both. He told me about his girl in Chicago and how much he liked her. I was interested and he told me lots about her and himself. By Christmas we were the best of chums, went everywhere together. I helped him buy her present. I slipped in a handkerchief for her from myself. I know this sounds silly, but I called him my big brother and I meant it. I sincerely think he meant it too.

In January, a college friend (H.) and myself rented an apartment. F. practically lived at my house. It was mine, for I took all the responsibility—cooked, washed, ironed, cleaned, paid the bills. F. had a friend T., who was in and out a great deal, too. I arranged my whole life to best serve those three people, H., T. and F. I worked hard and I loved it. I treated F. as I had been taught to treat my brother.

I undressed in front of him or dressed as the case might be. When I was tired, he rocked me to sleep or read me stories. He kissed me and I kissed him but there was no emotional strain of which I was conscience [*sic*]. His girl, G., finally came to Los Angeles. She came to my house here in San Bernardino on the average of every two weeks and stayed a week at a time. We had loads of fun. Then one time F. came back from Los Angeles where he had been with G. over the weekend, and said that he couldn't come over so much. She had made a fuss. I was too hurt and surprised for words. F. didn't understand and I didn't. We had never hidden one thing from her. I had always thought I was perfectly square and fair. The result was that I all of a sudden realized that I was only three years younger than F. and that I wanted him around. He only stayed away one week. I suppose I changed then. Anyway things began to develop into sexual emotions. I trusted F. to the very limit. All he had to say was, "Don't you believe in me, honey?" He finally dragged out of me the fact that I loved him. He didn't mean to hurt me. He was dreadfully sorry. It was as much my fault as his. I gave him every opportunity. I never said no.

Of course, he married G. I knew all the time he would. They live here in San Bernardino. We are supposedly very good friends. I like his wife and still respect and adore F. It hurts like everything to hear him call her "honey." Yet I'm glad they are happy. G. believes we have told her the truth that there is nothing and never has been anything between F. and myself but good, clean friendship. I want to have it that way.

I have started to sing in a church choir and teach a Sunday school class. I've joined a teachers' bridge club. I can teach school and I really like it. But at night all I really want to do is to stay home and dream about the good times I had last year. I'm so lonesome for F., I'm sick. I'm scared to death that I'll say or do something in front of G. that will let her know the real truth. I hate this hiding something. F. likes me and shows it. I want to be happy and good friends with them both.

I know I've been terribly foolish. But must I be ashamed of having loved him? Am I a bad girl? We had so much fun together. We understand each other so well. Was it all wrong? Can't I ever again be just sincerely and honestly his friend and nothing more? F. and I have talked it over. There seems to be nothing he can do. Most of the time I'm bright and cheerful because it hurts him so when I'm not. But I want to really feel that way inside. Can you, will you do anything to help me?

Very respectfully,

Dec. 2, 1930

My dear Miss

I have read very carefully every word of your letter of October 25 [*sic*] addressed to me in care of the *Ladies' Home Journal*.

It is quite obvious to me what has happened to you but I don't know whether I can make it clear in a letter but I shall try. You see you grew up loving your brother and thinking that he was the great and perfect lover. This made things very pleasant and happy for you at home but unfortunately we cannot all our lives stay children and live at home. There comes a time, and it should be much earlier than it occurred in your life, when we transfer our expectations for love from inside the family to outside the family. You have been extremely blind as to the significance of sex in the world and this is because you grew up in this beautiful nature of love, meaning by that nonsexual. Then you met this fine young fellow who was evidently a good deal like yourself and you had a typical love affair which you both refused to recognize in its real sense. He didn't want to recognize it as such because it would have hurt his conscience on account of the woman to whom he was engaged and you couldn't recognize it as such because you were brought up with a curious blindness about sex, and a sort of loyalty to your brother which prevents you from seeing men in a correct light.

You ask if you should be ashamed of having loved him. I don't think anyone ought ever to be ashamed of love. I don't think love is anything to be ashamed of under any circumstances. I think you ought to be a little ashamed of your ignorance but even that is not really your fault. It is something, however, which you can remedy. Your second question is, "Am I bad girl?" I haven't the slightest idea what a bad girl is. I think a bad girl is a term used by some people to call attention to the sins of other people and thereby distract attention from their own. Of course you are not a bad girl. If anything you are too good a girl. But your goodness is not on a good basis. You say you understood each other so well. As a matter of fact, you understood each other but you did not understand yourselves. "Was it all wrong!" you ask. There again I don't know what you are talking about. I don't know exactly what you mean by the word wrong. Evidently it turned out rather badly and from a pragmatic standpoint it must have been wrong. "Can you ever be his sincere and honest friend and nothing more?" You never have been his sincere and honest friend and nothing more. What I mean is that you have always been something more. But you will not continue to be; gradually I think you will adjust yourself, find another lover, and I hope deal much better with the situation as a result of this experience.

In the meantime I would certainly do a little reading if I were you and a little studying. Read some novels dealing with love problems, for example, read Theodore Dreiser's *An American Tragedy,* and a recent collection of essays called *A New Generation* edited by [V. F.] Calverton and [Samuel] Schmalhausen. Read Freud's book *Totem and Taboo* translated by [A. A.] Brill. When you get thru you will be a wiser and I think also a happier girl. I am awfully glad you wrote me because I think it may be the turning point which might otherwise be destined to a series of incredible and explicable disasters which you can just as well avoid.

Sincerely yours,

Worcester, Mass.
Nov. 18, 1930

Dear Doctor Menninger:

Because I need a man's point of view rather badly, I am writing you in the hope that you will give me a little advice, and I will try to put the situation briefly.

Two and a half years ago I met a young man my age who worked out of town but was in the practice of coming home every other weekend. He was considered by his friends as sophisticated and uninterested in girls so that I was surprised when he seemed to take an interest in myself and invited me to a party at his home. After that he came home practically every weekend and if we were not alone we went out with another couple, our best friends.

The third time we went out together he kissed me and I told him I did not care for it and it was three months or so before he did again and I allowed it because I had grown fond of him so that one might say we went in for heavy "petting" but at least we both kept our heads.

How can I describe his peculiar disposition? At times he was cold and distant like a stranger, then again sophisticated and cynical and at such times would speak about various men friends who had married and wished they hadn't or had changed because of it and saying what a burden children were. Then again he would be crazily boyish, up to all kinds of pranks, terrible tease. Thirdly he was the kind of man I adored, sympathetic, kind, would hold a newborn baby in his arms, speak about what a home means—just awfully nice.

However, he never spoke of marriage as between the two of us nor said he cared for me. He'd call me sweet, admire my new dress or tell me my hair looked nifty, etc. But still, I felt he did care but didn't want to—he was too accustomed to his independence. Then, too, his work wasn't to his satisfaction, hoped for changes which never came about and he was clever too but in the artistic line which doesn't pay any too well.

In a sense he treated me badly—for instance I would be expecting to see him or hear from him, but suddenly for two or three weeks not a word and then he would show up as though nothing had happened. I spoke to him about it after a few times and then he would be angelic for a while but act up again—you know, let me sit by the phone and wait! We had our first real quarrel a year ago, both acting very childish and obstinate—he wanted to go to a football game and I wanted to go to a party—all his little meanness came to my mind and I told him I never, never wanted to see him again (very melodramatic). He took me at my word and after a month I wrote him a comical note saying I did want to see him within a hundred years and he came back flying. Perhaps I would not have written but I knew it was a trying time for him as his father was very ill with cancer and his time was limited. I had to swallow a good deal of pride to write the note but considered it worth the pride.

Everything went smoothly then until the early spring when he began again not to say whether he was coming home or not and then if he happened to, would phone me. I tried to cure him by being busy when he called but it was awfully hard to do this. Finally we had a talk—he told me I hadn't trained him right from the beginning—I told him it was natural for a girl to save certain days for one man in particular—then he said something about my being busy and then I wouldn't be disappointed if he didn't phone—lots of words and not getting anywhere so that finally I told him to go home. He tried to tease me into a happier mood but was unsuccessful. Well, for two or three weeks after he tried to get me but I was always busy and he wrote crazy notes in Chinese with lots of exclamation points. Then his father died after an agonizing two weeks for the family. Having had trouble myself, it was only natural for me to write a note of sympathy to him, taking care not to mention in any way that I hoped to see him again.

He wrote in answer and was very dear—then through the spring and early summer he acted very well, asking for his dates, seeing me weekends and writing during the week.

To the best of my knowledge everything was smooth and I saw him as usual—the last weekend in July. During the following week I wrote him a comical letter, something about opportunity knocking and I was visiting relatives the next weekend and he could take out one of his other girls. Also that I might be busy every weekend during August as my Company gave us extra time off at the weekends.

A little about myself—my mother died when I was eighteen and since that time I had worked and kept house for my stepfather for seven years. My stepfather made things rather unbearable for me and as he was about to marry again, upon the advice of my relatives and friends, I left home and roomed out. All my relatives live out of town—I am absolutely alone but have some wonderful friends. It is only natural that when I get an opportunity I visit these out-of-town relatives.

To come back to the young man, since my supposedly comical letter, I have heard not absolutely one word of him. I can't understand it, I follow along every line of thought. Did he misconstrue my letter, was he offended because I was to be busy during the following month, did he merely take this opportunity to drop me because no longer interested, was it because his best boy friend and my best girl friend are getting really serious and he believed it the gentlemanly thing to allow me to think of him as a cad perhaps?

The end of Sept., again swallowing my pride or conceit, I dropped him a brief note of one sentence asking if he were well, how his work was and why hadn't I heard from him. No answer. Here, I suppose you'll say I should know that he is no longer interested. I've tried to give you an inkling into his character. He is extremely stubborn and would bite off his nose to spite his face. He has a jealous streak and the mere mention of a male cousin of mine makes him furious. I have reviewed the last evening we were together and I faintly recollect making a tactless remark about being at a certain place to dine and dance several times. He was not my escort but it was at one of those times when he had been acting up, as it were.

I am twenty-seven, have had other boy friends, so that this is not a case of infatuation. Recently I have tried to enjoy the company of other men but I can't forget the other. I have absolutely no news of him although I meet and talk with his sister frequently but he has always been close-mouthed about his affairs and I know he wouldn't care to have me discuss ours with his sister. She probably is in the dark also. His best friend for a year has been a long way off and they never correspond, both hating to write letters—they always received news of each other through we two girls.

Now the point to all this is that having gone through a good many sorrows myself, losing my mother, my home, and knowing the dreary aspect ahead without these loved things, can I swallow my pride for the third time and write a frank letter to him asking what it's all about?

Will you give me a man's point of view on all this—what shall I do or is there nothing to do? Am I to look elsewhere for my happiness and if so, how am I to know that I will not make a similar mistake on someone else? My friends tell me I am too kind, but it is because I appreciate kindness and it is such a little thing to be kind.

I haven't said or expressed what I wanted to, it's taken so much writing. Please do not publish this, my friends would only too quickly recognize the story as they read your column.

Am I not entitled, just a little, to know why our friendship has so suddenly ceased? I could reconcile myself if there were another girl for him or even if he were just disinterested in me, but it's wondering if I am at fault anywhere. One of my friends has said that if he cares, he'll come back, but if he had been wounded in any way or doubted me, wouldn't he hesitate being so obstinate anyway? I am very unhappy about all this—can you help me?

Sincerely,

Dec. 12, 1930

My dear Miss:

I have read with care your letter of November 18 addressed to me in care of the *Ladies' Home Journal*.

I should be glad to do what I can to give you a man's view as you call it. However, I hope it will be a little more than merely a man's view; I hope it will be the view of one who can look at these things from the standpoint of the abnormal psychology involved.

It strikes me that your boyfriend is trying his best to hurt you. I think you have described his character very well and summed it all up when you say that he is the kind of person who cuts off his nose to spite his face. Now a person who cuts off his own nose to spite his face will also be glad to cut off other people's noses to spite his face. Apparently this is what your friend likes to do.

Now in view of that fact, let us ask ourselves why it is that you are so anxious to have him. Do you want to be loved by someone who hurts you? Do you want a man to express his love to you by hurting you? Many women do. Many women put up with all sorts of abuse from men when it is quite unnecessary that they do so. They seem to expect that men should hurt them. Over in Europe it is done with fists and clubs. You know the old story, no doubt, which is a true one, about the Russian woman who complained that her husband didn't love her any more. The judge asked her why she thought so and the woman replied, "He hasn't beaten me for a week."

Now if you want to be like a Russian woman or a Romanian woman or whatever it was, I think I would swallow my pride and get back this fellow at all costs because he is apparently the kind of a chap who will give you plenty of pain. But if that is not the kind of a lover you want, I think I would take his silence and indifference for what he apparently intends it to be and look for a new lover. I don't think you will have any difficulty and I think you will be taking a great step in advance for your own mental health when you elect a different kind of a friend, and cease craving this one.

Sincerely yours,

Brooklyn, N.Y.
Jan. 21, 1931

Dear Dr. Menninger:

I am sure I do not know whether I should confide my troubles to you or to some "advice to the lovelorn." It is such a simple thing and yet one that has made me dreadfully unhappy and "blue."

I am twenty years old, I can imagine your smile at that, but for all my youth I have one earnest desire—marriage. I awake with it, live with it all day long, and then go to bed with it. My greatest horror is that I may live to be an "old maid!"

I know myself well enough to realize that unless I have some one close to me who cares a great deal about me I am an unhappy mortal. I am not self-sufficient, I do not enjoy going to lectures, plays, and musicals alone. I want some one near who will be both a comrade and a lover. I want marriage!

If I could only do something to alleviate this desire before it becomes an obsession. Please, Dr. Menninger, don't think that I am sexually inclined, that that is all that ails me, for I don't believe it is. I hate to be kissed and mauled unless it is someone for whom I really care. And I am not a lump of ugly clay. I am conceited enough to say that I am a good-looking, presentable girl.

This sounds a great deal like a lot of silly raving, but I had to get it off my mind.

If you can suggest anything to help me I should appreciate it a great deal.

Sincerely yours,

Feb. 7, 1931

My dear Miss:

I have read with interest your letter of January 21 addressed to me in care of the *Ladies' Home Journal.*

I don't think you are likely to ever get married unless you change your attitude toward it rather radically, perhaps I should say happily married. Most anyone can get married but it is quite another thing to get married in a way in which one doesn't have more regrets than happiness. If you go at it in this spirit that I have got to get married to someone quick expressed in your letter, you are certainly going to make a mess of things.

I think you are quite right in the latter part of your letter where you say the desire to marry has become an obsession. An obsession is an idea which comes to us for reasons quite other than the apparent one and has an entirely different significance than the apparent significance. In other words, I do not think that your desire to get married could be explained by the ordinary rational reasons for marriage. I think you want to get married for some unconscious and neurotic reason which is not at all clear to you. Hence I think you could get quite a little help by talking the matter over with a psychiatrist.

Sincerely yours,

Indiana
May 20, 1931

Dear Sir:

I am troubled with an emotional conflict which is ruining my life, and am taking advantage of my interest in your page in the *Ladies' Home Journal* to appeal to you for aid. I presume that you get many letters of the type which I am going to write to you, and hope that you have some solution for the troubles which I know are very real to young girls in my position.

I am a young girl, aged 22, a teacher in high school by profession, was graduated two years ago from the state university; I am deeply and passionately in love with a fine and noble young man, aged 24, who was graduated last year from the law school of the same university; he returns my love with the same depth and passion that I feel for him. We know each other very well, having been acquainted for four years. We did not fall in love at first sight, but were very much attracted to each other at once, and during the two years that we were both in college, this attachment deepened. We have been separated for two years. We are both serious-minded and ambitious and anxious to do right; we are happiest in each other's company and have to make ourselves associate with others for we know we should. We both love to read together and have the same tastes in books; we both are learning golf and all each other's faults, which are many, and we respect each other's good qualities. I am in temperament inclined to be impetuous, impulsive and romantic though I try to curb this nature and temper it; my lover is matter-of-fact, and willing to give up what he wants for what he thinks best, a thing not many young men are wise enough to do. You can see that I love and admire him a great deal, and that I consider us well-suited. I suppose that you even wonder why I am writing; but here is the fly in the ointment, or rather the dragon in the gravel-pit . . . neither of us have a cent of money and we cannot be married. This has caused us so much suffering that I sometimes wish we had just starved together, tho' of course that is an extremity of suffering compared to which our troubles are paltry. Anyway, they are real enough to me, and I am writing to you for a solution.

I presume that by now you have guessed the difficulties in our way, and have the key to the emotional disturbance that I mentioned. It is of course the eternal question of sex, and I am writing to you to know what we can do to solve it. Young people in love all have to face this question, of course, but most of their troubles are short-lived and the one I love and I have been separated for two years, and will be for I don't know how many more, so if you can give us some comfort it will be an aid.

He is a young lawyer, one year out of college; I do not need to add that, though he is doing very well and is thoroughly well-liked by the city-attorney under whom he is working, he is not making enough to buy us stale buns, let alone raisin bread! I am a young teacher, trying to teach school, and so bothered and torn-in-two by my very natural desires that I want to get some relief before the fall term. We are over a hundred miles apart, he in a medium-sized city of about 150,000 and I in a small town of less than 5,000. I am an only child at home and he is the only one now in his home, though he has one younger married sister. You can easily see the complications that beset us. I should explain that his father is 65 and irritable and that my lover will not have us make our home there, nor is it wise for young couples ever to live with another family, do you think? On the other hand, the years stretch out bleakly before us. I should tell you that in Indiana the married teacher is barred from teaching, so it is impossible for us to do as we would like . . . that is, marry and each continue working.

Now here is our emotional situation. We are man and wife in spirit. That is what we want to be, not lovers, for we want our love to last a lifetime. We have traveled together in the freedom which is possible today . . . we have visited each other for as long as two-week periods . . . we feel free to discuss any problem or to make any confidence . . . in other words, we are just an unmarried man and wife. We have never yielded fully to our love, for we have not considered it wise. But we are strongly sexed, evenly mated, passionately in love, and you can, I am sure, understand our situation. You can also understand that I can confide or obtain help from no one and that I wish professional advice.

Am I just making a mountain out of a molehill? Should we become lovers and think no more about it? I will confess that most of my friends have been lovers with their husbands, but they have not had the separation, nor the suspense that we have had. The irresponsible ones have just gone on a few wild parties and then been married, and the serious-minded ones, into which class I fall, have worried themselves to death about it as I have, but have had a speedy end to their miseries by marriage. Sometimes I think that such a solution would solve our situation beautifully, but you see I do not want in any way to cheapen our love or to have my lover tire of me which seems to be the probable end of any liaison. My lover, being a man, does not worry about the sexual end of our affairs at all and he urges me not to; he wants me to be happy and it worries him dreadfully to know that I am really quite miserable about the most satisfying relationship of my life. He tells me that it is best to satisfy our perfectly natural desires and not to worry about it; I agree with him but it is impossible for me to be so easy-going about a situation so fraught with dangers . . . our love is my life's work, you might say, and I want it to last! And we only satisfy our passion by substitutes; I hate substitutes, deceit, the eternal acting as if we were casual sweethearts when we are at heart man and wife. So you see my life is one long conflict. I believe that people should be happy and should use their intelligence to attain that state, but mine seems to have given me no help and I am appealing to you.

I should tell you that I had a thoroughly rounded college education. I am a member of Phi Beta Kappa, had all the social life and dates that any one girl could want, was a columnist on the university paper, in the university musical revue, member of Theta Sigma Phi, had the highest grade possible in practice teaching and the most hearty and flattering recommendations possible from the professors and deans. My personality is all that got me these honors, for I've never had money to spend on clothes. You can see that I had every reason to think that I would succeed in my profession, and you can see that it grieves me to realize that my personality is no longer vivacious, gay and irresponsible, but that I am un-natural, unhappy and, I fear, unadjusted. Only with my lover am I happy, and then not wholly, and we can be together only once every two or three months. He is of course devoting himself to his business and cannot get away often, nor do I urge him to neglect it for me. I am in my small-town home where I have few friends as most of them are married and moved away. Small towns are very dull places, sometimes!

I like my work as a teacher, and am fitted for it perfectly if I could only get my mind at rest. Knowing the theory of making your personality whole again by casting out what is troubling you, I tried to break up with my lover, and put him entirely out of my life, for the future apart looked hopeless to me. I felt quite normal for a few weeks, but I do not need to add that only his death or his marrying another person could really put him out of my mind and heart. He is not the kind of man who can be trifled with, but he understands me awfully well and I wrote him why I did as I did, and we are trying once again to come to a satisfactory agreement. We have tried to be just friends, but our times together are all alike, regardless of any resolutions to the contrary. First, we are intensely happy just to be together . . . then with kisses and caresses we are uplifted away from all our cares and worries . . . and then comes the reaction. Being a teacher, and an example to my pupils, I feel that my emotional life should be the correct one. My ultimate love, however, means more to me than my profession, and I am seeking now to bridge over these years when we must be apart. Am I just taking everything too hard? What do doctors advise in such cases? You can see that in a small town I must be extremely careful. I do not need to tell you that I suffer from nervousness and nervous indigestion, all of which I am sure is mental for I am strong and healthy, tho' I fear I am turning into a hypochondriac. Please help me right myself; no one guesses that I am anything but "normal" (whatever that is) for I lead an active life in my community in every way, but I am oh, so troubled. I should tell you that I have black hair and blue eyes . . . is that some sort of emotional type? Does that explain why I am taking my life so seriously? Does that give me a tendency to be morbid?

Please help me, Dr. Menninger. Would a secret marriage be the thing for us? There should be in society some provision for couples like us, but it seems that the world is so organized that we can have no compensations for what is really a strong and true love. Will everything come out in the wash, and is this just a temporarily hard period? I am willing to do anything that will solve my mental condition. I really try to conquer it myself, but here comes my love and tears me in two. Are there books you can recommend for me? Is there a course of action prescribed by psychiatrists for couples like us? Neither of us had any intimacies with others before our love . . . of course we kissed a few people . . . but this is the real thing and I am so proud to have a lover who never degraded himself and I don't want him to degrade himself for me either. What can we do?

I realize that you are a very busy man and doing lots of good for unadjusted people, but will you please answer me in whatever detail you consider necessary? Talk to me frankly, for I only want the truth and want to do what is best. Please treat this letter as absolutely personal, for I have lots of friends who might recognize it if printed. You may of course use the situation in your article if it will help the many thousand of other young people who probably share my difficulties.

Thanking you in advance, I am . . .

Jul. 6, 1931

My dear Miss:

I have read several times your letter of May 20th addressed to me in care of the *Ladies' Home Journal*. It is one of the best of its sort which I have ever received.

The first two pages I understand very well. You are separated from a man you love, you see him all too infrequently, you are both passionate, you cannot be married, you wonder if it is permissible for you to have sexual relations without offending your conscience or his or becoming pregnant or stirring up a scandal, or most important of all, losing his love.

Now the answer to such a problem from my standpoint would be that the only reason which you advance, namely that of losing his love, is the least important one because if you love each other enough to desire sexual intimacy as intensely and as sincerely as your letter makes it evident that you do, I do not think the danger of losing his love is very great. I think the only dangers to consider are the tangible ones of whether or not you are fairly confident of birth control measures, of the possibilities of avoiding scandal in causing yourself distress in your present location, etc.

You say that your lover feels that it would be best for you to satisfy your perfectly natural desires and have no worry about it and it is not quite clear to me how you differ with this except for the feeling that you might lose his love. I quite agree with you that frustration and substitutes of unsatisfactory sorts are much less mentally healthy than frank indulgence in sexual intercourse, providing you do not run real dangers from the latter and providing you do not have an unconscious sense of guilt which would interfere with your being completely honest and wholehearted in so doing.

The third page of your letter, however, gives me some misgivings as to what your real mental state about the matter is. It is not quite clear to me in other words why it is that you wanted to break off the love affair with your lover when you are quite sure that you loved him so much. It is also not clear to me why you must postpone your marriage so long. Where there is a will there is a way you know and while I agree with you that you should not handicap your future by getting married when too heavily in debt, however I do not think you have convinced yourself that it is absolutely necessary to wait so long for any good reason.

Furthermore, I do not think that because your husband had previous sexual experiences that he would have been degraded. I only mention this because from several things in your letter I rather suspect that you still attach to sexual relations a certain evilness or wickedness unless they be blessed with legal or at least emotional sanction. This is a very natural and widely prevalent attitude on the part of all of us because for so long sex has been so severely taboo.

I should think it would be very much better if you would take a very healthy-minded practical attitude toward the matter. If you want sexual relations and can avoid serious complications and dangers, regard that as a very natural thing to do without any regrets or remorse. A great many people take that position nowadays until one might almost say it is the prevalent mode of action altho it is not the prevalent official attitude of society. Society still condemns it officially and it is therefore necessary as you say to keep it strictly a personal and private affair.

I think you might get a great deal of satisfaction out of reading some books like Bertrand Russell's wife's book *The Right to Be Happy* and her husband's book *Education and the Good Life* and also his other book on *The Conquest of Happiness.* Read Mrs. Russell's book first.

I may say in closing that I feel quite certain that your feeling of great tenseness and anxiety about the matter would probably be rather speedily relieved if you and your lover could be together intimately for a time (it is probably dependent upon your highly charged erotic feelings), providing that you do not have about the matter a sense of guilt which would cause what you call a reaction. This is the reason that I never directly advise people to do this because I cannot take the responsibility of advising you to do something which you may unconsciously condemn in yourself so severely that it would do more harm than good.

I can only say that I would advise you to follow the dictates of your intelligence rather than of your emotions. What do you really think is the wisest thing to do?

Sincerely yours,

Texas
Oct. 5, 1931

Dear Dr. Menninger:

I am a girl twenty-four years of age. I am very restless and believe the reason for this is that I have nothing on which to pin my hopes, affections etc., aside from my family, which seems very insufficient at times. Allow me to picture myself as others see me, in so much as I have heard.

I have lots of girl friends. Girls like me from the beginning and like me more all along. I can really get over big with girls. I am "the life of the party" with girls. I am considered very witty. I have been told I am beautiful, but some of my friends are inclined to laugh this off. I really think I am quite ugly. I am tall (extremely, 5′8″) very, very dark, have freckles, which are fierce, and, of course, dark eyes and hair. People usually think my eyes and hair very pretty. Have nice well-kept teeth. I am considered sarcastic, although it is surely unintentional, and I guard against it. Taking things as a whole, I am considered very attractive. Please do not believe me *conceited,* as I really lack *self-confidence*[1] to a certain extent. But I am told often by various groups of friends that everyone who knows me likes me.

Now the big issue—why do men not like me? They seem to take one look and that is more than enough. They almost ignore me entirely. Of

---

1. Menninger has underlined the two phrases, noting in the margin, "One explains the other."

course, there have been exceptions to this. Several boys have seemed to really like me, but usually they are the type I do not care for at all. I like the athletic, real he-man type. I do not like to go with a boy unless I like him, I mean unless he appeals to me. I will not go with a boy when I do not like them, just to have a good time.

I believe in necking, drinking and smoking, although I do not smoke. This cannot be the reason they do not like me, as I have not always done these things, and it was the same.

Older men usually like me. The other girls' boy friends like me. Married men invariably like me. I *get over awfully big* with my friends' husbands, cousins' husbands etc.[2]

Boys, I have learned, class me either as a "stick" or as wild as possible. They seem disappointed either way.

One boy said I was too extreme, too sweet, or too sarcastic.[3] One said I was very clever, but also quite disgusting at times. Another said I was too, well, I suppose you would say, high-hat. That I expected to do everybody anyway and get by with it. I am very high-tempered and quite plain-spoken, and above *all* things I cannot stand to be domineered.[4]

There has been one man in my life, whom I thought I really loved, and whom I believe I still love, if I only had an opportunity. We lived at the same place, when I was away working. When I first met him he appealed to me very much, but he had practically none of the qualities I had always thought essential. He is twenty-nine and a butcher. Works in his uncle's grocery and market in a large city. He is Bohemian. Well, my family, friends and everyone I knew all but had fits to think I was interested in him. To make matters worse he was married when about nineteen, divorced in less than two years, and since that time has lived a while with first one immoral woman and then another. I have heard from several sources that before he married this woman, who was absolutely nothing, that he was very clean-minded and very innocent. He is rather a carefree sort of person, but I believe he hates the life he leads, and he has told me himself he hates these women, but it seems he just doesn't have spunk enough to get a new grip on life. Perhaps he thinks it is futile. I believe, were he to marry he would be a perfect husband. He is good-natured, never quarrels, etc. I would look at him and think I could see how utterly miserable he was and how hopeless his life seemed to him, even though outwardly he seemed very happy and carefree. That was it, he seemed too much that way don't

2. Menninger: "typical."
3. Menninger: "i.e., submissive and then hostile because of it."
4. Menninger: "rejection of feminine role."

you see? No one seemed to see this but me, and I cannot believe I was wrong. I want to go into great detail so you will understand perfectly and can give me your candid opinion—is it love or infatuation? I have been away from that city seven months and my feeling has not changed at all. He did not seem interested in me at first, but after a while did seem very interested. For fear he would see how hopelessly mad about him I was I could hardly act natural, was quite tongue-tied when he was about and when I did say something it always seemed sarcastic. He always thought everything I said was cute and funny, at first. Later, nothing I *ever* said was interesting or funny which made me more sarcastic, to show him I did not care, you see. All the time it was almost worrying me to death. Finally I took to going on drinking parties, etc., just the thing he hates. I knew he hated it, but I was tired getting no response from him. I was trying in such a big way to show him I didn't care that I made pretty much of an ass of myself I am sure.

He always seemed jealous of the boys I went with. Our relatives, whom we both lived with, told me I was too sarcastic, that he was afraid to be decent to me, lest I snap his head off. Which of course humiliated him, but it would happen every time in spite of all my efforts. Oh what fools we can make of ourselves. I ridiculed the women he went with. Well I must have been a hell-cat, right?[5] I wanted to love him and pet him and tell him how much I loved him and believed in him and how I expected him to throw up the life he leads and be worthwhile. I did on one or two occasions when I had had too much to drink. For all his way of living etc., he treated me with the highest respect. When I was away during vacation time he would bring his girls to the house, but not once when I was there. Why?

I had pneumonia while home for Xmas holidays, and only worked a short while afterwards, and came home rather unexpectedly on account of my sister's death. I have seen him once during this seven months, and he seemed glad to see me, nothing more. If I was, and still am, willing to give up friends, if necessary, anything for him, do I not love him, or is it because I cannot have him? He doesn't seem indifferent, he just seems at a loss as to what to do, if anything. Should I write him?[6] Should I forget him?[7] The boys I meet I am not interested in. Would I be foolish to marry one so out of my class socially, of different nationality, one whose ideas on life are so different from my own? I do not think so, but at times I am scared, and I cannot bring myself to pursue him enough to get him interested again. I

5. Menninger: "Yes."
6. Menninger: "Why not?"
7. Menninger: "Can you?"

heard that someone told him I had tuberculosis when I had to quit work. I was run-down, in a bad nervous state and did have a spot on my lung from the pneumonia but have fully recovered now. Sometimes I believe it is foolish to think he cares, and then I cannot see why he doesn't when I care so much for him. I did not intend to write this much, but what a relief to unburden one's mind, and I feel so confident you can help me.

One more question—with the above physical condition, would marriage or having children cause me to have tuberculosis? I have heard such but not from a reliable source.

Please advise me on these points and I will try to abide by your advice and will appreciate it greatly. Enclosed is a stamped, addressed envelope.

Your page in the *Ladies' Home Journal* is so very interesting I think you should really have twice the space. I'll have to speak to the editor.

Sincerely,

Jan. 18, 1932

My dear Miss:

I am very sorry to have been so long in answering your letter but the delay was unavoidable.

Your first question was "Why do men not like me?" Then you tell me of one man who seems to have liked you very much and you say you believe you love him, and yet according to your own story you were sarcastic to him, humiliated him on every occasion, and ridiculed him, in spite of all your efforts not to do so. I think this answers your question as to why men do not like you, because even if you do not show your hostility toward them quite so openly in every case, yet they probably feel it in your manner toward them.

The question then is: "Why do I have such hostility toward men? Why am I self-conscious and ill at ease with them?" This attitude probably dates back many years and perhaps originated in your childhood. I cannot trace its causes but perhaps you can and if you recognize it and understand it to some extent I believe you will be able to solve the problem of the particular man whom you love. I think at present the conflict within yourself is so great that you do not know what you wish to do concerning him. You say you are willing to give up friends, anything for him and yet you cannot bring yourself to pursue him enough to get him interested again. The apparent contradiction in these statements and the inconsistencies in your treatment of him represent the conflict between your love for him and your unconscious hostility toward him.

Sincerely yours,

Illinois
Oct. 5, 1931

Dr. Karl Menninger:

I am a school teacher. I have been criticized for having too idealistic views. I haven't minded the criticisms. I refuse to do what the crowd does just because the crowd does it. I don't drink or smoke. I have friends, very dear friends among different classes of people. I love to go places and do things but I can be just as happy with a book or a bit of sewing.

Last spring I fell very much in love with a man two years my senior. I am very sure of his love for me, yet there are circumstances that make me worry. He likes to go with the crowd and do as the crowd does. He enjoys a social glass of beer.[1] I have never seen him drunk and he says I never will. He would like to serve beer to his friends in our home. I am afraid I can never stand it. I shall always be afraid of the time when he might get drunk. I am a strong prohibitionist.

He has many fine qualities to offset this one.[2] I have never seen him angry. He is very patient with me when I lose my temper. He gave up his country and a comfortable income in Denmark to become an American and marry me. He works hard and makes a good living. Would I be lowering my ideals if I give in about his drinking?[3] He sometimes drinks as high as four glasses of beer in a day.

I want to thank you in advance for the help I am sure you can give me.

Sincerely,

Jan. 18, 1932

My dear Miss:

I am sorry that my answer to your letter of several weeks ago has been delayed so long. Perhaps you have decided your course of action before this, but if not I shall tell you what my opinion is.

In every successful human relationship a process of adaptation must go on. This adaptation means that one gives up certain prejudices, ideas and habits for the sake of the loved one and on the other hand accepts certain ideas and habits of the loved one with tolerance. The extent to which one can adapt himself depends largely on how much he loves. The question which you must answer therefore is: "How much do I love this young man? Do I love him or my prejudices most?" He has evidently already settled

---

1. Menninger has added in the margin, "Which do you love more, him or your prejudices?"
2. Menninger: "Don't agree that it is a fault"
3. Menninger: "raising."

this question in his mind, since as you tell me, he has already given up a great deal for you.

You will probably say, "But this is more than a prejudice on my part; it is a matter of principle." If the young man were trying to persuade you to drink and you believed it was wrong for you to drink then indeed it might be a matter of principle. In that case he would be doing just what you want to do to him, i.e., imposing *his* standards and *his* ideas upon you because he thought they were better than yours. But I gather from your letter that he is far too tolerant and kind to try to dominate you in this way. If you can be equally magnanimous toward him and toward the things in him which you find alien, I believe your ideals will be raised instead of lowered by your association with him.

Sincerely yours,

Mansfield, Ohio
Mar. 17, 1932

Dear Dr. Menninger,

Your articles in the *Ladies' Home Journal* each month have interested me for a long time. Your replies to the published letters seem wise and I am sure you, as a neutral person, have given much help to countless people. I am wondering if you can give me some valuable help.

My life would be classified under "wrong investment of love." I am finding it difficult to marry and yet it is the thing I want more than anything else in the world. I am 36 years of age, so you see I should have married 8 or 10 years ago. I have had several opportunities to marry but do not seem to fall for those who care for me. One trouble has been that I idealized one fellow with whom I grew up and he was killed in the war. For some years after, I compared all men I met to him. This man, a Princeton graduate, was a student by nature, musical, athletic enough and such an all-round fellow that no one seemed his equal. He is my ideal whom I have never forgotten.

My own home is a happy one. A bachelor in town once made the statement that he thought my parents the best mated and happiest pair in town. I appreciate my parents and my home, but I am not being developed by being deprived of the responsibility of my own home.

I have had advantages and traveled more than is the privilege of many. It is surprising that I am having this difficulty. When I was having a gay time during my High School years, one of the older residents said she thought I would be first in my crowd to marry. Some of my mother's friends said I was an ideal girl for I was not boy-crazy but was more of a comrade with boys. I am athletically inclined. During High School I was one of the best tennis players in town. I am rather a natural golf player, loved to ride a bicycle and horseback and play baseball. I am in splendid health and weigh 125 lbs., being 5'4" tall.

Upon being graduated from High School, I went east for 2 years. The war was on then. After school, I went to New York City, had a job, and lived in an apartment with 2 other girls. When the war was over, I came home. I wanted to do something and put my name in as a substitute for teaching. The Supt. gave me a job of assisting a 2nd grade teacher who had too large a school. The next 5 years, I taught a 2nd grade here. The next year, I went down to Miami, Florida, and easily obtained the position of teaching the 3rd & 4th grades. During this time, one summer I took a 3 months trip to Europe with two friends. After 6 years of teaching, I decided to make a change and go back into business. The woman secretary and policy clerk who had been in my father's office for years left at this time and suggested my taking her place.

Last summer, I spent my vacation in Oklahoma and learned to fly an airplane. I flew it just once alone before coming home. I enjoyed this experience immensely and may finish getting a license this summer. I might have stopped for an interview with you while on this trip last summer.

I realize that I should be intelligent enough to manage my own affairs. I should be more of a go-getter. I have a shy quality and am afraid I am too reserved. However I like to meet people and have many warm friends. I have many good friends among women. My family say I am more myself when married men are around than single men. My married friends' husbands like to play golf and bridge with me.

Now my question, Dr. Menninger, is—could you help me to find a man who would be a good mate for me. I feel that I could make a good home and be a good companion. I am fond of children and thoroughly enjoyed my years of teaching little children. I like a home above everything else, having always had a happy one but would not care to go so frantically as many women are doing today. I shall be willing to answer any questions you might ask me about other qualities and tendencies.

Yours very truly,

P.S. I am a Protestant, being a good Congregationalist.

Mar. 31, 1932

My dear Miss:

In your recent letter to me you asked me to help you find a man who would be a good husband for you, but I think what you really want is for me to help you see why it is difficult for you to find a mate for yourself. This I cannot do without knowing more about you. I know many reasons why girls find it difficult to fall in love and marry but each individual is a special problem and requires careful personal study.

For example, I might infer from your letter that your difficulty is one of conflicting loves. You will remember that in the *Journal* I have spoken of women who are so much in love with someone that they cannot give any love to a mate. I think you may be correct in saying that part of your trouble has been that you overidealized your first love. What you want to know is what you can do to overcome this tendency to remain attached to the past instead of going forward and forming new relationships.

I think that first you will have to study the situation very carefully and see that although you say you want to marry more than anything else in the world yet you have refused all your opportunities to do so. It is therefore reasonable to assume that you do not want to marry nearly as much as you think you do. When you realize this and understand the reason, which may or may not be the one I have suggested, you will be much more able to "manage your own affairs," as you say, than you are at present.

Sincerely yours,

About the Editors

Howard J. Faulkner and Virginia D. Pruitt are professsors of English at Washburn University in Topeka, Kansas. They have coedited two other volumes of Karl Menninger's letters, *The Selected Correspondence of Karl A. Menninger, 1919–1945* and *The Selected Correspondence of Karl A. Menninger, 1946–1965,* both available from the University of Missouri Press.